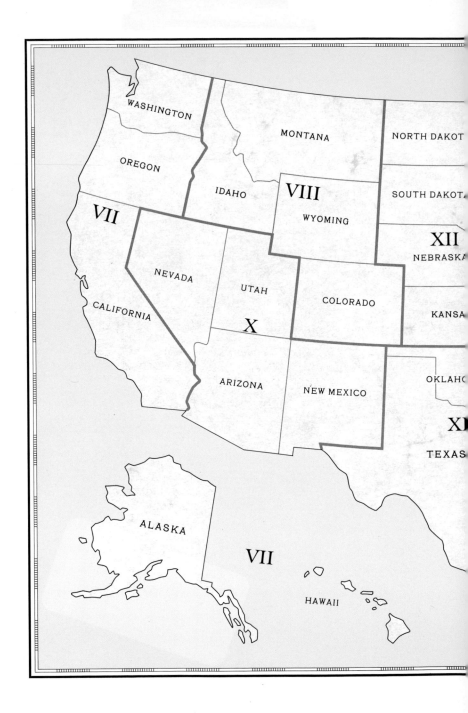

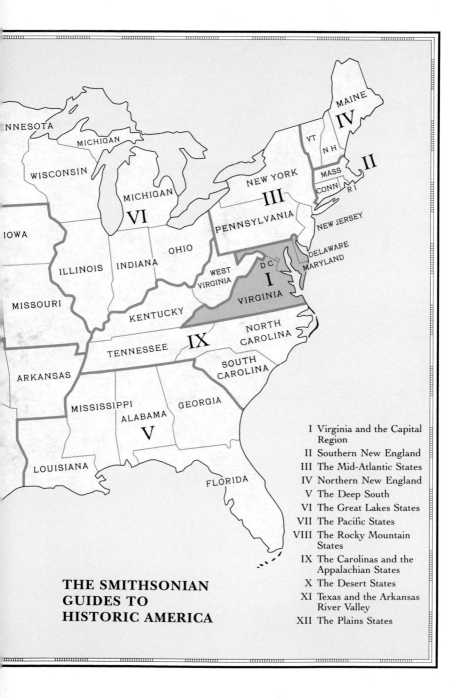

MAINE
IV
VT
N H
II
MASS
CONN
R I
NEW YORK
III
PENNSYLVANIA
NEW JERSEY
DELAWARE
MARYLAND
D C
I
VIRGINIA
WEST VIRGINIA
NNESOTA
MICHIGAN
WISCONSIN
MICHIGAN
VI
IOWA
OHIO
ILLINOIS
INDIANA
MISSOURI
KENTUCKY
NORTH CAROLINA
TENNESSEE
IX
SOUTH CAROLINA
ARKANSAS
MISSISSIPPI
GEORGIA
ALABAMA
V
LOUISIANA
FLORIDA

I Virginia and the Capital Region
II Southern New England
III The Mid-Atlantic States
IV Northern New England
V The Deep South
VI The Great Lakes States
VII The Pacific States
VIII The Rocky Mountain States
IX The Carolinas and the Appalachian States
X The Desert States
XI Texas and the Arkansas River Valley
XII The Plains States

THE SMITHSONIAN GUIDES TO HISTORIC AMERICA

THE
SMITHSONIAN
GUIDES TO
HISTORIC AMERICA

VIRGINIA AND
THE CAPITAL REGION

TEXT BY
HENRY WIENCEK

EDITORIAL DIRECTOR
ROGER G. KENNEDY
Director Emeritus, the National Museum of
American History of the Smithsonian Institution,
former Director of the National Park Service

Stewart, Tabori & Chang
NEW YORK

Due to limitations of space, additional photo credits appear on pages 399–400 and constitute an extension of this page.

Published in 1998 by Stewart, Tabori & Chang, A Company of La Martinière Groupe 115 West 18th Street, New York, NY 10011.

Front cover: main photo–Lincoln Memorial, Washington, D.C.
inset 1–Chesapeake Bay Maritime Museum, St. Michaels, MD.
inset 2–map by Guenter Vollath
inset 3–"Mock-Bird" by Catesby; Colonial Williamsburg Foundation, VA.
inset 4–Curtiss P-40E War Hawk, National Air and Space Museum, Washington, D.C.
Half-title page: Eagle, Washington, D.C.
Frontispiece: Executive Mansion, Richmond, VA.
Back cover: Cannon, Fort Harrison, Richmond, VA.

Series Editors: Henry Wiencek (first edition), Donald Young (revised edition)
Editor: Mary Luders
Photo Editor: Mary Z. Jenkins   **Photo Assistant:** Barbara J. Seyda
Art Director: Diana M. Jones   **Cover Design** (revised edition): Nai Chang
Designers: Joseph Rutt and Paul P. Zakris (first edition), Lisa Vaughn (revised edition)
Associate Editor: Brigid A. Mast
Cartographic Design & Production: Guenter Vollath
Cartographic Compilation: George Colbert   **Data Entry:** Susan Kirby
Text revisions throughout this edition by the series editor.

Library of Congress Cataloging-in-Publication Data

Wiencek, Henry.
    Virginia and the capital region / text by Henry Wiencek — Rev. ed.
       p. cm. — (The Smithsonian guides to historic America ; 1)
    "Text revisions throughout this edition by Donald Young"—T. p. verso
    Includes index.
    ISBN 1-55670-632-4
    1. Middle Atlantic States—Guidebooks. 2. Virginia—Guidebooks. 3. Washington Region—
Guidebooks. 4. Historic sites—Middle Atlantic States—Guidebooks. 5. Historic sites—Virginia—
Guidebooks. 6. Historic sites—Washington Region—Guidebooks. I. Young, Donald. II. Title. III. Series.
F106.W64   1998
917.504'43—dc21   96-53233

Distributed in the U.S. by Stewart, Tabori & Chang,115 West 18th Street, New York, NY 10011.
Distributed in Canada by General Publishing Co. Ltd., 30 Lesmill Road, Don Mills, Ontario, Canada, M3B 2T6.
Distributed in all other territories by Grantham Book Services Ltd., Isaac Newton Way, Alma Park Industrial Estate, Grantham, Lincolnshire NG31 9SD, England.
Sold in Australia by Peribo Pty Ltd., 58 Beaumont Road, Mount Kuring-gai, NSW 2080, Australia.

Printed in Japan

10 9 8 7 6 5 4 3 2

Revised edition

C O N T E N T S

INTRODUCTION   10

WASHINGTON, DC   18

NORTHERN VIRGINIA   98

RICHMOND AND ENVIRONS   146

WILLIAMSBURG AND THE HISTORIC
   TRIANGLE   186

THE SHENANDOAH VALLEY AND
   JEFFERSON'S VIRGINIA   224

ANNAPOLIS AND THE EASTERN SHORE   254

BALTIMORE AND NORTHERN MARYLAND   298

DELAWARE   350

NOTES ON ARCHITECTURE   386

INDEX   388

VIRGINIA AND THE CAPITAL REGION

INTERSTATE HIGHWAY
○ HISTORIC SITE
CIVIL WAR BATTLE ♣ PARK

PITTSBURGH

Ohio R.

70

79

Morgantown

48

OHIO

Ohio R.

WEST

77

VIRGINIA

79

CHARLESTON

A L L E G H E N Y

KENTUCKY

A P P A L A C H I A N

Roanoke

PKWY

RIDGE

Wytheville

New R.

BLUE

81

77

Dan R.

29

♣ Cumberland Gap N.H.P.

TENNESSEE

NORTH

Greensboro

0   80 Mi.

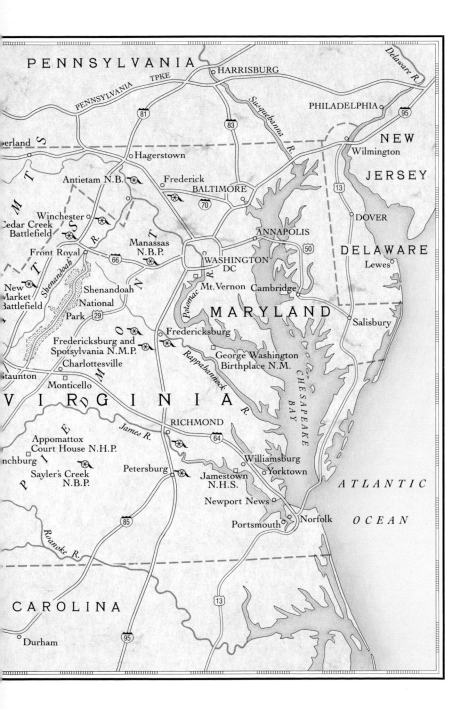

INTRODUCTION

ROGER G. KENNEDY

Washington, DC, the metropolis of the Chesapeake, is today America's imperial city, though it may have to vie for coverage on the nightly news with New York and upstart Los Angeles. Once before as well, the Chesapeake Region had an irresistible claim upon the nation's attention. In the 1780s, the most powerful political elite in the United States was the tobacco gentry of the Chesapeake, though they shared economic power with the burghers of Philadelphia and Boston and even with those of upstart New York.

As the United States commenced its career as an independent nation, Virginia and Maryland together exerted greater leverage upon the policies of the new American republic than any other states, except, perhaps, Pennsylvania and Massachusetts. Agriculture was the chief source of wealth, and the measure of the importance of the area was, roughly speaking, the amount of tobacco produced (whereas now it is the amount of paper consumed).

The power of the Chesapeake Region was built upon the cultivation of a drug. Tobacco, as we now know, though the Founding Fathers did not, is dangerous. It was also the most important factor in the life of this region in the first two centuries of European occupation. The British had learned from the Dutch, French, and Spaniards the general shape of the coastline of Chesapeake Bay. They explored the land and found it good for the cultivation of tobacco, the "sot-weed," which was native to the area, as it was to the West Indies. An exploring party sent out by Columbus to Cuba had reported in 1492 that its natives perfumed themselves by burning a dried leaf with a pleasant smell. Before a decade was past, other Spaniards noted the use of the same leaf for snuff and chewing. A hollow wooden tube in a "Y" shape, called a "tabaco," was held to capture the fumes and transmit them into the nostrils.

Tobacco culture in Maryland and Virginia was easily commenced, since the soil was fertile, and the plant throve amid stumps on barely-cultivated ground. The home market was avid and there was a rapid increase in cultivation, which brought prices down so rapidly in the early seventeenth century that many of the first generation of planters were bankrupted, while much of the land they planted became exhausted. Crops remained "sweet" only on newly-planted land, but there was land aplenty; the once-numerous Indians were reduced by disease and driven from the shores, though they took a long time to relinquish the mountains.

The seventeenth century was a violent time; there were constant Indian wars and battles among competing European settlements. Life was destabilized by vehement surges and declines in the marketplace—in periods of prosperity planters expanded their acreage, which resulted in overproduction and a fall in tobacco prices; their heavy debt at the planting season was relieved by a sudden gush of liquidity at harvest time, setting off the kind of gluttonous demand for fancy goods that is characteristic of unsteady and speculative economies. Nor was colonial life tranquil politically. Bacon's Rebellion broke out in Virginia in 1676, and the antipathies that erupted into religious wars in Europe spread into British colonies. Maryland was seized by anti-Catholic frenzies in the last decades of the seventeenth century.

Maryland had been a sort of "Holy Experiment" in proprietorship by Catholic aristocrats tolerant of Anglicans, Quakers, and Dissenters. It had extended all the way from the Anglican corporate colony of Virginia to the chartered Puritan colonies of New England. But turns of fortune in London brought about obligations on the part of an Anglican king to his brother the Duke of York, and to William Penn, the Quaker son of a powerful admiral. New York and Pennsylvania were lopped away from the Roman Catholic Calverts and their deputies, the Carrolls.

Little remains above ground to tell us what life was like during the first century of European settlement, or for the Native Americans of this region. Archaeologists have been busily reconstructing what they call "impermanent" structures from postholes and debris; St. Mary's City, the early capital of Maryland, has been quite completely explored, but the most tantalizing work is that recently undertaken at the Thunderbird site in the Shenandoah Valley. Faint markings, 11,000 years old, have been found of an oval structure, perhaps with a veranda (my interpretation, not that of the experts). The striking thing about the evidence at Thunderbird is the degree of permanency this sort of building implies; greater effort and expectations of longer occupancy are implied in it than in most of what remains from the first two generations of European occupation. As the plantation system settled down, Europeans built for a longer haul, and surrounded themselves with African settlements, as slave-quarters might be described.

Searching the tranquil terrain of the interior of the Delmarva Peninsula and "South Side" Virginia, we can find a few remaining medieval buildings that record the humble beginnings of plantation permanency. Amid ephemeral triumphs and frequent disasters, Indian Wars and slave risings, some Englishmen built little peaked houses, which, in their very antiquity, now bely their scrambling, harried, bloody-handed origins.

Upon the flat, rural, ageless, endless land there are still buildings that present to traveler's eyes something quite similar to what would have been seen in 1700. Among the most accessible examples of the medieval are Bacon's Castle, in Surrey County, built by Arthur Allen about 1665. St. Luke's Church, east of Smithfield, is nearby and was built around the same time. The Thoroughgood House, built around 1680 and several times restored, shows how the Gothic tradition persisted in the eighteenth century and beyond, into the revival period of the nineteenth century. Bremo Recess (a private house not open to the public in Fluvanna County) was composed in 1834 by people who still had memories of the medieval Williamsburg that preceded the classical town that has been restored for us.

Classical Williamsburg and plantation houses like Westover and Carters Grove replaced all that. They were a new order of things. We sometimes call them "Georgian," after the three King Georges of England, but their prototypes were Dutch, French, and Italian, as well as English. The Georgian-style house became, in the Chesapeake Region, the symbol of the success of the local tobacco culture. But we should be careful to view these Georgian houses skeptically—life was not so serene as all that. These balanced, red-brick-and-white-trim buildings were created by the system of institutionalized violence that was slavery.

The colonial period is reasonably clear to us because we have been busy "restoring" that era—it is a somewhat mysterious characteristic of our own time that we have chosen to lavish our most diligent care upon the preservation of our dependent, rather than our independent past. In the Chesapeake Region, which reached its apogee of relative importance before the new nation was launched, we have Williamsburg and Winterthur, Annapolis and New Castle, the James River plantations and societies of Early American Life. The tobacco-raising gentry are easily summoned to the stage, but they had less than a century to create the remarkable heritage of cultivated living we have so diligently preserved. The founders of some of the first families of Virginia, having arrived as indentured servants, worked the land in the 1600s. Their successors, a new group—Carters, Burwells, Byrds, Beverleys, and others—rose to eminence only after 1720 or so and remained eminent, in economic terms, for only fifty years thereafter.

Tobacco had accounted for as much as half the total exports of the thirteen original colonies but declined in importance after independence. Annapolis, the capital city of the tobacco culture, was soon to be eclipsed by Baltimore, barely a village in the 1790s. Baltimore's merchants were beginning their boisterous intrusions into the wheat country behind Philadelphia, to draw off the business of its prosperous German farmers from the senior and somewhat smug Quaker community. The new wheat and corn economy nourished bakeries, distilleries, and retailing; wheat, unlike tobacco, gave rise to a multitude of mercantile subcultures and to the rapid industrial growth that was appearing along the tributaries of Delaware Bay, the Brandywine and the Schuylkill. Though these streams were barely twenty miles from the head of the Chesapeake, they were a million miles, culturally, from its lower reaches, dominated by the planters of the James, the York, and the Rappahannock. Cities and industry burgeoned in the North and cotton began its reign over the expanding South; by 1850, the "sot-weed" accounted for less than thirteen percent of American exports.

Prescient men like Thomas Jefferson had always lamented the pernicious effects of a reliance upon tobacco cultivation through the deployment of slave labor. He called the combination of the two "a culture productive of infinite wretchedness....men and animals on those farms are barely fed, and the earth is rapidly impoverished." The great planters were able to find funds to pay for fertilizers, but most others could not; large estates engrossed more and more unprofitable land. Yet they did not thereby become richer, merely more extended. Jefferson's own Albemarle County was "worn out, washed and gullied," and a British traveler reported that that washing was so severe that the rivers, carrying the earth in the spring run-off "appeared like a torrent of blood."

Another torrent washed out of Virginia and Maryland after 1780, a torrent of its most vigorous talent. The denuded and

OVERLEAF: *A pitch-and-tar swamp, Jamestown Island.*

increasingly sterile soil of the Tidewater could not support even the levels of population of the 1770s, and the consequences of "natural increase" had to be decanted elsewhere. Yeomen departed in tens of thousands. More than a third of the white children born in Virginia and Maryland around 1800 emigrated to the West. Three hundred thousand slaves were sold to planters in the New South; some Virginians fell into the detestable practice of breeding human beings for sale.

As early as 1816, a committee of the Virginia legislature lamented that while "many other states have been advancing in wealth and numbers...the ancient Dominion...has remained stationary. A very large proportion of her western territory is yet unimproved, while a considerable part of her eastern has receded from its former opulence. How many sad spectacles do her lowlands present of wasted and deserted fields, of dwellings abandoned...of churches in ruins!" This was not the work of the War Between the States; the destruction of the tobacco economy of the Virginia, Maryland and the Chesapeake was well underway before Robert E. Lee was born. During his lifetime, the decline of his native region was rapid, lamented, but, apparently, irreversable.

Long before the War Between the States, as Virginia and Maryland were losing ground to their quickly-growing neighbors, they were already changing character, though not in ways celebrated in legends of an imaginary ante-bellum world. Crop diversification and fertilizing were undertaken. So was diversification into heavy industry. In Delaware, industrial growth initiated by the genius of the duPonts and their affluent, well connected, and charming partner, the long-forgotten Pierre Bauduy, spread outward from Wilmington.

Richmond was becoming the Ruhr of the South, a steel and iron town presaging Pittsburgh. The Confederacy's strategy in the war was founded on the central economic importance of that slave-driven industrial city. It was not only to protect its capital city that the South fought so hard. It was also desperate to keep its Bellona and Tredegar Iron Works, its armory, navy yard, ordnance laboratory, its munitions industry and its uniform-making plants. It is often forgotten that those plants were largely state enterprises, created by taxing the rural economy to create an industrial base to compete with that of the North. Aside from the Tredegar Works, they were managed in a kind of war-time state socialism.

As one contemplates the economic map of the region today, it is striking how much power and population is concentrated in those regions of Virginia which seemed most depressed in the immediate antebellum years, Fairfax County, now a huge suburb of the Federal City, and the resurgent maritime complex around Norfolk and Newport News. It has been the ironic fate of Virginians, who developed the most eloquent and consistent theoretical basis for opposition to the expansion of federal power, and supplied the crucial economic and intellectual leadership of a great war fought against that expansion, to find themselves the chief beneficiaries of the growth of the federal bureaucracy. Regiments of civil servants are now bivouacked in suburbs where once the ring of forts precariously protected the Federal City from the armies of the South. Now, there sprout the girders and cranes of the feeder-exurbs. Corporate offices, like the cells of mud-wasps, are every day being laid among steel combs about Tyson's Corner, Manassas, and along the Dulles Corridor. However they may lament the passing of the rural delights of Montgomery and Fairfax Counties, and the rapid replacement of pastures by parking lots and paddocks by industrial parks, Maryland and Virginia landowners and developers are enjoying what used to be called "unearned increment" as the Federal lava ineluctably inundates the landscape.

There remain, today, few unsullied sylvan scenes from Fredericksburg to Frederick and from Port Tobacco to Annapolis. Baltimore remains a real city, but it is now continuous with Washington; Richmond, only barely beyond the commuting distance of federal bureaucrats, is once again under siege.

Yet, farther afield, there remain vestiges of aboriginal America. The largest stretch of virgin timber betwen the Catskills and the Smokies is to be found in Ramsey's Draft, west of Staunton, near Headwaters, Virginia. There are patches of old-growth hemlocks along the headwaters of the Hazel and the Thornton Rivers, in Shenandoah National Park, and high up, near Skyland, in "Limberlost." Ravaged West Virginia still can show surprises in the alpine tundra of Dolly Sods and the Cranberry glades. A surveyor's error has left a wedge of virgin spruce near Gaudineer Tower, and there is a good "climax stand" in fifty acres along Route 50.

At the extremes of the region, one can still feel the proximity of the primitive past. Atop 5500-foot Mount Rogers one is well above the encroachments of the twentieth or even the nineteenth centuries, and in the swamps south of Norfolk nothing much has changed for a thousand years. The water-snakes glide, the great trees add another ring, the insects rise at sundown, and the most exciting activity of the day is photosynthesis.

CHAPTER ONE

WASHINGTON, DC

Washington, DC, the youngest of the great Eastern cities, was willed into existence by the fledgling federal government in 1790. The site, at the marshy confluence of the Potomac and Anacostia rivers, was chosen as part of a larger political compromise over the federal assumption of state debts from the Revolutionary War. Maryland and Virginia ceded their sovereignty over one hundred square miles of land; but the ownership of the land remained in private hands. The area was sparsely settled but for the small port town of Georgetown, begun in the 1750s and, downriver a little, Alexandria.

George Washington appointed a committee to supervise the design of the city and its principal buildings. As Major Pierre Charles L'Enfant, a French officer of engineers, conducted a thorough survey of the terrain, Washington negotiated the purchase of the land. He persuaded the owners to agree to a plan that seemed quite reasonable: They would be paid for lots to be occupied by federal buildings; but they would retain ownership of lots earmarked for private housing and commercial development, sharing the profits they made on this land with the government—profits that were expected to be substantial. Finally, tracts to be used for roads and parks would be deeded to the government gratis.

When L'Enfant's plan was unrolled before the owners' committee, they were thunderstruck. The plan called for broad avenues crisscrossing the city in a network of diagonals; where the avenues met there were to be spacious squares or circles; and from the site of the future Capitol extended a mile-long, four-hundred-foot-wide mall—the owners had agreed to part with all such lands for nothing. Washington soothed them with visions of the large profits they would reap from future sales of other lots to private and commercial interests.

L'Enfant's design was an inspired one. Based on Baroque planning ideas, and closely derived from that of Versailles, the plan combined a grid pattern for streets, with grand avenues (to be named after states) sweeping through the city. The plan was both practical and aesthetically pleasing. It not only allowed for rapid access to the center from the periphery, but it provided long, majestic vistas down the avenues to the circles or squares that would be occupied by statues, fountains, and other monuments of public pride. L'Enfant proposed to place the Capitol on Jenkins Hill, from which Pennsylvania Avenue would run northwest to the

A View of Washington *drawn by E. Sachse, 1832.*

president's house. It was at Jefferson's suggestion that L'Enfant included a mall rolling westward from the foot of the hill.

The government was scheduled, by law, to occupy the city by 1800, and work began in the early 1790s on the Capitol and the president's house, but the growth of the city was painfully slow, as it lacked manufacturing or commercial enterprises to attract money or citizens. The government and a few farmers were the only employers. In 1808 a visitor wrote that, "all around are premature symptoms of decay . . . so many houses built, not inhabited, but tumbling into ruins." During the War of 1812, a British column descended on the city and put all the public buildings but one (the Patent Office) to the torch. Dismayed by the ruins, Congress voted on the question of abandoning the city; the motion lost by only nine votes.

Official Washington was rebuilt, but the rest of the city continued to languish in the early nineteenth century. It was known derisively as "The City of Magnificent Distances." An Irish poet had some sport with a couplet: "This embryo capital where fancy sees / Squares in morasses, obelisks in trees." In 1842 Charles Dickens visited and found "spacious avenues that begin in nothing and lead nowhere . . . public buildings that need but a public to be complete."

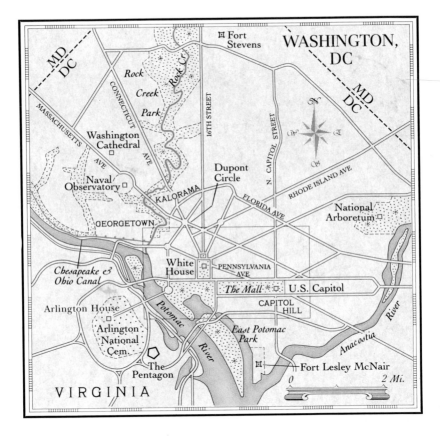

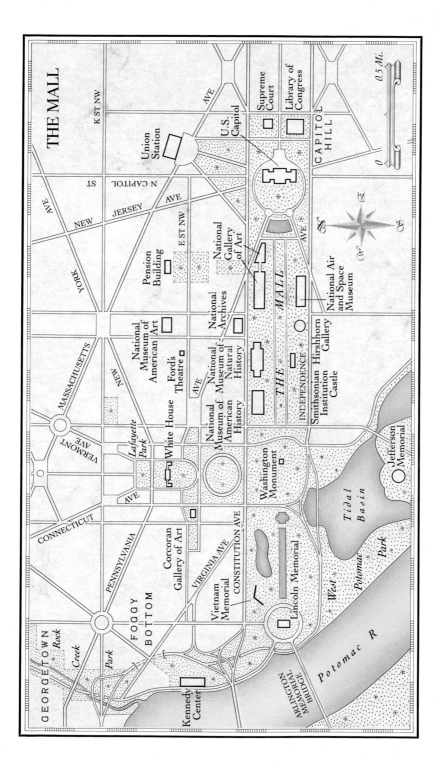

THE MALL

K ST NW

Union
Station

N CAPITOL ST

NEW   JERSEY   AVE
YORK
AVE
AVE

MASSACHUSETTS

NEW

VERMONT AVE

Lafayette
Park

White House

CONNECTICUT

AVE

PENNSYLVANIA

CONSTITUTION AVE

VIRGINIA AVE

Corcoran
Gallery of Art

Vietnam
Memorial

FOGGY
BOTTOM

GEORGETOWN

Rock   Creek   Park

Kennedy
Center

National Museum
of American Art

Ford's
Theatre

E ST NW

Pension
Building

National
Archives

National
Gallery
of Art

AVE

National
Museum of
Natural History

National
Museum of
American History

AVE

Washington
Monument

THE   MALL

INDEPENDENCE   AVE

Smithsonian
Institution
Castle

Hirshhorn
Gallery

National Air
and Space
Museum

U.S.
Capitol

Supreme
Court

Library of
Congress

CAPITOL
HILL

N

Lincoln Memorial

ARLINGTON
MEMORIAL
BRIDGE

West   Potomac   Park

Tidal
Basin

Jefferson
Memorial

Potomac R.

0   0.5 Mi.

During the Civil War, Washington became a huge hospital. Wounded soldiers were housed in public buildings and were tended by the newly formed National Sanitary Commission, precursor of the Red Cross. The writers Walt Whitman and Louisa May Alcott were among the volunteer nurses.

At the outbreak of the war the city was virtually undefended until the arrival of a New York regiment on April 25, 1861, and in July of that year the Confederates could have entered the capital with little opposition after their victory at Manassas. In July 1864, General Jubal Early failed to take the city only because he delayed his attack, giving Grant enough time to bring up reinforcements. The fighting that month reached Fort Stevens at the city's outskirts. Lincoln himself observed the fighting by poking his head foolishly over the parapet. Actually, much against his will, Lincoln spent his entire presidency in the company of armed guards. His first inauguration, which preceded the outbreak of the war, was watched over by a corps of riflemen. During the war he rode about the city escorted by cavalry with drawn sabers. Ironically, he was shot at Ford's Theater when his lone bodyguard stepped away.

It was not until the early 1870s that Washington began to be transformed into a true city. This was largely the work of one man, Alexander Shepherd, a close friend of President Grant. As vice president of the board of public works, Shepherd dispatched crews throughout the city to entrench sewer, water, and gas lines, lay sidewalks, and grade roads. He cared little for the niceties of a bureaucracy, a budget, or the law, but he could get things done. Road grading was carried out with little or no regard for the houses along the road: Homeowners found that the new street might be several feet below their front door—or several feet above. When a railroad refused to accommodate the new grade of Maryland Avenue, Shepherd simply tore up the tracks; when merchants refused to vacate a square, he demolished their stalls. During Shepherd's three-year reign he filled in the abandoned and dangerous Washington Canal, paved over one hundred miles of streets, including Pennsylvania Avenue, and planted tens of thousands of trees.

Shepherd's public works campaign coincided with, and spurred, a short-lived black renaissance in the city. From its very foundation the capital city has been a testing ground for the nation's race relations. One of the men who laid out the city was

OPPOSITE: *Detail showing the ceremonial lighting of the chandelier from Samuel F. B. Morse's painting,* The Old House of Representatives.

Benjamin Banneker, a successful black farmer in his sixties who was an accomplished engineer, musician, astronomer, and almanac writer. (Banneker sent a copy of his almanac for the year 1792 to Jefferson, who judged him a "very respectable mathematician.")

Nevertheless, Banneker's contributions to the creation of the city sank from public memory. In the first half of the nineteenth century, Congress and the city council enacted numerous laws and regulations to restrict the rights of blacks: They could be fined or whipped for attending meetings, entering the Capitol grounds, possessing abolitionist literature, or being on the street after 10:00 PM. Cursing, gambling, drinking, or swimming in the Potomac were also punishable offenses for blacks. Slaves were marched in chains down Pennsylvania Avenue to auction blocks on the Mall and behind the White House.

During and just after the Civil War, freed slaves flocked to the capital, where the black population in 1867 reached nearly forty thousand, about a third of the city's total population. Though a black middle class began to emerge, most lived in poverty, and a great many died quickly when disease swept through their shanty settlements. At a relief center, a visitor found "a cloud of darkness, poverty, rags, hunger, cold, and suffering." Their plight was lessened in the late 1860s and 1870s when the great public works programs gave employment to thousands of black laborers. A black-owned bank, newspaper, and hotel (the city's most elegant) flourished. An act of Congress funded Howard University, which was established in 1867, the same year that blacks were enfranchised in the city. In 1870 segregation in public places was made illegal. Frederick Douglass, elected to the city council, was an official pallbearer at the funeral of Vice President Henry Wilson. For a brief time Washington was known as "the colored man's paradise." But fears that blacks would use their vote and economic power to "take over" the city led to a resurgence of discrimination and segregation. Blacks found themselves banned from places of public accommodation; they were shut out of the skilled jobs and professions that had lately brought them out of the shanties. A race riot tore the city in 1919; the capital's segregation laws were expanded in the 1920s. When the Lincoln Memorial was dedicated in 1922, blacks watched the ceremony from across a road, kept in their place by a barrier of ropes.

Racial antipathies fanned the decades-old anxiety that the government would pull up stakes and leave. Shepherd's rebuilding program was launched partly to keep the government in Washington; there had been calls to move it to St. Louis, Chicago, Cincinnati, and Kansas City. But the public structures erected in the last decades of the nineteenth century changed that: After decades of neglect and political tug-of-war, the Washington Monument was finished in 1884, and the Old Executive Office Building, erected in 1888, and Library of Congress, completed in 1897, were both sumptuous symbols of the government's commitment to the city.

At the turn of the century a commission appointed by Senator James MacMillan undertook another public works project—the still-neglected Mall. It called for the construction of the Lincoln and Jefferson memorials and the extension of the Mall to the Potomac. With Theodore Roosevelt's help, the commission was able to remove railroad tracks and a depot from the Mall. To replace the depot, the architect Daniel Burnham, one of the commissioners, designed the monumental Union Station as the city's proper gateway a short walk from the Capitol. The next great phase of building took place in the 1920s under President Coolidge, whose administration constructed the Federal Triangle buildings. The Mall, site of the Smithsonian Institution since the 1850s, has become one of the world's great museum centers. The city as a whole boasts more than a score of museums devoted to history, the arts, natural history, and technology, but its great attraction is, of course, the pageant of democratic government. Portions of the Capitol and the White House are open to visitors year-round.

This chapter begins at the Capitol and the Capitol Hill district to the east, then proceeds to the Mall, the White House area, Federal Triangle, the downtown sites, Georgetown, Dupont Circle, and Kalorama. A **visitor center** (1450 Pennsylvania Avenue, NW 202–789–7000) provides maps, brochures, and information about current exhibits in the city.

C A P I T O L   H I L L

U.S. CAPITOL

The Capitol has been the seat of the United States Congress since 1800. Thomas Jefferson was the first president to be inaugurated here, in the Senate Chamber in 1801. In 1829 Andrew Jackson began the tradition of taking the oath of office outdoors on the East Portico.

The building has undergone many changes since 1800. The Capitol seen today is more than twice the size of the original, with a much higher dome. Pierre L'Enfant chose for its site a high point overlooking the city, Jenkins Hill, which he called a pedestal awaiting a monument. Proposals were submitted in 1792 for the design for the building; the last of these—which arrived three months after the "competition" was scheduled to terminate—came from a West Indian physician, Dr. William Thornton. He produced a design Thomas Jefferson called "simple, noble, beautiful, excellently distributed," which "captivated the eyes and judgment of all." Thornton's plan called for a modest dome atop a cubical central section, itself containing a rotunda and flanked by wings to accommodate the chambers of the House and Senate. Because Thornton had probably never designed a complete building before (he had provided elevations of a much smaller building in Philadelphia and may have offered suggestions for a planter's house on the island of St. Croix), some modifications had to be made. For example, after examining the plans, Jefferson pointed out that many parts of the building would not receive sufficient light and air, but work went ahead, and George Washington, wearing Masonic regalia, laid the cornerstone in 1793. The wings were begun first, amidst disputes between Thornton and a succession of other architects called in to improve his plans, and Congress was able to move into the North Wing in 1800. In 1803 Jefferson appointed Benjamin Henry Latrobe as surveyor of public buildings. Under him, the House wing was completed and linked to the North Wing by a wooden walkway. One of Latrobe's refinements was to decorate column capitals with carved corncobs and tobacco leaves, symbols of the New World's agriculture.

OPPOSITE: *The Capitol of the United States of America.* OVERLEAF: *Statuary Hall, home to the House of Representatives until 1857.*

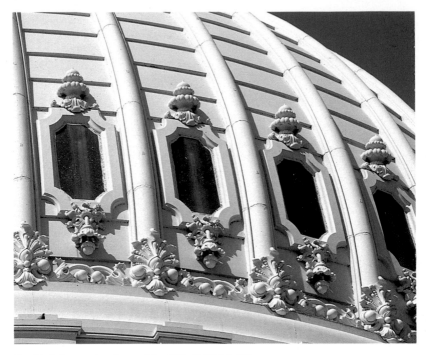

Detail of the massive dome of the U.S. Capitol building.

On August 24, 1814, during the War of 1812, the British burned the Capitol along with all of the city's public buildings except the Patent Building. Reputedly, Rear Admiral Cockburn stood on the speaker's chair before a mock assembly of soldiers and presented the motion, "Shall this harbor of Yankee democracy be burned?" (Cockburn joined in the looting of the building, as evidenced by a treasury report that was taken by him and returned to the U.S. government in the 1940s.) A heavy downpour on the night of the burning doused the flames, saving the building's walls.

In 1819, after Latrobe had rebuilt the wings, President Monroe replaced him with Charles Bulfinch of Boston. At the president's request, Bulfinch built a larger dome than either Thornton or Latrobe had envisioned.

The next major work took place in the 1850s under Thomas U. Walter. He built new wings with larger chambers for the House and the Senate to accommodate the representatives from new states, thereby doubling the length of the building. To compensate for the increased width—and to satisfy a growing taste for the neo-

The interior of the Capitol dome, with paintings by Constantino Brumidi.

Baroque—Walter replaced the dome and added a massive drum encircled by pilasters and columns. He designed the new cast-iron dome with two shells, an inner shell and an outer shell—an engineering method used in the U.S. only once before (in St. Louis).

Much of the mural decoration of the Capitol was designed by Constantino Brumidi, who had fled political upheaval in Italy in the 1850s. He worked twenty-five years "to make beautiful the Capitol of the one country on earth in which there is liberty." The **Brumidi Corridor** in the Senate wing is an exuberant display, with American portraits, flora, fauna, and inventions incorporated into a Roman decorative scheme. His work did not meet with universal approval, however: Samuel Clemens assessed it as "the delerium tremens of art." Frederick Law Olmsted designed the grounds between 1874 and 1892. In 1961 the east front of the building was brought forward thirty-two-and-one-half feet and given a new facade of Georgia marble.

The main entrance to the Capitol, leading to the Rotunda, is the **Columbus Portal**—a massive pair of bronze doors, weighing ten tons, and depicting episodes from the life of Columbus in high relief. The doors were modeled in the 1850s by Randolph Rogers, an American artist living in Rome, and cast in Munich.

Ninety-five feet in diameter, and 180 feet high, the **Rotunda** is the symbolic center of the Capitol and the city; in L'Enfant's plan, the north–south and east–west axes of the city cross in this room. Eight historical paintings encircle the Rotunda, four by John Trumbull: *The Declaration of Independence, The Surrender of General Burgoyne at Saratoga, The Surrender of Lord Cornwallis,* and *Washington Resigning His Commission as General of the Army.* Trumbull, who was in his sixties when he completed the paintings, had served briefly in the Continental Army and knew many of the people he painted. In 1816 he appealed to Jefferson for the Capitol commission, writing, "future artists may arise with far Superior Talents, but time has already withdrawn almost all their Models; and I . . . was one of the youngest Actors in the early scenes of the War." Trumbull had also been given a rare privilege: Years before, Washington had posed for him on horseback so that the artist could make accurate sketches.

A statue of Abraham Lincoln in the Rotunda was based on sketches made by a seventeen-year-old artist, Vinnie Ream. Lincoln agreed to sit for her because she was poor but talented. In 1865 Constantino Brumidi painted the fresco on the canopy under the Rotunda dome, *The Apotheosis of George Washington.* He also worked on the nine-foot-high frieze depicting events in the nation's history, starting with Columbus's landing in the New World. The final portions of the frieze were completed in 1953, with a depiction of the Wright Brothers flight at Kitty Hawk. In 1865 Lincoln's body lay in state in the Rotunda, beginning a tradition.

Below the Rotunda are a **crypt and a tomb** originally intended to hold the remains of George Washington, but his family declined to allow the remains to be removed from the tomb at Mount Vernon. The Capitol tomb (not accessible) holds the bier upon which lay the body of Lincoln as well as those of all others who have lain in state in the Rotunda. A marble block in the crypt portrays three women notable in the struggle for women's rights: Susan B. Anthony, Elizabeth Cady Stanton, and Lucretia Mott.

Statuary Hall, an echoing, semicircular marble chamber with marble columns and a coffered ceiling, served as the House chamber until 1857. In 1864 Congress invited each state to send two statues of notable citizens for display here. The weight of the accumulated marble sparked fears that the floor would collapse,

G.P.A. Healy's depiction of Daniel Webster delivering his argument, "Liberty and Union, now and forever, one and inseparable!" to the Senate in 1830 (detail).

and in 1934 some of the statues were moved to other parts of the building. In 1848 former president John Quincy Adams collapsed from a stroke at a spot in the hall now marked with a bronze plaque; carried from the chamber, he died in an adjacent room.

The Supreme Court sat at the Capitol until 1935, first in the **Old Supreme Court Chamber** (1810 to 1860), then in the **Old Senate Chamber.** Latrobe modeled both rooms in the shape of amphitheaters. In 1844 Samuel F. B. Morse sent the world's first telegraph message—"What hath God wrought"—from the Old Supreme Court chamber to Baltimore.

The **Old Senate Chamber** was the scene of the historic debates that preceded the Civil War, as Henry Clay, Daniel Webster, and John C. Calhoun argued the issues of slavery and states' rights. The debate over allowing slavery in the new western states erupted into violence here in 1857 when Representative Preston S. Brooks of South Carolina attacked Senator Charles Sumner of Massachusetts with a cane. In 1859 the Senate moved to its new chamber.

LOCATION: Capitol Hill. HOURS: 9–4:30 Daily. FEE: None. TELE-PHONE: 202–225–6827.

Just southwest of the Capitol grounds, on Independence Avenue, is the **Bartholdi Fountain,** a bronze statuary group depicting three women designed in 1876 by Frédéric Auguste Bartholdi, the sculptor who later created the Statue of Liberty.

SEWALL-BELMONT HOUSE

Built in 1800 for Robert Sewall, the Sewall-Belmont House has important associations with the early political life of the capital and with the women's rights movement. From 1801 to 1813 it was occupied by Secretary of the Treasury Albert Gallatin. He was in the habit of working at home, and it is likely that the details of the financing of the 1804 Louisiana Purchase were pieced together here. In 1929 the house was acquired by the National Woman's Party and renamed in honor of Mrs. Alva Belmont, a major supporter. It was the residence of Alice Paul, the party's founder, and today is the party's headquarters. Saved from demolition in the 1950s, the house has been restored and furnished with items of several periods. On display are portraits of prominent women, such as Susan B. Anthony and Elizabeth Cady Stanton, as well as desks used by Anthony and Henry Clay.

LOCATION: 144 Constitution Avenue NE. HOURS: 10–3 Tuesday–Friday, 12–4 Saturday–Sunday. FEE: None. TELEPHONE: 202–546–3989.

SUPREME COURT BUILDING

The U.S. Supreme Court did not have a building of its own until this structure was completed in 1935. Constructed of white marble, it was designed by the architect Cass Gilbert of St. Paul, Minnesota, and New York. Its central portion is a temple in Greek style, with a portico of Corinthian columns. A sculptural group in the pediment represents the themes of Liberty, Authority, Order, Council, and Research. The faces of the Council figures, right to left, are former Chief Justice Charles Evans Hughes, the sculptor, Robert Aitken, Cass Gilbert, and Elihu Root. Former Chief Justices John Marshall and William Howard Taft appear as the Research figures. The interior contains two beautifully designed rooms, the Great Hall and the Courtroom, both featuring classical colonnades.

LOCATION: 1 First Street NE. HOURS: 9–4:30 Monday–Friday. FEE: None. TELEPHONE: 202–479–3000 or 479–3211.

OPPOSITE: *The U.S. Supreme Court, designed by Cass Gilbert.*

LIBRARY OF CONGRESS

The Library of Congress is the largest library in the world. Its books, pamphlets, documents, manuscripts, official papers, photographs, and prints aggregate to some 107 million items—a number that swells day by day—housed on 535 miles of shelves.

Congress authorized a library in 1800, which amounted to three thousand books and a few maps when it was destroyed when the British burned the Capitol in 1814. To replace it, Thomas Jefferson sold the government his private library of almost 6,500 volumes—the finest in the nation at the time. The collection, again housed in the Capitol, had grown to 55,000 when a fire destroyed more than half of it. In 1866 a portion of the Smithsonian Institution's library was added to the Library of Congress, and in the following year the government entered an international program by which copies of U.S. documents were exchanged for those of other nations. The copyright law of 1870 ensured the library would always be up to date by requiring publishers to send two copies of each book published to the library in order to obtain copyright.

By 1870 the collection had outgrown its Capitol quarters. A suggestion to raise the Capitol dome and fill it with bookshelves was rejected, and in 1873 Congress authorized a competition for the design of a library building. A variety of disputes delayed construction for more than a decade, but the library's Thomas Jefferson Building was finally opened in 1897.

The Neoclassical design of the building and its interior reflect the ebullient spirit of the Columbian Exposition of 1893. A team of fifty painters, sculptors, and other artisans created one of the most lavish interiors in America. The **Main Entrance Hall** is a spectacle of soaring arches, columns, statuary, and a profusion of painted, sculpted, mosaic, gilded, and stenciled decoration. In all, there are 112 murals in the building, and columns of Numidian marble support a 125-foot-high dome in the octagonal **Reading Room.** Although the decoration has not been to everyone's taste—a critic in 1934 called the library "a dreadful medley of waste and maudlin virtuosity"—more recent critics tend to be kinder and see the library as an expression of the exuberance of the Gilded Age.

LOCATION: 10 First Street. HOURS: 8:30–9:30 Monday–Friday, 8:30–6 Saturday. FEE: None. TELEPHONE: 202–707–8000.

OPPOSITE: *Scholars in the main reading room of the Library of Congress, watched over by philosophers and tourists alike.*

FOLGER SHAKESPEARE LIBRARY

Founded by Henry Clay Folger, the library houses the largest collection of Shakespeare items in the world, including seventy-nine copies of the First Folio. Folger, who died in 1930, did not live to see the library's opening in 1932. He was the president and chairman of the board of the Standard Oil Company of New York as well as an avid and discriminating collector of Shakespeareana. In his pursuit of things Shakespearean, he was aided by his wife, Emily Jordan Folger, a scholar of English literature. The Exhibition Hall is decorated in the Elizabethan style with oak panelling and a vaulted plaster ceiling. Among the Shakespearean items on display is a model of the Globe Theatre, which took a decade to build.

LOCATION: 201 East Capitol Street, SE. HOURS: 10–4 Monday–Saturday. FEE: None. TELEPHONE: 202–544–7077.

The Elizabethan-style theatre, above, and library, opposite, of the Folger Shakespeare Library.

The District east of the Capitol contains many examples of nineteenth-century residential architecture, two parks with statues of note, and a Gothic Revival church by Benjamin Henry Latrobe. The area was fashionable from the late 1870s until World War I and is becoming so once more. From the rear of the Capitol, Maryland Avenue leads to **Stanton Square,** named for Lincoln's secretary of war and holding a statue of General Nathanael Greene (1887) sculpted by Henry Kirk Brown. A native of Rhode Island, Greene was one of America's finest commanders during the Revolutionary War. He saw action at Bunker Hill in Boston, and distinguished himself as commander of American forces in the South. From Stanton Square, Massachusetts Avenue leads to **Lincoln Park,** with a statue, entitled *Emancipation* (1876) of Lincoln and a freed slave. The model for the slave was Archer Alexander, the last man captured under the Fugitive Slave Act, a federal law that provided for the return of runaway slaves to their owners.

Among the notable buildings to be seen in this district are the townhouses along **East Capitol Street** from 5th Street to Lincoln Park and on **11th Street** from the park to C Street. **Maples House** (619 D Street, private) dates to the 1790s. The houses on 6th Street between South Carolina Avenue and G Street date to the middle of the nineteenth century. The oldest house on these blocks, **Carbery House** (423 6th Street, private) was built in 1813. **Christ Church** (620 G Street) was designed by Latrobe and built in 1806. The house at 636 G Street was the birthplace of John Philip Sousa (1854–1932), the composer known as "the March King" for such stirring works as "The Stars and Stripes Forever." He was the leader of the Marine Corps Band from 1880 to 1892. Just two blocks away, the **Marine Barracks** (8th and I streets, 202–433–6060) provide quarters for today's Marine Band. The **Marine Commandant's House,** designed by George Hadfield and built in the early 1800s, has an unusual double bow-front design.

Three blocks south, on the northern bank of the Anacostia River, is the **Navy Yard** (M Street between 1st and 11th streets), established here in the first decade of the nineteenth century. The **Navy Museum** (Building 76, 202–433–2651) has a large display of ship models, dioramas, weaponry, gun turrets, navigation equipment, uniforms, and other historical exhibits, such as a hut used by Admiral Byrd in the Antarctic and items recovered from the ill-fated Antarctic expedition of Captain Robert F. Scott in 1910. The museum has a fully rigged fighting top from the USS *Constitution,* the deep-diving bathyscaphe *Trieste,* and a submarine room with working periscopes. A two-acre park at the museum displays naval guns. The **Marine Corps Historical Center** (202–433–3534) displays uniforms, weapons, photographs, letters, and other items illustrating the two-century history of the corps. There are special exhibits devoted to the Civil War and the Marine Band, and changing exhibits of combat art.

ANACOSTIA MUSEUM

The Anacostia Museum in the southeastern historic district of Anacostia was first opened in 1967 as an experiment in bringing a museum to the people rather than the people to a museum, and to have a museum of, not just in, a neighborhood. Over the years, however, the Anacostia Museum has expanded its focus to become a national museum devoted to the history and culture of Afro-Americans. In 1987 it moved into a new building better able to serve and house its national scope.

Exhibits cover a vast variety of topics that touch on Afro-America: black churches, the Harlem Renaissance, the Middle Passage, and black aviators among them. Both art and culture are included in the exhibits that are created by the museum staff and often become part of the Smithsonian Institution's traveling exhibition program. The museum also houses a research library on Afro-American art, history, and culture, which is open to scholars.

LOCATION: 1901 Fort Place SE. HOURS: 10–5 Daily. FEE: None. TELEPHONE: 202–357–2700.

CEDAR HILL

Cedar Hill was the home of black human rights leader Frederick Douglass from 1877 until his death in 1895. A former slave, Douglass came to Washington in 1872. He edited the newspaper *New National Era*, served as the District of Columbia's marshall and recorder of deeds, and was named minister to Haiti in 1889. His twenty-one-room house, located on an eight-and-one-half-acre hilltop site with spectacular views of the city, has been restored. Many of Douglass's personal items have been preserved here, including his two-thousand-volume library. A brief film narrates his life as a champion of civil rights.

LOCATION: 1411 W Street, SE. HOURS: April through October: 9–5 Daily; November through March: 9–4 Daily. FEE: None. TELEPHONE: 202–426–5961.

L'Enfant's "Grand Avenue," a mile-long mall lined with museums and monuments, stretches

T   H   E   M   A   L   L

In L'Enfant's plan for the capital he included a mile-long mall, which he called a "Grand Avenue," to be bordered by private houses. Where imaginary lines drawn from the Capitol and the president's house intersected, there was to be a monument to George Washington. But, for eighty years, L'Enfant's Grand Avenue was a muddy, malodorous symbol of official inaction. A guidebook written in the 1840s pointed out "the large tract of waste ground" west of the Capitol. "It is not generally known," the writer continued, "that this is the national mall." The land was so marshy

from the Capitol to the Lincoln Memorial.

in places that the Washington Monument could not be built on its intended spot, lest it topple. When the Lincoln Memorial was proposed, the speaker of the house grumbled that it would be in the middle of "a damned swamp." During his renovation of the city in the early 1870s, Alexander Shepherd neglected the Mall; in fact, he allowed railroad tracks and a depot to be built on it. The unfinished Washington Monument was a national disgrace and the focus of political wrangling until the 1870s. At the start of the twentieth century, the MacMillan Commission did the draining and landscaping necessary to bring dignity, at last, to this stretch of green, now a splendid avenue of museums and memorials.

GRANT MEMORIAL

At the eastern end of the Mall, at the foot of the Capitol lawn, a 250-foot-long sculpture group pays tribute to Ulysses S. Grant. The cavalry group is a vivid tableau of seven horsemen charging into battle. To the south is an artillery group, with three horses hauling cannon through mud. Presiding over this turbulent battle scene is Grant, rendered in a calm pose. The memorial was done by Henry Merwin Shrady, who took immense pains to model the men and horses realistically. He began work in 1901, finished two decades later, and died two weeks before the dedication in April 1922. At the time it was the largest cast sculpture in the country.

NATIONAL GALLERY OF ART

The National Gallery of Art, chartered by Congress in 1937, was the creation of Andrew W. Mellon, a member of the Pittsburgh banking and steel family, who served as secretary of the treasury in the early 1920s. Mellon had collected paintings with the idea of donating them to a national museum, and he encouraged others to do the same. The museum's art works are all gifts from private collectors or are purchased with donated funds, though the museum's operations are funded by the federal government.

The West Building showcases paintings by Italian, Spanish, German, Flemish, Dutch, French, British, and American artists. Many of the greatest European masters are represented—Botticelli, Leonardo da Vinci, Raphael, Titian, El Greco, Vermeer, Rembrandt, Rubens, and Van Dyck. The museum has an exceptional collection of nineteenth-century French works by Manet, Monet, Renoir, Van Gogh, and others. There are galleries devoted to sculpture, French furniture and decorative arts, tapestries, and ecclesiastical arts. The American collection of portraits, landscapes, still lifes, and other works from the eighteenth century to the present includes paintings by John Singleton Copley, Gilbert Stuart, Rembrandt Peale, Thomas Sully, Thomas Cole, John Singer Sargent, Thomas Eakins, and James Abbott McNeill Whistler. A separate gallery displays the Garbisch collection of American folk art paintings of the eighteenth and nineteenth century.

The East Building, which opened in 1978, houses changing exhibitions and the museum's collection of twentieth-century art,

Van Gogh's Farmhouse in Provence, Arles, *1888, from the collection of the National Gallery of Art (detail).*

with sculpture and paintings by Picasso, Matisse, Moore, Calder, Rothko, Pollock, Motherwell, and others.

The classical West Building was designed by John Russell Pope, and the contemporary East Building by I. M. Pei.

LOCATION: 4th Street and Constitution Avenue NW. HOURS: 10–5 Monday–Saturday, 11–6 Sunday. FEE: None. TELEPHONE: 202–737–4215.

SMITHSONIAN INSTITUTION

The Smithsonian administers fourteen museums and galleries in Washington, DC (nine on the Mall), the National Zoo, and the Cooper-Hewitt and American Indian museums in New York. Its museums conduct research and gather collections in the fields of history, natural history, art, technology, the social sciences, aviation, ethnology, and others. This premier institution of American learning owes its existence to an Englishman, James Smithson (1765–1829), who never set foot in America. Illegitimate son of the duke of

Behind the Smithsonian "Castle," the Enid A. Haupt gardens form the roof of the Institution's

Northumberland, Smithson willed his estate of some $550,000 to the United States to found "an establishment for the increase and diffusion of knowledge." "My name," he wrote, "shall live in the memory of man when the titles of the Northumberlands and Percys are extinct and forgotten." After a good deal of disagreement about what precisely should be done with the Smithson bequest, Congress decided to establish, in 1846, an institution to carry out scientific research.

LOCATION: The Mall. HOURS: 10–5:30 Daily. Later in summer; verify by phone. FEE: None. TELEPHONE: 202–357–2700.

new underground National Museum of African Art and Arthur M. Sackler Gallery.

The Smithsonian Building

The Smithsonian's first home was designed by James Renwick, Jr. in the manner of a twelfth-century Italian Romanesque castle. Built in 1855, the Renwick building, popularly called the "Castle," originally housed laboratories, offices, a lecture hall, art gallery, and science museum. Scientists conducting research at the Smithsonian were offered living quarters in the tower. The institution's first secretary, Joseph Henry, moved his family into the second floor and carried on research concerning electricity and magnetism, which he applied to the design of electromagnets, electric meters, and the telegraph. When Samuel F. B. Morse demonstrated the first telegraph, Henry immediately realized its application to weather forecasting. He organized a network of 150 weather observers, who telegraphed weather data to the Smithsonian. Since weather usually moves from the west, the western observers were sometimes able to alert the eastern and northern regions to approaching storms. When dangerous weather patterns were observed, officials flashed warning signals to coastal authorities from the Smithsonian tower. Henry's network inspired the formation of the U.S. Weather Bureau.

The building now houses many of the offices of the institution and the Woodrow Wilson International Center for Scholars. Just inside the Mall entrance is the tomb of James Smithson, with exhibits about his life.

Arts and Industries Building

The red brick and Ohio sandstone building, designed by the Washington firm of Cluss and Schulze in a High Victorian style, opened in 1881, just in time for the inaugural ball of President James A. Garfield. It was built to house exhibits that had been displayed at the Centennial Exposition in Philadelphia, and the name of the building refers to the theme of the exposition. In the nation's bicentennial year, 1976, the museum was partially restored to its original appearance.

Above the entrance, a statue depicts the figure of Columbia protecting the seated figures of Science and Industry. In the rotunda, a fountain surrounded by plants provides a serene setting. Some of the interior preserves the appearance of the Centennial period. Prominent exhibitions included presentations mounted by the National Museum of the American Indian and the Center for African American History and Culture. Programs for young children are given at the Discovery Theater.

Hirshhorn Museum and Sculpture Garden

The collector Joseph Hirshhorn donated his extensive collection of nineteenth- and twentieth-century art to the Smithsonian in 1966. Although Hirshhorn focused his efforts on modern art, he also gathered significant works by painters Thomas Eakins and John Singer Sargent. European artists represented in the museum include Rodin, Degas, Matisse, Picasso, Giacometti, Miro, and

Balthus. Hirshhorn's collection of sculpture is displayed on an outdoor plaza and in a sculpture garden.

National Air and Space Museum

Twenty-three areas of exhibits trace the history of aviation. In the museum's dramatically designed galleries, aircraft hang overhead on wires, as if in flight. Films shown on large screens portray the history of flight and convey a sense of adventure.

The Smithsonian Institution has long had an interest in flight. Its third secretary, Samuel P. Langley, was himself an inventor of experimental aircraft in the 1890s. Spanning an exciting century, exhibits feature aircraft and spacecraft that are landmarks in aviation history. In this gallery are the Langley Aerodrome #5, designed by Samuel P. Langley, that made a ninety-second, unmanned flight in 1896; the Wright Brothers' craft, in which Orville Wright made the first manned flight at Kitty Hawk in 1903; and Charles Lindbergh's plane, the *Spirit of St. Louis*, in which he made his historic solo flight across the Atlantic. The U.S. space program

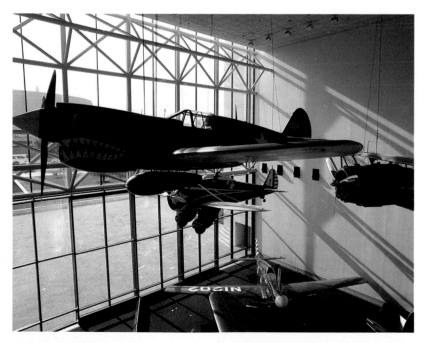

A Curtiss P-40E War Hawk bares its teeth in the National Air and Space Museum's gallery, Milestones of Flight.

is represented by a host of exhibits, including *Friendship 7,* in which John Glenn became the first American to orbit the earth in 1962, and the *Apollo 11* command module that brought Neil Armstrong and his crew back from the first moon landing.

Other galleries display the *Apollo–Soyuz* spacecraft that carried American and Soviet astronauts; a Minuteman ICBM; and a World War II German V-2 rocket. The gallery on jet aviation also displays an example of World War II-era technology, the Messerschmitt Me 262, along with later developments of the jet. Among the displays of helicopters and their precursors, the autogiros, is a Pitcairn AC-35, designed in 1935 with blades that fold back so that the craft could function as both car and autogiro. Aerial espionage photographs are displayed along with a U-2 spy plane. A rocketry and space-flight gallery traces the development of rocket engines, space suits, and other space technologies. Other galleries are devoted to World Wars I and II, naval aircraft, balloons and airships, the *Apollo* moon landing program, and other facets of air and space history. Visitors may touch a moon rock. The museum's Paul E. Garber Facility in Suitland, Maryland can also be toured.

National Museum of Natural History

Opened in 1911, the museum has collected over 121 million items in the broad categories of anthropology and natural history, which include fossils, meteorites, minerals and gems, stuffed and live animals, and a wide range of art and artifacts from around the world. Exhibits are augmented by dioramas, films, and murals. The museum building, erected in 1910, centers on a rotunda that displays a thirteen-foot-high, mounted African elephant.

Portions of the museum's large fossil collection are displayed in a series of galleries. There are exhibits on ancient marine life and the development of seeds, flowers, and trees. The dinosaur area includes an eighty-foot-long skeleton unearthed in Utah in the 1920s. From the Ice Age, a 28,000-year-old bison found frozen in Alaska, a saber-toothed cat found in the LaBrea tar pits in Los Angeles, a mastodon, and a mammoth are all on exhibit.

The hall of Eskimo and Indian cultures preserves an Arapaho teepee made from buffalo hides, a canoe made from bark, lacrosse sticks, pottery, and other artifacts. Dioramas recreate scenes from the daily life of various Indian cultures.

OPPOSITE: *An African elephant greets visitors to the Smithsonian's National Museum of Natural History.*

From the collection of the National Museum of American History: Above, engraved American glassware made near Frederick, Maryland, ca. 1785. Below, an 1890 tri-color camera that produced color pictures through three simultaneous exposures with three colored filters.

Top, the printing telegraph, patented in 1873 by inventor Thomas Edison. Bottom, three Islamic astrolabes and a Persian Qibla indicator, used to determine the position of the holder, the stars, and Mecca.

A series of rooms display art and artifacts from cultures of the Pacific, Asia, and Africa. Some Pacific items were gathered on the famous U.S. Exploring Expedition of 1838 to 1842, led by Charles Wilkes. The most imposing exhibit is a huge stone head from Easter Island. An exhibition on African history and culture opened in 1997. Clothing, sculpture, ceremonial objects, and crafts illustrate the life, rituals, and achievements of the world's cultures.

The hall devoted to marine life features two aquariums containing plants and animals, one from the Maine coast, the other a Caribbean coral reef. There are models of sharks, porpoises, and, hanging from the ceiling, a blue whale over ninety feet long.

The hall of gems contains stones distinguished for their size and beauty, including the most famous in the world, the blue "Hope Diamond," believed to have been cut from an even larger Indian gem stolen in 1792. The hall of minerals displays nuggets from the 1849 California gold rush, and a gallery devoted to geology explains volcanoes and earthquakes, and displays meteorites and moon rocks.

The ancient cultures of Mesopotamia, Egypt, the Aegean region, and Rome are represented in the museum through royal artifacts, mummies, and art objects.

National Museum of American History

This museum's most impressive display is just inside its Mall entrance: the original "Star-Spangled Banner" that flew over Baltimore's Fort McHenry while Francis Scott Key watched its bombardment. The morning after the bombardment, Key wrote the patriotic song that became the national anthem. In order to preserve it, the flag is kept behind a curtain that is lowered for two minutes every hour on the half hour to reveal the flag. This "second" floor is devoted to social and cultural history, the first to the history of science and technology, the third to other national collections such as stamps, coins, and musical instruments.

Also on the second floor is the exhibition entitled "After the Revolution: Everyday Life in America 1780–1800," which examines the daily life of American families: On display are furnished rooms from their houses, and objects associated with blacks, Indians, and a diversity of white families from such communities as Longmeadow, Massachusetts and Isle of Wight County, Virginia.

This exhibit, along with "Field to Factory" across the rotunda, reflects the museum's emphasis on the lives of ordinary Americans.

On the first floor, "Engines of Change" traces the development of the American Industrial Revolution from 1790 to 1860 through some 250 artifacts. Notable is the John Bull locomotive, the world's oldest self-propelled vehicle still in operating condition, imported from England in 1831. Also on display are tools, parts of a sawmill, a re-created clockmaker's shop, and items sent from the U.S. to the first world's fair, held in London in 1851. Entries include a piano, an artificial leg, and a McCormick reaper, the machine that helped make large-scale farming practical.

The **East Wing**'s first floor has exhibits on early machinery, maritime history, railroads, automobiles, and clocks. On the third, among the military and naval items on display, are George Washington's uniform and camp gear, a Revolutionary War gunboat that sank in 1776 and was raised in 1935, and an exhibition called "A More Perfect Union," about the internment and military heroism of Japanese Americans during the Second World War.

The third floor of the **West Wing** houses collections of musical instruments, ceramics, glass, and a variety of items illustrating the history of communications, such as newspapers, photographs, cameras, stamps, and televisions.

Freer Gallery of Art

Charles Lang Freer (1854–1919) made his fortune manufacturing railroad cars and was also an avid collector of art. He particularly admired the work of James Abbott McNeill Whistler and befriended the artist. Under Whistler's influence Freer began to collect Oriental art. He donated his collection to the Smithsonian, providing funds for a Renaissance-style museum building that opened in 1921. The museum's renowned collection of Asian art includes bronzes, ceramics, and paintings. The museum's other theme is the career of Whistler: Well over a thousand of his prints, pastels, oils, and watercolors are housed in the Freer. The centerpiece of the Whistler collection is the magnificent Peacock Room, named for the peacocks Whistler painted in turquoise and gold. Whistler designed the room for the home of a Liverpool businessman and called it *Harmony in Blue and Gold*. The **Arthur M. Sackler Gallery**, linked to the Freer by an underground passage, displays Chinese bronzes, jades, lacquerware, metalwork, and paintings.

The National Museum of African Art and the Arthur M. Sackler Gallery

This building is primarily below ground. It is topped with six copper domes and a copper roof, and is paved with "Columbia Pink" granite flooring. All the architectural detail in the National Museum of African Art is circular or curvilinear, in contrast to the Sackler Gallery's angular design. The African museum emphasizes traditional arts of Africa south of the Sahara, both ancient and contemporary, created in wood, metal, ceramics, cloth, and ivory. Exhibits in the Sackler Gallery trace the development of Asian and Near Eastern arts from ancient to contemporary times. Beautiful works by living artists share space with wondrous discoveries at archaeological digs. Asian culture is celebrated in dance and music, and in films and theatrical performances.

Cotton wrapper, Ghana, from the National Museum of African Art.

Contemporary account of the 3,300 pound capstone set into place on the Washington Monument, December 6, 1884.

WASHINGTON MONUMENT

At just over 555 feet in height, the Washington Monument is the tallest masonry structure in the world. The monument bears little resemblance to the original design by Robert Mills, who envisioned a high shaft (but not an obelisk), encircled by a shrine 100 feet high and 250 feet in diameter.

Congress refused to appropriate money for the project but allowed the private Washington National Monument Society to take over. The cornerstone was laid in 1848 with the same trowel George Washington had used to lay the cornerstone of the Capitol. Volunteers hauled the cornerstone from the navy yard to

the site, singing "Hail, Columbia" and "Yankee Doodle," but fund-raising lagged. States were asked to donate funds; Alabama offered to send a stone instead, and the society then solicited other blocks for the interior, engraved with tributes.

A block sent by Pope Pius IX was stolen by anti-Catholic "Know Nothings" of the American Party in 1854. The latter took control of the project in 1855, but their inept management halted construction. For twenty years the shaft stood unfinished at 150 feet, sharing space with a government slaughterhouse.

In 1876, Congress appropriated $200,000 to finish the monument. The shaft had tilted because the foundation was unsound. Engineers laid a new, thirteen-foot-thick concrete foundation beneath the old one, pulled down the courses laid by the Know Nothings, and resumed laying the marble. At the urging of the U.S. minister in Rome, George Marsh, builders scrapped the Mills plan for a colonnade at the base. Up rose a simple, dignified obelisk, built according to measurements sent from Rome by Marsh, who presumably commissioned a measurement of an obelisk there. The first builders had used Maryland marble. Massachusetts marble was used for twenty-six feet, then builders reverted to Maryland stone. The marbles weathered to different tones, creating a ring where work resumed. The monument was capped in 1884 with an 8.9-inch-high pyramid of aluminum (then a rare commodity) and with platinum lightning rods. Inside, by the 898 steps, are 189 tribute blocks sent by states, nations, organizations, and localities.

KOREAN WAR VETERANS MEMORIAL

Nineteen men, dressed for battle, move cautiously forward. They appear to be on patrol, ready to fight at any moment. But they are not alive; the figures are made of stainless steel. They are the centerpiece of the memorial, which occupies 2.2 acres by the Lincoln Memorial Reflecting Pool. Some 54,000 Americans died in the so-called Forgotten War (1950–1953). A 164-foot granite wall bears the words, "Freedom is not free," and is etched with photographic images of nurses, mechanics, chaplains, and other support personnel who backed up the fighting men.

OPPOSITE: *The Washington Monument. The break in the color of the stone marks the pause in its construction between 1855 and 1876.*

A portion of the Vietnam Memorial, inscribed with the names of the more than 58,000 Americans killed or missing in the Vietnam War. OPPOSITE: *The Lincoln Memorial.*

VIETNAM VETERANS MEMORIAL

The memorial to the 58,202 Americans killed or missing in the Vietnam War is a broad V of black marble, inscribed with the names of the dead and missing. Dedicated in 1982, it was designed by an architectural student, Maya Lin, whose plan was chosen in a competition. A bronze sculpture by Frederick Hart depicts three servicemen. The **Vietnam Women's Memorial,** in a nearby grove of trees, consists of a bronze statue of three servicewomen aiding a wounded soldier.

LINCOLN MEMORIAL

Two years after Lincoln's assassination, Congress explored the possibility of building a memorial, but the idea languished. It was not until 1911, some fifty years later, that a memorial commission under President Taft selected a site—in the middle of a swamp—and an architect, Henry Bacon. Bacon's plan called for a flat-roofed Greek temple of white Colorado marble, surrounded by thirty-six Doric columns. The sculptor Daniel Chester French

fashioned one of the most famous monumental images in America, a nineteen-foot-high figure of the president seated, grasping the arms of his chair, his face slightly downcast. Stone carvers worked for four years to fashion the statue from twenty blocks of Georgia marble. The ceiling panels, treated with beeswax, are translucent, and seem to glow softly in strong sunlight.

Bronze plaques inscribed with Lincoln's Gettysburg Address and his second inaugural speech are in the north and south halls, with Jules Guerin's murals of *Emancipation* and *Reunion*. The memorial played a part in race relations. The 1922 dedication ceremony was segregated; even Booker T. Washington, who gave a speech, had to watch from a roped-off section. In 1939 the black contralto Marion Anderson sang at the memorial for 75,000 after she had been prevented from appearing at Constitution Hall by the Daughters of the American Revolution. In 1963, Dr. Martin Luther King, Jr., gave his "I Have a Dream" speech on the memorial steps. At the edge of the Tidal Basin, the **Franklin Delano Roosevelt Memorial**, occupying 7.5 acres of statues, waterfalls, gardens, and alcoves, was opened in 1997. Four open-air rooms depict FDR at different stages of his life. One sculpture show unemployed people in a bread line during the Great Depression; another evokes the president's role as leader of the fight against fascism during World War II. Eleanor Roosevelt is present, as well as the president's pet dog Fala. Disabled Americans complained that Roosevelt should be shown in a wheelchair, which he used for the last 23 years of his life after being stricken by polio.

THOMAS JEFFERSON MEMORIAL

The capital's memorial to the third president and the author of the Declaration of Independence is a domed and colonnaded enclosure with a nineteen-foot-high statue of Jefferson by Rudolph Evans. It was dedicated April 13, 1943 by President Franklin Delano Roosevelt. The design by John Russell Pope echoes the domes Jefferson placed on his own house, Monticello, and on the rotunda of the University of Virginia (as well as Pope's for the National Gallery). The walls of the memorial bear excerpts from the two documents for which Jefferson most wanted to be remembered, the Declaration of Independence and the Virginia Statute for Religious Freedom.

The Jefferson Memorial. The sculpture is by Rudolph Evans.

THE WHITE HOUSE

The White House has been the official residence of the president since November 1, 1800, when the second chief executive, John Adams, moved into the unfinished building. Although universally known as the White House, the building was first called the President's House, and later the Executive Mansion. Not until Theodore Roosevelt's administration in 1901 did the name "White House" appear on presidential stationery.

Construction began in 1792. At Thomas Jefferson's suggestion, a competition was held to design the house. The commissioners in charge wrote that they desired "a grandeur of conception, a Republican simplicity, and . . . true Elegance of proportion." (Under the pseudonym "A.Z.," Jefferson himself may have submitted a

The South Portico of the White House, the official residence of the president of the United States.

proposal inspired by a sixteenth-century Italian villa by Palladio, the Villa Capra Rotunda.) The winner was James Hoban, an Irishman who had emigrated to this country in the early 1780s, whose design was based partly on Leinster House and other eighteenth-century houses in or near Dublin.

Early occupants considered it to be large; Abigail Adams remarked upon its "grand and superb scale." Jefferson found it expedient to suggest that he thought it "big enough for two emperors, one Pope, and the grand lama," though his own recommendations for public buildings were equally grand. The White House entertainments of Dolley Madison earned her the reputation as the most gracious of Washington's hostesses. It was said that "her bonhomie could not be surpassed." She also possessed courage: In August 1814, during the War of 1812, as an invading British column approached the capital, she supervised the hasty packing of official papers and what few personal possessions she could gather. As the sounds of enemy cannon fire grew nearer, she delayed her escape until a Gilbert Stuart portrait of George Washington could be cut away from its frame and packed. (The picture is seen today in the East Room.)

The British set fire to the building; although a heavy rain-storm put out the fire, the building had been gutted. After the war, under Latrobe's direction and with Hoban as contractor, it was rebuilt. President Monroe purchased new furnishings in France, some of which are still at the White House today.

The First Families of the nineteenth century decorated the White House in the prevailing styles of their times, adding creature comforts brought about by advancing technology: Thomas Jefferson built two waterclosets upstairs; Andrew Jackson installed the plumbing for running water; James K. Polk put in gas lights; Martin Van Buren installed central heating; Rutherford B. Hayes a typewriter and telephone; James A. Garfield the first elevator; and Benjamin Harrison introduced electric lights.

Modernization of the building, always performed with haste and employing shortcuts, weakened its structure, as supporting floor beams were burrowed through to make way for pipes and electrical conduits. Because the house was not only the president's home, but his office as well, the building endured the stress of hundreds of daily visitors. Beginning in 1867, various plans were suggested for expanding the building, or demolishing it to make way for a larger one. But when Theodore Roosevelt took office in 1901 he declared flatly, "the President should live nowhere else than in the historic White House."

Mrs. Roosevelt asked Charles McKim of McKim, Mead & White to examine the building and make recommendations. Appalled by the deterioration he found, McKim undertook a hasty renovation of the structure and a revision of the rooms to give them the appearance of the early 1800s. McKim moved the grand staircase to enlarge the State Dining Room and stripped away Victorian ornamentation, such as frescoes and encaustic tile floors. He greatly enhanced the Neoclassicism of James Hoban's original decorative scheme. At the same time, McKim's firm added an office structure to the West Wing so that the White House proper was thenceforth reserved for residential and ceremonial purposes.

In 1923 President Coolidge spurned a half-million-dollar request to repair the dangerous roof: "If it's as bad as you say it is, why doesn't it fall down?" Finally President Truman was persuaded of the need for large-scale repairs. From 1948 to 1952 a massive rebuilding project involved disassembling the rooms and gutting the building. The interior was then pieced together over a steel structural frame. Mamie Eisenhower conceived the idea of furnishing the house with antiques. In the early 1960s Jacqueline Kennedy

The Red Room, a state reception room.

again restored the interior along historical lines and brought to reality the idea of filling the state rooms with appropriate antiques and reproductions.

The state interiors of the White House have been open to the public since 1801. Today there are two types of tours: The regular tours encompass rooms on the first floor (the East Room, Green Room, Blue Room, Red Room, State Dining Room, and the entrance hall); the V.I.P. tour includes, in addition, ground-floor rooms: the library, Vermeil Room, China Room, the Diplomatic Reception Room, and the groin-vaulted corridor.

The **East Room** was redecorated in 1902 with a parquet floor and classical pilasters and plasterwork. The color scheme of gold and white was chosen by McKim and Mrs. Roosevelt. In Hoban's plan it was called "the Audience Chamber," and it still serves as the room for large public functions and entertainments. In Jefferson's administration this was the living quarters of his secretary, Meriwether Lewis, later the famed explorer of the West. The

The Blue Room, decorated in the Empire style, with the Green Room beyond.

bodies of Abraham Lincoln and four other presidents have lain in state here. The room contains the portrait rescued by Dolley Madison of George Washington by Gilbert Stuart. The room also has a striking portrait of Theodore Roosevelt by John Singer Sargent.

The **Green Room,** decorated today as a Federal-style parlor, features early nineteenth-century New York furniture by Duncan Phyfe, Chinese export porcelain, and one of three marble mantels ordered by President Monroe, who used it as a card room. It was named the "Green Drawing Room" during the tenure of John Quincy Adams. Among the art works on display are a 1767 portrait of Benjamin Franklin painted in Paris by David Martin, portraits of John Quincy Adams and his wife by Gilbert Stuart, and George Caleb Bingham's painting *Lighter Relieving a Steamboat Aground.*

The **corridor colonnade** displays changing exhibits of White House memorabilia, as well as fine examples of American furniture, including chairs designed by the Salem, Massachusetts architect, Samuel McIntire. The **Library** is a panelled room decorated in early nineteenth-century style, featuring portraits of five Indian chiefs who visited President Monroe in 1822 and shelves holding first editions of books given to the president by writers and publishers. The furnishings include chairs by Duncan Phyfe, a chandelier that belonged to the family of James Fenimore Cooper, and a pair of Argand lamps given to General Henry Knox by Lafayette.

The **Vermeil Room** is named for its display of gilded silver dating from the Renaissance to the early twentieth century, presented to the White House in 1956. A French marble mantel and Turkish rug both date to 1830. Also on display here is a drawing by Jean-Honoré Fragonard, *The Apotheosis of Franklin,* an allegorical work in which Avarice and Tyranny are routed.

The **China Room** was set aside in 1917 by Edith Galt Wilson to display the china collection started in 1889 by Caroline Harrison. The **Diplomatic Reception Room** is an oval room furnished in the manner of an early nineteenth-century drawing room, with a scenic wallpaper depicting the American landscape in the 1830s.

The **Blue Room,** also an oval reception room, has been decorated in the Empire style to recall the French furnishings ordered in 1817 by Monroe and auctioned by President Buchanan in 1860. Of the original group, a settee and seven chairs remain. There are portraits of John Adams (1793) by John Trumbull, Thomas Jefferson (1800) by Rembrandt Peale, Andrew Jackson (1819) by John Wesley Jarvis, and John Tyler (1859) by George P. A. Healey, as well as views of the harbors of Boston and Baltimore painted in the 1850s by Fitz Hugh Lane.

The **Red Room,** used for state receptions, also features Empire-style furnishings made between 1810 and 1830 by the New York cabinetmaker Charles-Honoré Lannuier. Hanging are an 1804 Gilbert Stuart portrait of Dolley Madison and Albert Bierstadt's 1870 *View of the Rocky Mountains.*

The **State Dining Room** was enlarged to its present size in the 1902 renovation. It features a large portrait of Lincoln, painted four years after the president's death, by George P. A. Healey. The style of the room is predominantly Neoclassical, but the stone mantel is decorated with a pair of carved bison heads, requested by Theodore Roosevelt to replace the original lion's heads.

LOCATION: 1600 Pennsylvania Avenue. HOURS: 10–12 Tuesday–Saturday. FEE: None. TELEPHONE: 202–456–7041.

DAUGHTERS OF THE AMERICAN REVOLUTION

Just west of the White House ellipse stands the massive Beaux-Arts Memorial Constitution Hall, part of the National Society Daughters of the American Revolution's headquarters complex, and home of the DAR's Decorative Arts Collection. The collection, started in 1890 by the Revolutionary Relics Committee, now comprises more than 30,000 objects that reflect the culture and craftsmanship of the country's formative age. The museum gallery also houses an outstanding collection of ceramics and silver used in America and features changing exhibitions on a variety of topics and themes.

Aside from displays in the gallery, there are thirty-three **period rooms** furnished by individual states to evoke distinct regional styles throughout U.S. history. Examples include a whaling station parlor indicative of Monterey, California; an Oklahoma kitchen of nineteenth-century conveniences; and New Jersey's room, framed with timbers of the British frigate *Augusta*.

DAR Headquarters also houses the Americana Room, containing a collection of more than five thousand historical documents and imprints on early America and the DAR. The DAR library of genealogy and local history occupies the Society's original meeting hall. It is open to the public and contains much unique material on American family history in 140,000 books, a quarter of a million files, and a microform collection. A historical research library specializes in references on the Revolutionary era and DAR history.

Sunday. *Period rooms* 10–3 Monday–Friday, 1–5 Sunday. FEE: None. TELEPHONE: 202–879–3241.

CORCORAN GALLERY OF ART

Founded in 1859, the Corcoran Gallery is among the oldest art museums in the country, housing one of the finest collections of American art from the Colonial period to the latest works by contemporary artists. Originally in the building now known as the Renwick Gallery, the Corcoran moved in 1897 to its present marble, Beaux-Arts-style building designed by Ernest Flagg. This private museum was founded by William Wilson Corcoran, who had established the Riggs Bank in Washington. Corcoran himself collected a wide range of American art, augmented in 1925 by the donation of Senator William A. Clark's collection of European art. Among the notable American painters represented in the collection are John Singleton Copley, Gilbert Stuart, Rembrandt Peale, Thomas Sully, Samuel F. B. Morse, Frederic E. Church, John Singer Sargent, Thomas Eakins, and Winslow Homer. Also displayed is Hiram Power's once-controversial statue, *The Greek Slave*.

LOCATION: 17th Street NW and New York Avenue. HOURS: 10–5 Wednesday–Monday, 10–9 Thursday. FEE: Donation. TELEPHONE: 202–638–3211.

OLD EXECUTIVE OFFICE BUILDING

One of the grandest of the capital's nineteenth-century government buildings, the Old Executive Office Building was finished in 1888. At the time, it was the city's largest structure, and one of the country's most exuberant expressions of the Beaux-Arts style. Originally it housed cabinet offices, but today it is used mainly by the president's staff. The interior was lavishly decorated by an Austrian architect, Richard von Ezdorf. The building's finest room is probably the Indian Treaty Room, elaborately ornamented with Italian marble, tiles, and wrought iron. It was the scene of hundreds of historic signings, although none were with Indian tribes.

LOCATION: Pennsylvania Avenue and 17th Street NW. HOURS: Tours by appointment, Saturday morning. FEE: None. TELEPHONE: 202–395–5895.

RENWICK GALLERY

Designed by James Renwick in 1859 and completed in 1874, the building was erected to house the Corcoran Gallery, the first private art museum in the city. Renwick's design was in the Second Empire style, with curved mansard roofs. Inside, William Wilson Corcoran's collection of paintings and statuary was exhibited in plush surroundings. A large stairway ascends from the first floor to the Grand Salon, now refurbished. The Octagon Room was designed to exhibit a sculpture by Hiram Powers called *The Greek Slave*. Considered shocking in its day, the statue of a nude woman with her wrists enchained (now housed at the new Corcoran Gallery) was viewed by men and women separately. The Corcoran

OPPOSITE: *A portion of the facade of the Renwick Gallery, from 1873 to 1897 home to the collection of W. W. Corcoran.*

RUBENS

moved down the street in the 1890s, and the building was used by
the U.S. Court of Claims. The restored Renwick Gallery is now part
of the Smithsonian Institution and is devoted to the decorative arts
and crafts. Changing exhibits of twentieth-century American art
are presented regularly, and the Grand Salon displays nineteenth-
century paintings of the type Corcoran collected.

LOCATION: Pennsylvania Avenue and 17th Street NW. HOURS:
10–5:30 Daily. FEE: None. TELEPHONE: 202–357–2531.

LAFAYETTE SQUARE

When the White House was completed, it stood virtually alone;
facing it on its northern side were a farmhouse, barn, orchard, and
a family burying ground. The first building to go up nearby was
Latrobe's St. John's Church in 1816, followed two years later by
another Latrobe design, Stephen Decatur's house. Lafayette
Square, a seven-acre park with beautiful plantings, was originally
known as President's Square. It was renamed for the French war
hero in 1825 when he made a tour of the country, visiting every
state in the Union, and collecting gifts of land and cash over an
eighteen-month period.

There are five statues in the park, one honoring Andrew
Jackson (at the center) and, at the corners, four heroes·of the
Revolution who had come from Europe to aid the American cause:
Lafayette, Rochambeau, von Steuben, and Kosciuszko. The Jack-
son statue, cast in 1853, was the first equestrian statue made in the
U.S. It was considered a marvel in its day because the sculptor,
Clark Mills, had been able to balance the figure of a rearing horse
on its hind legs. The houses bordering the park have been occupied by some of the capital's most distinguished residents: Stephen
Decatur, Dolley Madison, Henry Clay, Daniel Webster, Henry Adams, John Hay, and various foreign ambassadors. On the night
Lincoln was shot, Secretary of State Seward was stabbed, not fatally, by one of John Wilkes Booth's co-conspirators in a boarding
house that no longer stands. This tour of the buildings around the
park moves clockwise from the southeastern corner.

The **Blair-Lee House** (1651 Pennsylvania Avenue, private),
built in 1824, was purchased in 1836 by Francis Preston Blair, a
friend of Andrew Jackson. In this house Robert E. Lee was offered
the command of the Union armies by Montgomery Blair, a close
advisor of Lincoln, just after the outbreak of the Civil War. Torn by

conflicting loyalties, Lee refused and later took command of Virginia's forces. The government-owned house is used for visiting dignitaries.

Decatur House

The eminent naval hero Stephen Decatur built this house with prize money he won fighting the Barbary pirates and the British. It was designed by Benjamin Henry Latrobe. Two floors of the house are open to the public, with six restored rooms. The first-floor decor reflects the Federal period when the Decaturs were in residence. There are several items that belonged to Decatur on display, such as a ceremonial sword and a punch bowl presented to Decatur's father. The second floor is refurbished in Victorian style, as it was when occupied by the Beale family. Beale was the man who spread the news of the California gold discovery across the nation.

Victorian parlor in the Decatur House.

At the age of 25, Decatur performed "the most bold and daring act of the age," in the words of British Admiral Lord Nelson. On the night of February 16, 1804, Decatur piloted a ketch with seventy volunteers into Tripoli harbor and set fire to the captured American warship *Philadelphia,* so that it could not be used against the U.S. During the War of 1812, Decatur captured the British ship *Macedonian* after an hour-long battle.

Decatur and his wife, Susan, lived in their new house for only fourteen months. In 1820 Decatur was shot in a duel with Commodore James Barron, who maintained that Decatur had hindered his naval career. Decatur, wounded in the abdomen, was carried back to his house from Bladensburg, Maryland, and died after a day of agony. At the time of his death he was one of the most admired men in the country; Congress adjourned for his funeral. Susan Decatur, left impoverished at her husband's death, moved to Georgetown, and this house was occupied by the French ambassador and his wife, the Baron and Baroness Hyde de Neuville.

LOCATION: 748 Jackson Place. HOURS: 10–2 Tuesday–Friday, 12–4 Saturday–Sunday. FEE: Yes. TELEPHONE: 202–842–0920.

At the north end of the square, the **Hay-Adams Hotel** stands on the site of houses built for Henry Adams and John Hay by Henry Hobson Richardson in 1885. Hay served as secretary of state under both William McKinley and Theodore Roosevelt. Adams, a descendant of the two Adams presidents, was a historian and the author of *The Education of Henry Adams,* and a monumental history of the administrations of Thomas Jefferson and James Madison.

St. John's Church is known as the church of the presidents: Every president from Madison to Clinton has attended services here. (President Kennedy, as a Roman Catholic, did not actually participate in religious services but did visit the church.) Not only did Latrobe design the building, he also played the organ and sang in the choir. He was quite pleased with the building, writing in a letter that, "I have just completed a church that made many Washingtonians religious who had not been religious before." The bell was cast from captured British cannon. The adjacent parish house was built in the 1820s and served as the British Embassy.

Two private buildings, the **Cutts Madison House** and **Benjamin Ogle Tayloe House,** both dating to the 1820s, face the eastern side of the park on Madison Place. After President Madison's death, the Cutts Madison House was given to Dolley Madison by her brother-in-law, in payment of a debt.

The **Treasury Annex** at the southeastern corner of the park was built in 1919 by Cass Gilbert, who also designed the **United States Chamber of Commerce** building (1925) at the northwestern corner. In his designs for these buildings, Gilbert echoed the style of the Treasury Building.

TREASURY BUILDING

Next door to the White House stands the Treasury Building, occupied by the Department of the Treasury, which manages all aspects of national finances, from regulating the banking system to providing security protection for the president. Designed by Robert Mills in the Greek Revival style, it was built over the years 1836 to 1869 on the site of two former Treasury buildings destroyed by fire. Its four wings are of granite, though the original east wing was

One of the seventy-four granite columns raised into position for the Treasury Building in 1861. The construction took thirty-three years to complete.

of sandstone, replaced in 1910 with granite to match the subsequent wings. A statue of Alexander Hamilton, the first secretary of the treasury, stands in front of the entrance to the south wing; a statue of Albert Gallatin, the fourth and longest serving secretary of the treasury, stands at the north wing entrance.

As part of a project to restore the building to its 1860–1880 style, the Cash Room, originally built as a bank, has been restored to the marble, plaster, and gilt splendor that surrounded statesmen when Ulysses S. Grant held his inaugural ball there in 1869. In contrast to the tenor of Grant's gala, the building had been used as barracks for the Union Army during the Civil War. For two months after Lincoln's assassination, Andrew Johnson used offices in the building as his presidential headquarters. Throughout, the offices are home to an impressive collection of WPA oil paintings and works on paper; in the corridors hang portraits of all the secretaries of the treasury.

LOCATION: Pennsylvania Avenue and 15th Street NW. HOURS: Guided tours by reservation only. FEE: None. TELEPHONE: 202–622–2000.

Facing each other across 15th Street are two memorials to war heroes, **Pershing Park,** honoring General John J. Pershing, who led U.S. forces in World War I, and the **Sherman Monument,** commemorating the Civil War general, William Tecumseh Sherman. The statue, by Carl Rohl-Smith, is on the spot where Sherman stood in 1865 to review his victorious army.

FEDERAL TRIANGLE

Bounded by Pennsylvania Avenue, Constitution Avenue, and 15th Street NW, Federal Triangle is the site of nine government buildings erected in the 1930s, the District Building (1908), and the **Old Post Office Building** (1899). The Post Office was supposed to have been demolished in the 1930s as part of the Triangle's master plan, but lack of funds saved the grand Romanesque structure from the wrecker's ball. Today it is a complex of offices and shops. The only significant historic site in the Triangle is the **National Archives** (8th Street NW and Constitution Avenue, 202–501–5000), that displays the original Declaration of Independence, the Constitution, and the Bill of Rights.

OPPOSITE: *The National Archives, keeper of the country's heritage.*

FORD'S THEATER

President Lincoln was shot here at 10:15 PM on April 14, 1865, by John Wilkes Booth. He was watching a performance of a comedy, *Our American Cousin*. After shooting the president, who was sitting in the box at the right of the stage, Booth leapt down to the stage, caught his spur in the flag that draped the presidential box, and broke a bone in his leg. Shouting, "*Sic semper tyrannis!*" ("Thus always to tyrants!"), he made his escape on a horse waiting for him by the stage door. The president, wounded in the head, was tended by a young surgeon in the audience, Dr. Charles A. Leale, who ordered Lincoln carried to the nearby Petersen house rather than risk further injury in a carriage ride to the White House over rough mud streets. Booth outlived the president by only eleven days. He was shot in Port Royal, Virginia and died on April 26.

The theater was purchased by the government shortly after the assassination and used as offices and as the Army Medical Museum. It was restored in the 1960s. Box 7, where Lincoln was shot, has reproductions of the furniture, including the president's rocking chair, there on the night of the shooting. Also on exhibit are the murder weapon (a single-shot derringer), the flag that covered Lincoln's coffin, and other items associated with the president, such as the clothing he was wearing when he was shot, a life mask, some of his books, and personal memorabilia.

LOCATION: 511 Tenth Street NW. HOURS: 9–5 Daily. FEE: None. TELEPHONE: 202–426–6924.

PETERSEN HOUSE

Lincoln died in this house at 7:22 the morning after he was shot. The house belonged to a German immigrant named William Petersen, a tailor who ran it as a boarding house. The ground-floor bedroom where Lincoln died has been restored, along with the front parlor where Mrs. Lincoln waited through the night, and the back parlor where Secretary of War Edwin Stanton interviewed witnesses to the shooting. The government purchased the house in 1896. It was first restored in the 1930s.

LOCATION: 516 Tenth Street NW. HOURS: 9–5 Daily. FEE: None. TELEPHONE: 202–426–6924.

Two American artists, Mary Cassatt in a self-portrait, left, and John James Audubon, right, from the collection of the National Portrait Gallery (both details).

NATIONAL PORTRAIT GALLERY

The National Portrait Gallery, established in 1962, displays an enormous range of portraiture. The collection is both an artistic and historical treasure house, displaying sculptures, paintings, and photographs of men and women who have contributed to American political, military, scientific, and cultural developments. The second floor houses the famous Gilbert Stuart portraits of George and Martha Washington (exhibited on an alternating basis with the Museum of Fine Arts in Boston) as well as the Hall of Presidents, with portraits of every chief executive from George Washington to the incumbent; two galleries of eighteenth- and nineteenth-century leaders in government, the military, law, literature, and the arts; halls of explorers, scientists, and inventors; and the Meserve Gallery, which displays a large collection of Mathew Brady's photographs. The gallery is a part of the Smithsonian Institution.

LOCATION: 8th and F streets NW. HOURS: 10–5:30 Daily. FEE: None. TELEPHONE: 202–357–2700.

NATIONAL MUSEUM OF AMERICAN ART

The National Museum of American Art houses a collection of paintings, sculpture, photographs, prints, and other works dating from colonial times to the present. Its early paintings include works by John Singleton Copley, Benjamin West, Charles Willson Peale, and Gilbert Stuart. Later nineteenth-century collections include landscapes by Albert Bierstadt, Thomas Moran, and Winslow Homer. Twentieth-century art is on the third floor, with contemporary works shown in the huge Lincoln Gallery, designed in 1852 by Robert Mills. Lincoln's second inaugural reception was held in this room. The museum is a part of the Smithsonian Institution.

The museum's collection originated with the work of a private collector, John Varden, who began gathering a variety of historical artifacts in 1829. In 1841 his collection was merged with that of the National Institute and displayed in the Patent Office Building.

LOCATION: 8th and G streets NW. HOURS: 10–5:30 Daily. FEE: None. TELEPHONE: 202-357-2700.

The Museum of American Art and the Portrait Gallery share the **Old Patent Office** that was saved from demolition in the 1950s and given to the Smithsonian Institution. The central portion of the south facade was designed by W. P. Elliot and Ithiel Town. Robert Mills added the east and west wings in the 1850s.

The Greek Revival **Tariff Commission Building** (701 E Street NW), which now houses the International Trade Commission, was also designed by Robert Mills. It was begun in 1839 and completed just after the Civil War.

NATIONAL BUILDING MUSEUM

Occupying one of the most impressive buildings in the capital, the National Building Museum commemorates and celebrates the American building arts. Beginning in 1881, the designer, General Montgomery C. Meigs, combined the inspiration of Italian Renaissance architecture with the know-how of nineteenth-century industrial design to create the massive brick, iron, wood, and terra cotta building for the Pension Bureau. Over 15,000,000 bricks make up the exterior that is encircled by a 1,200-foot-long terra cotta frieze of Civil War soldiers on an endless march.

The interior boasts one of the finest great halls in the country. First used as the site of Grover Cleveland's inaugural ball—before the building was even complete—it has hosted many inaugural affairs as well as other gala functions. Eight Corinthian columns of marbleized brick rise seventy-five feet and extend twenty-five feet in circumference. The first-floor arcade is ringed with seventy-two Doric columns of terra cotta. The second-floor arcade echoes the first with cast-iron Ionic columns, while the third-floor parapet is topped with seventy-six terra cotta urns. The fourth floor is encircled by a wrought-iron railing. Above, in niches just below the center court cornice, 244 busts replicate eight statues representing members of the building profession.

Built between 1882 and 1885, the building housed the Pension Bureau until 1926. After that time, a number of proposals for the space were considered, among them filling the inner courtyard with fifteen stories of steel filing for archival storage, and using it as a drill hall for the National Guard. In 1967 the idea for a National Building Museum was proposed, and 1980 saw its creation. In 1985 the galleries opened to the public and now house two permanent displays—"Washington: Site, Symbol & City," and "The U.S. Pension Building"—as well as other exhibits that focus on the nation's historic and contemporary building achievements.

LOCATION: Judiciary Square NW (F Street between 4th and 5th). HOURS: 10–4 Monday–Saturday, 12–4 Sunday. FEE: None. TELEPHONE: 202–272–2448.

One of Washington's finest architectural landmarks is the **District Court House** (Indiana Avenue between 4th and 5th streets), designed by George Hadfield as the city hall. It was completed in 1849, almost a quarter of a century after Hadfield's death. A central portico with eight Ionic columns is flanked by projecting wings with smaller colonnades. Hadfield, an Englishman, had been recommended to George Washington by the expatriate painters Benjamin West and John Trumbull as a candidate for superintendent of the construction of the Capitol. He arrived in the city in 1795. His talent was equal to that of the other architects who worked on the creation of the federal city; but his career was not a successful one. Quarrels with the Capitol commissioners, who refused to pay him for his extra work designing executive offices,

OVERLEAF: *The immense central hall of the old Pension Bureau, now part of the National Building Museum.*

brought him into political disfavor. Hadfield's sister, Maria Cosway, persuaded her close friend Thomas Jefferson to use his influence on Hadfield's behalf. Through Jefferson he did receive some commissions, but the unlucky architect passed his years in poverty and died in 1826. Some of his best work no longer remains; his surviving buildings in and around Washington are the commandant's house at the Marine Barracks, a handsome mausoleum in Georgetown's Oak Hill Cemetery, and Arlington House, a building that was among the most influential examples of Greek Revival architecture in nineteenth-century America.

NATIONAL GEOGRAPHIC SOCIETY

Founded in 1888 "for the increase and diffusion of geographic knowledge," the National Geographic Society today boasts a membership of over ten million and has supported more than 3,400 explorations and research projects. The archaeological discoveries of Louis and Mary Leakey (and their son Richard), the arctic and antarctic expeditions of Admiral Byrd and Robert E. Peary, the biological and sociological research on apes of Jane Goodall, and the underwater experiments and observations of Jacques Cousteau are but a few of these endeavors. Peary's sled and a ten-foot globe are among the many permanent exhibits at the Society's **Explorer's Hall** that also sponsors traveling exhibitions on such diverse subjects as holography, wolves, and the Sistine Chapel. In addition to the *National Geographic,* the Society publishes three other magazines as well as numerous books, maps, atlases, videos, and films. Special lecture series are also offered.

LOCATION: 17th and M streets NW. HOURS: 9–5 Monday–Saturday, 10–5 Sunday. FEE: None. TELEPHONE: 202–857–7588.

Across M Street from the National Geographic Society is the **Charles Sumner School** (202–727–3419), named in honor of the abolitionist senator from Massachusetts. It was built in 1871–1872 as a primary and grammar school and to house offices of the Superintendent and Board of Trustees of the Colored Schools of Washington and Georgetown, and has continued to provide educational opportunities for blacks in the District of Columbia. Designed by architect Adolph Cluss, the Gothic Revival building has been successfully restored in the 1980s. The school maintains a museum, research library, concert center, conference facility, and resource center focusing on public education in the District.

OCTAGON HOUSE

This architecturally distinguished house, now owned and maintained by the American Institute of Architects Foundation, has been restored with furnishings of the early nineteenth century. The unusual shape was required to make maximum use of an odd-shaped lot. It was designed by William Thornton and built in 1801 for John Tayloe. President Madison and his wife, Dolley, stayed here for six months in 1814 and 1815 after the White House was burned by the British. The house was an important social and political gathering place in the early nineteenth century.

> LOCATION: 1799 New York Avenue NW. HOURS: 10–4 Tuesday–Sunday; Guided group tours by appointment. FEE: Yes. TELEPHONE: 202–638–3221.

Nearby is **St. Mary's Church** (728 23rd Street NW, 202–333–3985), designed by James Renwick in the Gothic style for a black parish of the Episcopal Church. Among its attractions are hand-carved oak pews and stained glass windows.

The Octagon House, designed by Dr. William Thornton, original architect of the U.S. Capitol. It has been the headquarters of the American Institute of Architects since 1902.

Federal townhouses lining a quiet Georgetown street.

G E O R G E T O W N

The architectural historian Elbert Peets, writing in the WPA guide to Washington, used an arboreal metaphor to describe the difference between the looks of Washington officialdom and quaint old Georgetown: "Washington is like an oak in its prime that stands beside a beautiful old dogwood, always in flower." Georgetown's grace derives from its prim streets of brick houses, an elegant contrast to the imposing colonnades of the capital. A century older than the capital, Georgetown was settled about 1700 and received a large influx of Scottish immigrants during the next fifty years. In 1751 it was named George, later lengthened to George Towne. Its main occupation was shipping tobacco and other agricultural products.

Georgetown's last bid for commercial power was the construction of a canal to carry the products of the hinterland—grain, flour, coal, stone, and lumber—to docks on the Potomac. This was a fine undertaking, but soon railroads successfully competed with canals. Built between 1828 and 1850, the Chesapeake & Ohio Canal ran 184 miles between Georgetown and Cumberland, Maryland. The entire canal is preserved as the **Chesapeake & Ohio Canal National Historical Park.** One of the original 74 locks is preserved in Georgetown. The canal information center is in the Foundry Mall (between 30th and Thomas Jefferson streets, 202–653–5190). Boat trips are offered April through October.

Georgetown University, the oldest Catholic college in the country, was founded here in 1787 as Georgetown Academy. Inside the main entrance on 37th Street NW is a statue of the founder, John Carroll, the first Roman Catholic bishop in America and the first archbishop of Baltimore.

Good examples of Federal houses can be seen along **N Street,** particularly number 2606–2608, and Cox's Row, number 3327–3329, built in 1817. Two of the finest examples of Federal architecture in the district are Evermay and Tudor Place. **Evermay** (1623 28th Street NW, private) was built about 1800 by Samuel Davidson, a real estate speculator who was part owner of the land upon which the White House stands. He was protective of his privacy, so much so that in 1810 he published an advertisement warning "all persons, of whatever age, color, or standing in society . . . particularly . . . all amorous bucks with their dorfies, and all sporting bucks with their dogs and guns," to avoid his property. As for innocent gapers, he wrote, "I do not admit mere curiosity as an errand of business."

The **Old Stone House** (3051 M Street NW, 202–426–6851) is the city's oldest house, erected in 1765 by a cabinetmaker named Christopher Layman. The walls are fieldstone; the gables are finished in brick. Six rooms—the kitchen, workshop, back parlor, front parlor, and two bedrooms—have been restored and furnished with eighteenth-century items.

Other architectural sites of interest include the post office at 1221 31st Street, designed by Ammi B. Young and built in 1858 as the **custom house** for the port of Georgetown. At the entrance to **Oak Hill Cemetery** is the 1850 Gothic-style **Renwick Chapel** (R and 29 streets NW, 202–337–2835), designed by James Renwick. Within the cemetery, George Hadfield designed the 1826 **Van Ness Mausoleum,** a beautiful, circular brick tomb surrounded by a colonnade inspired by Rome's Temple of Vesta. **St. John's Episcopal Church** (Potomac and O streets NW) was built in 1809 and much altered in the nineteenth century.

DUMBARTON HOUSE

Headquarters of the National Society of the Colonial Dames of America, Dumbarton House is a superbly restored museum of the Federal period. The two-story brick mansion, in the style of Virginia and Maryland country seats, was built about 1805. In 1813 Charles Carroll, of the Maryland Carrolls, purchased the house. According to legend, Carroll and Dolley Madison stopped here for tea during her escape from the White House when the British burned the city in 1814. Eight rooms have been restored and filled with an excellent collection of furniture. The house displays personal items owned by the Washington, including Martha Washington's jewelry and china used by her daughter, Eliza Custis Law.

LOCATION: 2715 Q Street NW. HOURS: 10–1 Tuesday–Saturday. FEE: Yes. TELEPHONE: 202–337–2288.

The north vista, Dumbarton Oaks.

The Pebble Garden at Dumbarton Oaks includes a sheaf of wheat composed of Mexican stones.

DUMBARTON OAKS

Renowned collections of Byzantine art and pre-Columbian art are displayed at Dumbarton Oaks, one of the nation's most beautiful small museums. The main house, a two-story brick mansion, was erected in 1801 and much enlarged in the nineteenth century. Some of the additions were removed in the 1930s, but the house retains a late-nineteenth-century mansard roof. John C. Calhoun lived here during his term as vice president (1825–1832). In 1920 the house and its grounds were purchased by Mr. and Mrs. Robert Woods Bliss. A diplomat and heir to a substantial fortune, Bliss was a serious collector of Byzantine and pre-Columbian art. His wife hired the landscape designer Beatrix Farrand to create a ten-acre formal garden amidst the fifty-four acres they owned. In 1940 the Blisses donated the property and their collections to Harvard University. The house was the site of a 1944 conference of the Allied powers that led to the establishment of the United Nations.

LOCATION: 1703 32nd Street NW. HOURS: *Collection:* 2–5 Tuesday–Sunday; *Gardens:* April through October: 2–6 Daily. FEE: Yes. TELEPHONE: 202–342–3200.

TUDOR PLACE

In 1805 Martha Washington's granddaughter, Martha Custis Peter, bought a city block's worth of Georgetown property and retained the Capitol's architect, Dr. William Thornton, to design the high-style Neoclassical mansion. The house was completed in 1816.

The north facade, facing the formal gardens, is quite plain, while the south side of the house, overlooking sloping lawns, is punctuated by an impressive circular portico topped by a dome. The Neoclassical exterior of the large house is echoed by its interior detailing. The furniture, china, portraits, books, and household items reflect the Peter family's continuous ownership and the corresponding years of American culture; some furnishings were brought from Mt. Vernon. Since the Peter family was connected to such historical figures as George Washington, Lafayette, and Robert E. Lee, Tudor Place welcomed esteemed guests. Henry Clay, Daniel Webster, and John C. Calhoun's names are among those in the visitor's book.

Extensive gardens surround the house. Originated in the Federal period, the gardens still sport many of the lawns, specimen trees, and plantings that date to the early nineteenth century.

LOCATION: 1644 31st Street NW (intersection of Q and 31st streets). HOURS: Tours, Tuesday–Saturday. FEE: Yes. TELEPHONE: 202–965–0400.

DUPONT CIRCLE AND KALORAMA

The Dupont Circle area and the district to the northwest, Kalorama, comprised the city's fashionable residential area from early in the nineteenth century to the 1930s. The Kalorama district, a private estate in the 1700s, was given its name ("beautiful view" in Greek) by the writer Joel Barlow, who purchased the estate in 1807 and had its house remodeled by Latrobe. Later, millionaires who had made their fortunes in distant enterprises and wished to make an impression upon the capital built their mansions here, Massachusetts Avenue being a favorite address. Many of their houses are now occupied by foreign embassies and can be seen only from the street. This tour begins at Dupont Circle and proceeds northwest into Kalorama, an area bounded by Massachusetts and Connecticut avenues NW and Rock Creek Park.

Dupont Circle was named in 1882 for Admiral Samuel Francis duPont, a hero of the Civil War. DuPont won a victory in November 1861 when he captured Port Royal Sound, South Carolina. He repeatedly ran his fleet of seventeen vessels past a pair of Confederate forts, trading cannon fire with the shore batteries until the forts surrendered, and Port Royal became an important base for the Federal navy. A marble **fountain** by Daniel Chester French depicts allegorical figures representing Sea, Stars, and Wind.

Southwest of Dupont Circle, at New Hampshire Avenue and 20th Street NW, the **Historical Society of Washington, DC** (202–785–2068) has a library of books, manuscripts, prints, and photographs relating to the city's history. Of equal interest is the building itself, a Richardsonian Romanesque mansion built in the 1890s for Christian Heurich, a highly successful brewer. The Heurichs' original furnishings and their exuberant decorating scheme, featuring ornately carved woodwork, plasterwork, stenciling, and painting, have been preserved in three floors of rooms open to the public.

Just off Dupont Circle at Massachusetts Avenue and 20th Street NW is the **Blaine Mansion** (private), built in 1881 for James G. Blaine, who served as secretary of state under Benjamin Harrison and ran for president three times. On the same block, at number 2020, the **Indonesian Embassy** occupies a mansion built in 1903 for the Colorado gold magnate Thomas F. Walsh. The next block of Massachusetts Avenue is the location of the Phillips Collection and the Larz Anderson House.

PHILLIPS COLLECTION

The Phillips Collection, the nation's first permanent museum of modern art, displays an outstanding collection of nineteenth- and twentieth-century Western European and American paintings. It concentrates on French Impressionist and American Modernist painters, including Renoir, Van Gogh, Bonnard, Braque, O'Keeffe, Rothko, and Hartley. The museum was founded in 1921 by Duncan Phillips, an heir to the Jones & Laughlin Steel Company fortune. Situating the collection in his townhouse, he said it would be "a public gallery with its main stress on living painters"; but it would also exhibit works by deceased artists whose work "would be forever modern." Since its opening, the collection has been an important study center for American artists.

LOCATION: 1600 21st Street NW. HOURS: 10–5 Monday–Saturday, 12–7 Sunday. FEE: Yes. TELEPHONE: 202–387–2151.

The stair hall at the Larz Anderson House, the Massachusetts Avenue mansion of the Society of the Cincinnati.

LARZ ANDERSON HOUSE / SOCIETY OF THE CINCINNATI

The Society of the Cincinnati was founded in 1783 by American and French officers who had served in the Revolutionary War. The first president general of the society was George Washington. The society was named for the sixth-century BC Roman war hero Cincinnatus, who was twice appointed dictator during military crises, and who relinquished his power to return to farming after the crises had passed. Membership in the society is limited to some male descendants of Revolutionary officers. Thomas Jefferson and John Adams were among the prominent Patriots opposed to the establishment of the order, seeing it as the seed of an aristocratic, military clique inimical to the ideals of a republic.

Mr. and Mrs. Larz Anderson (he was the great-grandson of a founder of the society) built the house between 1902 and 1906. It has a gilded French parlor and a sixty-foot-long ballroom with a musicians' gallery supported by marble columns. The house is still largely furnished with the Andersons' furnishings. Paintings by

American artists such as Gilbert Stuart, John Trumbull, and George Catlin, a large library of books relating to the Revolution, exhibits of military items including miniature soldiers, and dioramas are also found here.

LOCATION: 2118 Massachusetts Avenue NW. HOURS: 1–4 Tuesday–Saturday. FEE: None. TELEPHONE: 202–785–2040.

Proceeding northwest, Massachusetts Avenue comes to **Sheridan Circle,** where a statue by Gutzon Borglum (the creator of the Mount Rushmore monument) honors the Civil War hero, General Philip H. Sheridan.

Three embassies on the circle were originally private residences. On the south, the **Turkish Embassy** (1606 23rd Street) was built in 1915 for Edward H. Everett, who made a fortune from the patent on the bottle cap. The **Philippines Ambassador's Residence** (2253 R Street) was designed by Waddy Wood for General Charles Fitzhugh and built in 1904; and an office of the **Egyptian Embassy** (2301 Massachusetts Avenue) was formerly the Joseph Beale House. Northeast of the circle, at 22nd and Decatur Place NW, is the **Codman House,** designed by the noted architect and interior designer Ogden Codman, the coauthor, with Edith Wharton, of *The Decoration of Houses.*

MUSEUMS OF JEWISH HERITAGE

The **National Museum of American Jewish Military History** (1811 R Street NW, 202–265–6280), governed by the Jewish War Veterans of the U.S.A., honors the service of Jewish Americans to the United States. Collections include photographs, uniforms, firearms, medals, and personal papers and other documents. The **B'nai B'rith Klutznick National Jewish Museum** (B'nai B'rith building, 1640 Rhode Island Avenue, 202–857–6583) has collections of Israelite archaeology and the gamut of recorded Jewish history. Folk art and ceremonial art are also represented. Classes for adults and children, as well as films, lectures, and concerts are offered. Organized trips are conducted to places of Jewish interest.

After they left the White House, Woodrow Wilson and his wife, Edith Galt Wilson, moved into the **Woodrow Wilson House** (2340 S Street NW, off Massachusetts Avenue, 202–387–4062), designed by Waddy Wood. Wilson died here in 1924, but Mrs.

Wilson lived in the house until her death in 1961 and left the house to the National Trust for Historic Preservation. They have maintained it as it was when the Wilsons occupied it. Next door is the **Textile Museum** (202–667–0441), displaying a large collection of textiles and rugs from all over the world, started by George Hewitt Myers in the 1890s when he was a student at Yale.

WASHINGTON NATIONAL CATHEDRAL

Officially named the Cathedral Church of Saint Peter and Saint Paul, the National Cathedral was begun in 1907. It was erected by the Protestant Episcopal Cathedral Foundation, chartered by Congress in 1893 to establish "a cathedral and institutions of learning for the promotion of religion and education and charity." The church stands on an eminence with a commanding view of the city, amid fifty-eight acres of grounds. Designed by the British architect George F. Bodley, with the assistance of Henry Vaughan of Boston, the cathedral is in the fourteenth-century English Gothic style, with flying buttresses and ribbed vaulting. Construction was not completed until 1990.

> LOCATION: Massachusetts and Wisconsin avenues NW. HOURS: 10–4:30 Daily; Guided tours: 10–3:15 Monday–Saturday, 12:30–2:45 Sunday. FEE: None. TELEPHONE: 202–537–6200.

Rock Creek Cemetery (Rock Creek Church Road and Webster Street NW) is the site of one of the masterpieces of Augustus Saint-Gaudens—his memorial to Marion Hooper "Clover" Adams. The wife of historian Henry Adams, she committed suicide in December 1885. In November 1886, Adams and the artist John LaFarge met with Saint-Gaudens to discuss a memorial. Saint-Gaudens scribbled down his ideas: "Adams / Buddha / Mental repose / Calm reflection in contrast with the violence or force in nature." The enigmatic bronze sculpture of a seated figure with a hood obscuring the face was installed in 1891 in a setting designed by Stanford White. Saint-Gaudens called it *The Peace of God* but wanted to keep the title a secret. Alexander Woollcott called it "the most beautiful thing ever fashioned by the hand of man on this continent." Some thought it pessimistic or atheistic. Adams himself wrote, "Like all great artists, St. Gaudens held up the mirror and no more."

OPPOSITE: *The great nave of the Washington cathedral, a construction of elegance and grace.*

CHAPTER TWO

NORTHERN VIRGINIA

OPPOSITE: *Mount Vernon, the home of George Washington.*

In 1607, thirteen years before the Pilgrims set foot on Plymouth Rock, one hundred Englishmen and four boys came ashore in Virginia and established Jamestown, the first permanent English settlement in the New World. They held the first legislative assembly in America in 1619. Despite poor planning and leadership, greed, disease, laziness, starvation, and mayhem, the Jamestown settlers managed to keep their foothold in the wilderness. Had Jamestown failed, it is doubtful the Pilgrims would have found the financial backing to establish their colony. The Pilgrims, in fact, were headed for a landfall south of the Hudson River, within Virginia territory, when they wandered off course and ended up on Cape Cod.

Virginia's original boundaries, set by royal fiat, were enormous, as evidenced by the colonies and states that were later formed by the dismemberment of Virginia: the Carolinas were made separate in 1629, Maryland in 1632; after the Revolution the future states of Kentucky, Ohio, Indiana, Illinois, Michigan, and Wisconsin were severed from Virginia and organized as the Northwest Territory. West Virginia was separated as a Unionist state during the Civil War through a legal maneuver whose constitutionality some Virginians continue to question.

The first American rebellion against royal authority took place in Virginia in 1676, when Nathaniel Bacon led a band of armed men in an attempt to unseat Governor William Berkeley. The immediate cause of the unrest was Berkeley's failure to attack his fur-trading partners, the Susquehannock Indians, who had been roughing up intruding white settlers; but Bacon also insisted that Berkeley had ignored the right of the people to petition for redress of grievances. Bacon's men burned Jamestown, which thereafter rapidly lost its population and importance. In 1699 a new capital was established at Williamsburg.

The destruction of Jamestown closed a short chapter in the colony's history. The London financiers who backed the Jamestown settlement had envisioned it as an urban headquarters for gold hunting and exploration, but it never went beyond being a farming village. Following the example of John Rolfe, who had been taught by the Indians, the settlers began to cultivate tobacco and ship it to Europe in place of the gold they were unable to find. The smoking habit quickly gripped the Old World, making tobacco the basis of Virginia's economy for centuries. In the seventeenth and eighteenth centuries English settlers established tobacco plan-

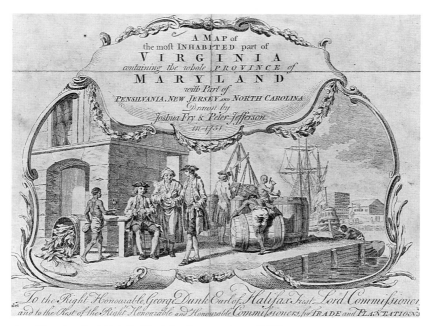

A map's cartouche depicts the Virginia tobacco trade ca. 1775.

tations along Virginia's four major rivers, the James, York, Rappahannock, and Potomac.

Because tobacco cultivation required large amounts of land,
the plantations were spread out, and because Virginia had a network of navigable rivers, each plantation could become a virtually
self-sufficient economic unit. Each had its own riverfront wharves
where oceangoing ships arrived to pick up tobacco and deliver
manufactured goods from England. As a result, few towns of any
size developed. Williamsburg, seat of the colonial government and
the College of William and Mary, was almost deserted much of the
year. Its permanent residents were few; planters came to town for a
few weeks when the House of Burgesses and Governor's Council
were in session.

Virginia provided much of the military and political leadership to the cause of independence. The roster of Virginia's political
leaders is like a roll call of American heroes—Washington, Jefferson, George Mason ("the Pen of the Revolution"), Patrick Henry,
and the five Lee brothers of Stratford Hall. The Congress named
George Washington commander-in-chief of the Continental Army

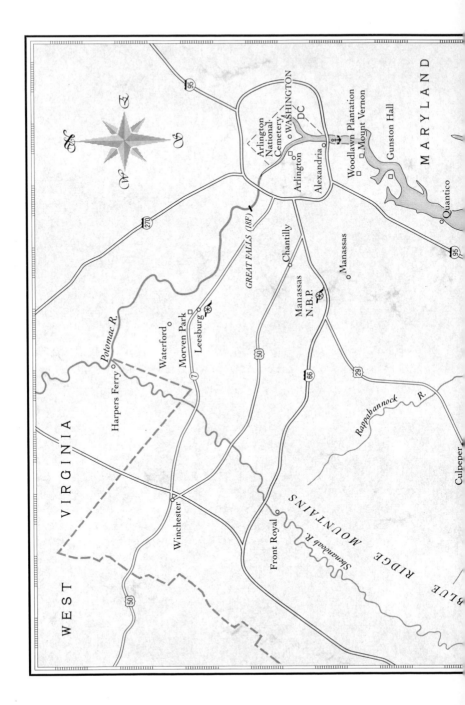

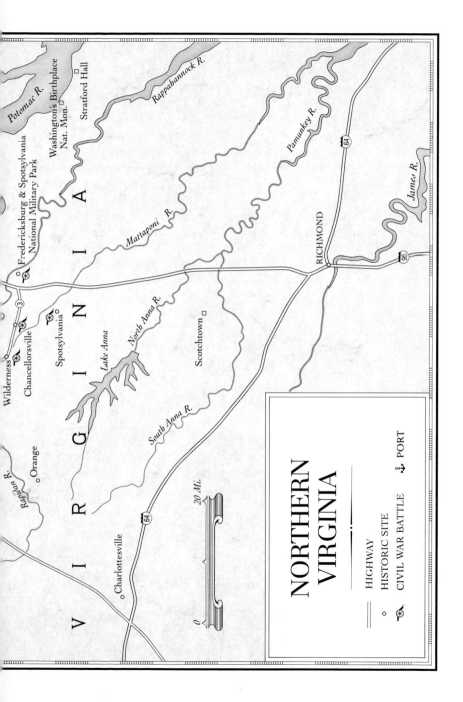

Potomac R.

Rappabannock R.

Washington's Birthplace
Nat. Mon. □

Stratford Hall

Pamunkey R.

64

James R.

Fredericksburg & Spotsylvania
National Military Park

Mattaponi R.

RICHMOND

95

3

Wilderness

Chancellorsville

Spotsylvania

North Anna R.

Lake Anna

Scotchtown □

V I R G I N I A

Rapidan R.

Orange

South Anna R.

64

Charlottesville

20 Mi.

0

NORTHERN VIRGINIA

— HIGHWAY

○ HISTORIC SITE

⚓ PORT

⚔ CIVIL WAR BATTLE

in 1775; he was a powerful politician of immense personal presence, and he had experience fighting the French and the Indians
on Virginia's frontier. Two other Virginians who served notably in
the army were Daniel Morgan and "Light-Horse" Harry Lee, both
brilliant field commanders, if somewhat temperamental and errat-
ic. The lawyers and orators of Williamsburg played as large a role
in shaping revolutionary thought and policy as their counterparts
in Boston's cradles of liberty, Faneuil Hall and Old South Church.
At the outbreak of the Revolutionary War, the Virginia militia, clad
in shirts bearing the slogan "Liberty or Death," chased Governor
Dunmore from the colony. Norfolk was reduced to ashes by British
shells and Patriot torches. Thereafter the fighting took place in the
northern states and the Carolinas, until Lord Cornwallis invaded
Virginia from the Carolinas, in 1781. In October of that year, he
was trapped at Yorktown, between a French fleet and a Franco-
American army.

At the birth of the republic Virginia was the wealthiest and
most populous state, at the zenith of its fortunes, but its Tidewater
and Piedmont soils were approaching exhaustion. The young and
energetic began a mass migration to the Shenandoah Valley and
beyond, rapidly depleting the population of the eastern part of the
state. Between 1820 and 1860 Virginia fell from the first state to
fifth in population. Although Richmond enjoyed a manufacturing
boom from tobacco products, flour, and iron, much of the country-
side was a wasteland of exhausted farms. The failure to build
canals and railroads to link the hinterlands with the cluster of ports
at Hampton Roads left commerce to languish. Progressive Virginians decried the sorry state of commerce, the educational system,
and agriculture; some contended that slavery was not only inhu-
mane, it was inefficient. By the 1820s, Virginia planters were sell-
ing their slaves to cotton plantations farther south and west.

Reformers praised the go-getting spirit of northern entrepre-
neurs and small farmers, but one Bostonian who visited Richmond,
the Reverend William Ellery Channing, found the "generous confidence of a Virginian" preferable to the "selfish prudence of the
Yankee." In Virginia, he wrote, "I find great vices, but greater
virtues than I left behind me. . . . They *love money less* than we do. . . .
Their patriotism is not tied to their purse strings. Could I only take
from the Virginians their *sensuality* and their *slaves,* I should think
them the greatest people in the world."

In 1861 Virginia wavered between the Union and the Confe-

deracy. Many of its foremost men, like Robert E. Lee, were opposed to secession. But when war came, Lee went with his state,
which cast its lot with the South. Richmond was selected as the
Confederate capital because of its ironworks, flour mills, and, some
said, its fine hotels. That honor proved to be Virginia's curse, as
Richmond became the strategic target of the Federal armies. Many
of the Civil War's major battles were fought in Virginia: First and
Second Manassas, the Peninsular War, Fredericksburg, Chancellorsville, and the series of terrible battles in 1864 and 1865 that led
to the fall of the Confederacy—Wilderness, Spotsylvania, Cold
Harbor, and the siege of Petersburg.

Virginia made a slow recovery from the war, hindered by a
large debt and the devastation of farmlands and factories. Tobacco
production remained one of the pillars of the agricultural and
manufacturing economy, as small-scale farms turned to the cultivation of high-quality leaf in fertilized soil. In the 1880s railroad lines
linked the Hampton Roads with West Virginia coal fields; and
Richmond's mills began to revive. The turn of the century saw the
beginnings of a literary flowering with the publication of first
novels by two young writers of the post-bellum generation, Ellen
Glasgow and James Branch Cabell.

In the 1920s the sleepy, virtually forgotten old capital of Williamsburg was rescued from decay by the efforts of a local minister
and John D. Rockefeller, Jr. The town was painstakingly restored
to its eighteenth century condition in a process of historical redisco-
very and reinterpretation that continues today. Throughout the
state, private and public groups have preserved eighteenth- and
nineteenth-century houses and battlefields. This chapter treats the
northern part of the state, beginning with Arlington and looping
through Leesburg and Manassas, moving back to Alexandria and
Mount Vernon, then proceeding south to Fredericksburg and the
Northern Neck, the long peninsula between the Potomac and Rappahannock rivers.

ARLINGTON HOUSE

Arlington House, also known as the Robert E. Lee Memorial, was
the home of George Washington Parke Custis, Martha Washington's grandson, whom George Washington adopted. The house
was designed by George Hadfield, a British architect who came to
Washington to work on the Capitol. Custis desired a building in the

The morning room at Arlington House is dominated by G. W. P. Custis's huge Battle of Monmouth, *originally painted for the U. S. Capitol.*

Greek style, and Hadfield obliged him with a monumental Doric portico plainly visible from Washington, DC. Construction on the south wing began in 1801; the main portion was completed in 1817. Custis made the house a virtual museum of Washington memorabilia. He displayed personal items he had inherited—china, silver, furniture, and portraits—as well as military items he bought at auction, such as camp tents and the flags surrendered by the British at Yorktown.

In 1831 Custis's daughter, Mary, married Robert E. Lee. The Lees always regarded this house as their permanent home. In April 1861 Lee was at Arlington when he made his decision to resign his commission in the army and serve with the forces of Virginia. The federal government seized the property, on the technicality that the taxes on it had not been paid in person by the owner, and established Arlington National Cemetery on the grounds.

The house is furnished with many items owned by the Lees, along with some Custis furnishings. The morning room displays some of the historical paintings Custis created to glorify the deeds of his adoptive father, including a huge canvas depicting Washington at one of his greatest triumphs, the Battle of Monmouth.

LOCATION: Arlington National Cemetery. HOURS: April through September: 9:30–6 Daily; October through March: 9:30–4:30 Daily. FEE: None. TELEPHONE: 703–557–0613.

ARLINGTON NATIONAL CEMETERY

Arlington National Cemetery was established during the Civil War and contains numerous monuments and statues memorializing the dead of every conflict since. The first burials took place on May 13, 1864. A granite monument to the unknown dead of the Civil War stands over a mass grave of 2,111 Federal soldiers. The mast of the *Maine,* which blew up in Havana harbor before the Spanish-American War, is preserved here near a memorial to the Rough Riders who died in the charge up San Juan Hill. Soldiers who fell in World Wars I and II, Korea, and Vietnam are buried in the **Tomb of the Unknowns.** Two presidents are buried at Arlington, William Howard Taft and John F. Kennedy. The Memorial Amphitheater holds services on Easter, Memorial Day, and Veterans Day.

LOCATION: Arlington, off George Washington Memorial Parkway. HOURS: April through September: 8–7 Daily; October through March: 8–5 Daily. FEE: None. TELEPHONE: 703–607–8052.

GREAT FALLS PARK

Located along the Great Falls of the Potomac River, the park preserves the ruins of a canal built by the Patowmack Company between 1785 and 1802 to skirt the falls, which prevented navigation. George Washington was one of the prime movers behind the canal's construction, believing it would turn the region into a prosperous center of commerce for the products of the Ohio River valley. Washington's close friend Light Horse Harry Lee invested heavily in the canal, and built the town of Matildaville, named for his first wife, as a speculative real-estate venture.

LOCATION: 9200 Old Dominion Drive, Great Falls; four miles west of Route 495 on Route 193. HOURS: 7 a.m.–dusk Daily. FEE: Yes. TELEPHONE: 703–285–2966.

OVERLEAF: *Stately rows of grave markers at the Arlington National Cemetery.*

Colvin Run Mill (south of Great Falls Park on Route 743, 703–759–2771) is a working gristmill, built about 1800 and in use until 1934. Demonstrations of milling techniques are given, and the adjacent miller's house may be toured. **Sully Historic Site** (Route 28 north of Route 50, Chantilly, 703–437–1794) was the plantation home of Richard Bland Lee, a younger brother of Light Horse Harry Lee. This Lee was also a congressman, and a founder of Phi Beta Kappa. His 1794 farmhouse, where he entertained Washington and Madison, has been restored.

LEESBURG

Chartered in 1757 as Georgetown, the town was subsequently renamed in honor of Thomas Lee of Stratford Hall and became the seat of Loudoun County. **The Loudoun Museum** (16 Loudoun Street SW, 703–777–7427) displays a small collection of artifacts of local history. Its visitor center, at Loudoun and Harrison streets, provides maps for walking tours of the town's nineteenth-century historic district and the **Ball's Bluff** battlefield. On October 21, 1861, two Union columns, under General Charles Stone and Colonel Edward Baker, attempted a reconnaissance of Leesburg. Baker, an inexperienced commander, came up against a strong Confederate position atop Ball's Bluff, mismanaged the attack, and died along with many of his men. The defeat was almost as serious a blow to Northern confidence as the first Battle of Bull Run in Manassas. The battlefield (Route 837, north of Leesburg) has been set aside as a park, with a cemetery.

Morven Park

Originally a small stone farmhouse built in 1781, the Morven Park mansion was greatly expanded in the early nineteenth century by Thomas Swann, the governor of Maryland, and by his son, Thomas, Jr., whose additions transformed the once-modest farmhouse into an imposing country seat. Virginia governor Westmoreland Davis occupied the house from 1903 to 1922, expanded it further, and decorated the rooms in a variety of European styles. There is a French drawing room, a Jacobean dining room, and a Renaissance great hall, where Davis gained a reputation for lavish entertaining in a state accustomed to generous hosts. Mrs. Davis collected the tapestries, silver, porcelain, and paintings displayed in the house.

OPPOSITE: *Weaver's cottage in Waterford, the oldest community in Loudoun County.*

The estate includes the **Museum of Hounds and Hunting,** tracing the history of the sport to which Virginians have been addicted since the colony was founded. Also on the grounds is a carriage museum with one hundred antique vehicles on exhibit.

LOCATION: North of Leesburg on Old Waterford Road, off Route 7. HOURS: April–October: 12–5 Tuesday–Sunday; November: 12–5 Saturday, Sunday. FEE: Yes. TELEPHONE: 703–777–2414.

The beautiful, well-preserved rural region west of Leesburg was settled in the 1730s by Quakers from Pennsylvania, Maryland, and New Jersey. In contrast to the plantation system they found in the colony, the Quakers worked small family farms, partly because they refused to use slave labor. The area around the town of **Lincoln** is dotted with their distinctive, stone farm buildings. **Waterford,** north of Leesburg, was a Quaker milling community established about 1733 and is a National Historic Landmark. Economic decline in the late nineteenth century preserved it as a virtually unspoiled example of an agricultural town.

OATLANDS

Oatlands was another outpost of the Carter family, descendants of "King" Carter. In 1798 George Carter won thirty-five hundred acres of land here in a lottery held by his father to divide his property, and subsequently George decided to join the emigration of young Tidewater planters to the fertile lands of northern and western Virginia. In 1804 he began construction of the mansion, a portion of which was completed in 1810. In the late 1820s, he added the three-story Corinthian portico, had the brick facade covered with stucco, and, inside, had some rooms decorated with Adamesque plaster work. For a brief time during the Civil War the house was a barracks for Confederate troops. In 1897 Carter's son sold the house to Stilson Hutchins, founder of the *Washington Post.* The furnishings seen today, reflecting the tastes of the early twentieth century, are those of the William Corcoran Eustis family, who purchased Oatlands in 1903. Mrs. Eustis supervised the design of the mansion's beautiful gardens, in the Italian Renaissance style.

LOCATION: Route 15, six miles south of Leesburg. HOURS: April through December 25: 10–4:30 Monday–Saturday, 1–4:30 Sunday. FEE: Yes. TELEPHONE: 703–777–3174.

MANASSAS NATIONAL BATTLEFIELD

The two Civil War battles that took place here in 1861 and 1862 are known in the North as First and Second Bull Run, after a creek that runs just outside of the town of Manassas; in the South they are called First and Second Manassas. The engagement here in 1861 was the first major battle of the war, in which Thomas J. Jackson won his nickname, "Stonewall."

Manassas, less than thirty miles from Washington, where a railroad junction connected lines from the Shenandoah Valley and the deep South, was held by about 20,000 Confederate troops. Under intense pressure to produce a victory before the Confederate Congress met in Richmond on July 20, Lincoln ordered an attack on Manassas, even though his army was not yet prepared. He reasoned that the troops on both sides were untested: When General Irvin McDowell urged delay until he could train his men, Lincoln replied, "You are green, it is true, but they are green, also; you are all green alike." Confederate spies in Washington warned of the impending attack, allowing General Pierre Beauregard to prepare. In addition, McDowell's army moved slowly and was delayed by supply problems.

The initial Union attack, launched in the early morning of July 21, met with success. A column of ten thousand men crossed Bull Run on the Confederate left flank and pushed the Southerners back throughout the morning. Confederate reinforcements halted the Union advance at Henry House Hill. (Judith Henry refused to leave her house on the hill and was killed by artillery fire.) Here the legend of Stonewall Jackson was born. He lined up his men along the top of Henry House Hill and refused to budge. Reputedly, General Barnard Bee called out to his South Carolinians, "There is Jackson standing like a stone wall!" The remark has generally been taken as a tribute, but Bee may actually have been complaining about Jackson's refusal to move forward. Bee did not survive the battle to clarify his remark. But if Jackson did not move forward, neither did he move back: His brigade halted the Northern advance, taking heavy casualties. In the afternoon Beauregard hurled fresh reserves at the exhausted Northerners, who retreated at the first "Rebel yell." The retreat turned into a panic-stricken run, but the tired Southerners were not able to press their advantage.

The Confederate success at Manassas inflated the confidence

The Stone Bridge, where the First Battle of Manassas began.

of the Southern public and politicians, causing them to underesti-
mate for a time the strength and determination of the North. For
the North, the defeat was a profound shock. New York newspaper-
man Horace Greeley, one of the most fervent promoters of the
war, wrote a letter to Lincoln advising him to consider treating for
peace on any terms the South might offer. But the more lasting
effect was to convince the North that the war would not be won
easily and that greater effort was called for. The day after the battle
Lincoln summoned Major General George B. McClellan and put
him in charge of the Army of the Potomac. Although McClellan
later proved indecisive in the field, he possessed great organizational talents and made the Northern army into a strong fighting
force. Another lasting effect was to instill in Lincoln an exaggerat-
ed fear of a Southern thrust at Washington.

The second battle at Manassas, August 26 to September 1,
1862, began after Stonewall Jackson's corps reached Union supplies stockpiled at Manassas, took what they could, and retreated a
few miles west to a system of ditches that had been dug for a

Manassas, the site of two Civil War battles. OVERLEAF: *McClellan's army at Manassas Junction, which was left devastated by retreating Confederates.*

railroad. Union general John Pope confidently attacked Jackson's position, believing that the Confederates were in retreat. He found the Southerners well-entrenched and ready to fight. When the Northern attack stalled, General Longstreet attacked its flank with devastating effect. The fighting that day ended at Henry House Hill, where the Northerners were able to gather themselves and stop the Confederate advance. The next day the Union army pulled back to Washington, having suffered heavy losses. Encouraged by the victory, Lee embarked on the invasion of Maryland that culminated in the Battle of Antietam.

The facilities of the 4,500-acre national park include an audiovisual presentation, an electric map tracing the fighting, and maps for automobile tours of the fields. A statue of Stonewall Jackson is atop Henry House Hill, where he made his famous stand.

LOCATION: 6511 Sudley Road, Manassas. HOURS: Mid-June through August: 8:30–6 Daily; September through mid-June: 8:30–5 Daily. FEE: Yes. TELEPHONE: 703–361–1339.

ALEXANDRIA

Alexandria, settled in the 1670s, became a flourishing tobacco port in the early decades of the eighteenth century. In 1748 George Washington, then a teenager, was one of the surveyors who laid out Alexandria's grid of streets. Wheat replaced tobacco as the town's most profitable commodity, and by the 1790s Alexandria was the seventh busiest port in the country. For five decades Alexandria was part of the capital district, included in Virginia's 1791 grant to the federal government, but ceded back to the state in 1846. At the outbreak of the Civil War Alexandria was occupied by federal troops, became capital of the small part of Virginia under federal control, and was turned into a stronghold—the anchor of the system of fortifications that defended Washington.

The city preserves a historic district, called **Old Town;** many eighteenth-century houses (private) can be seen along **Prince Street.** Washington built a townhouse at **508 Cameron Street** in 1765. The original building was demolished in 1850; a replica (private), based on a sketch made by a neighbor, stands on the site

Eighteenth-century houses on Prince Street, left, and Queen Street, right, in Old Town Alexandria.

The elegant Georgian Colonial facade of Carlyle House.

today. One of the town's finest nineteenth-century townhouses is the three-story, brick **Fairfax House** (607 Cameron Street, private), built in 1816. In 1830 it was purchased by Thomas, Lord Fairfax, a member of the family that had held a royal patent to vast tracts of Virginia land before the Revolution.

The city's visitor center is located in **Ramsay House** (221 King Street, 703–838–4200), a modern reconstruction of an eighteenth-century house. The **Lyceum** (201 South Washington Street, 703–838–4994), a temple-form building erected in 1839, has a small museum of local history.

Carlyle House Historic Park

John Carlyle emigrated to Virginia from Scotland in 1741, prospered as a tobacco merchant, and joined the colony's elite by marrying a member of the wealthy Fairfax family. In 1753, at the age of thirty-three, he completed this imposing stone mansion. Its design recalls that of the smaller country houses of the Scottish low country—one of which is Craigiehall, which Carlyle may have seen illustrated in an architectural pattern book. Surrounded by a hotel complex in the nineteenth century, the house was restored in the 1970s and furnished with eighteenth-century items. One room has been left unfinished to show details of its construction.

Carlyle House was the site of an important conference in 1755, during the French and Indian War. General Edward Braddock met here with five of the colonial governors to plan strategy and push for funding of the war. He was turned down and wrote a letter to London planting the idea of taxing the colonists to pay for their defense. Haughty and argumentative, Braddock refused to agree with a young militia officer, George Washington, that the French in America would not fight in the same fashion as the French in Europe. On the subject of persuading the colonials to raise funds and supplies for their own defense, Washington himself said it would be easier to raise the dead. Braddock's failure to adopt the guerrilla tactics of the New World led to a disastrous defeat, and his own death, in the forests of Pennsylvania.

LOCATION: 121 North Fairfax Street. HOURS: 10–4:30 Tuesday–Saturday, 12–4:30 Sunday. FEE: Yes. TELEPHONE: 703–549–2997.

Completed in 1773, **Christ Church** (118 North Washington Street, 703–549–1450) retains much of its original woodwork. The galleries were added by 1787 and the tower and cupola were completed by 1820. George Washington was a pew owner and worshiped here when in the area. Washington's pew and that used by Robert E. Lee are marked with silver plaques, as is the place at the chancel rail where Lee was confirmed on July 17, 1853. Lee worshiped here prior to the Civil War and attended services here the day before leaving for Richmond to accept a Confederate command.

Washington was a patron of the establishment preserved as **Gadsby's Tavern Museum** (134 North Royal Street, 703–838–4242). There are restored eighteenth-century bedrooms and a reproduction of a handsomely panelled ballroom, the original of which was removed from the building in 1917 and installed in the American Wing of the Metropolitan Museum of Art in New York.

The **Boyhood Home of Robert E. Lee** (607 Oronoco Street, 703–548–8454) was the residence of the future Confederate hero and his family from 1811 to 1816 and again from 1820 to 1825, when Lee began his studies at West Point. His father, Light Horse Harry Lee, moved the family to Alexandria when his eldest son, Henry, assumed the management of Stratford Hall, the Lees' grand country seat in Westmoreland County. It has been restored

Ballroom of Gadsby's Tavern, where Washington celebrated two birthdays.

with furnishings of the early nineteenth century. The **Lee-Fendall House** across the street (614 Oronoco, 703–548–1789), built in 1785, was home to thirty-seven Lees. It is furnished with Lee possessions based on an 1852 inventory.

The **Old Presbyterian Meeting House** (321 South Fairfax Street, 703–549–6670), built in 1774, may be viewed by appointment. The meetinghouse was the site of the funeral sermon for George Washington; in the graveyard is the Tomb of the Unknown Soldier of the Revolutionary War.

The **Stabler-Leadbeater Apothecary Shop** (105–107 South Fairfax Street, 703–836–3713), established in 1792, is one of the oldest in the country. It displays antique handblown bottles and prescriptions it filled for eminent Virginians. Robert E. Lee was at the shop in 1859 when he was handed his orders to suppress John Brown's uprising at Harpers Ferry.

Benjamin Henry Latrobe designed the Gothic-style **St. Paul's Episcopal Church** (228 South Pitt Street, 703–549–3312), consecrated in 1818. The interior was patterned after Christopher Wren's St. James, in London. It is said that when Federal forces occupied the city at the start of the Civil War, the rector was carried

A restoration of George Washington's Grist Mill, a source of flour that he claimed was "equal

out of the church by Northern troops because he refused to pray for Lincoln. During the war the church was used as a Federal hospital.

The **George Washington Masonic National Memorial** (101 Callahan Drive, 703–683–2007) pays tribute to Washington the Mason with a tower over 300 feet tall, completed in 1932. In the museum within, there is a display of historical items including the Washington family bible and the clock from his bedroom at Mount Vernon, the pendulum of which Dr. Elisha Dick stopped at the moment of Washington's death. The Memorial Hall also has two large murals and a seventeen-foot-high statue of the president

in quality to any made in this country."

wearing his Masonic apron. Washington was the master of a lodge and wore his regalia when laying the cornerstone of the Capitol.

Fort Ward Museum and Historic Site (4301 West Braddock Road, 703–838–4848) preserves earthworks and a gun emplacement built during the Civil War for the defense of Washington, DC. A small museum on the grounds displays Civil War items.

The **George Washington's Grist Mill** (Mount Vernon Memorial Highway, 703–339–7265) is a reconstructed eighteenth-century mill that originally stood in Front Royal. Washington built a mill on this site in 1770. The three-story stone mill has exhibits about milling techniques.

MOUNT VERNON

Mount Vernon was the home of George Washington from 1754 until his death in 1799. His father, Augustine, had built a four-room cottage on the property, a 2,300-acre tobacco plantation that was inherited first by George's half brother Lawrence; it came into George's possession in 1761. Over the years Washington enlarged his landholdings—he eventually owned about eight thousand acres in this area out of a total of more than ninety thousand—and with the house, he had one of the finest plantations in Virginia. At the time of his marriage to Martha Dandridge Custis, a widow with two children, he raised the roof to create a new story for additional bedrooms. In the 1770s he doubled the size of the house by adding the study and the large dining room. On the river facade—the house stands on a bluff 126 feet above the Potomac—he built an 8-columned portico that runs the width of the house.

Although Washington was often said to have a plain, "republican style of living," Mount Vernon reveals his keen awareness of the ways in which architecture proclaims status. His remodelings brought the house toward the balance of an English Palladian villa. The wooden facades were carved and sprinkled with sand to give them the appearance and texture of stonework. He arranged the outbuildings in the Palladian fashion, with two curved colonnades reaching out to embrace the subsidiary buildings and the long bowling green in front. His hand was upon all the design, construction, and interior decoration, as well as the landscaping of the extensive gardens, though some of it was executed during the war years, when he was otherwise occupied.

He furnished the interior with pictures imported from England before the Revolution. His letters to his London agent show a sensitivity to decorative fashions, although he did not wish to buy anything too elaborate. The small dining room has a chimney piece carved with leaves and scrolls designed after an English pattern book, and its ceiling's plaster decorations were done by the same itinerant stuccadore who created the ceilings at Kenmore, in Fredericksburg. The west parlor, painted Prussian blue, has another sculpted chimney piece, emblazoned with the Washington coat of arms, and a copy of the well-known 1772 portrait by Charles Willson Peale. Washington posed for Peale at Mount Vernon, wearing his Virginia Regiment uniform.

OPPOSITE: *The passage, or central hall (top), and study (bottom), Mount Vernon.*
OVERLEAF: *Mount Vernon Plantation, above the Potomac River.*

Mount Vernon's magnificent large dining room, two stories high, occupies the house's north end. The ceiling is decorated with plaster festoons and agricultural motifs, such as a scythe, a sheaf of wheat, and a pick and shovel. The room's marble chimney piece was a gift from a British admirer who emigrated to the United States after the Revolution. The study, at the south end of the house, contains a bookpress where he stored his papers, a portrait of Lawrence Washington, a copy of the Jean Antoine Houdon bust of Washington, and a reading chair with a built-in fan. On the second floor is a private stairway to the library, and six plainly furnished bedrooms, in one of which Washington died on December 14, 1799, from a throat infection contracted while inspecting his farms during a snowstorm.

One of the most intriguing historical relics in the house is the key to the Bastille, displayed in a crystal case in the passage. It was sent from Paris by Lafayette, who ordered the destruction of the "fortress of despotism" during the French Revolution.

On the grounds of the estate are restored outbuildings, slave quarters, a monument to Mount Vernon's slaves, and a museum with changing exhibits about the Washingtons. The simple tomb where Washington and his wife are buried is located south of the vineyard lot. It was Washington's wish to be buried on his own property, and his descendants turned aside efforts by Congress to have the remains transferred to a state tomb at the U.S. Capitol.

Since 1858 Mount Vernon has been the property of the Mount Vernon Ladies' Association of the Union, which was formed to acquire and preserve the estate when the opportunity to purchase it was offered to the federal government and the state of Virginia by the president's heirs. Through gifts and purchases the Association has acquired many original furnishings.

LOCATION: South of Alexandria on the Mount Vernon Memorial Highway. HOURS: April through August: 8–4 Daily; September through March: 9–4:30 Daily. FEE: Yes. TELEPHONE: 703–780– 2000.

Woodlawn, a short distance from Mount Vernon (Route 1, 703– 780–4000), was the home of Nelly Custis Lewis, Martha Washington's granddaughter, and her husband, Lawrence Lewis, Washington's nephew. This elegant brick house, remodeled by William Thornton, one of the architects of the U.S. Capitol, and completed in 1806, displays furnishings of the Federal period.

Pohick Church (9301 Richmond Highway, Lorton, 703–550– 9449) was the church where George Washington worshiped, and

Gunston Hall, one of the great houses of pre-Revolutionary Virginia.

which he may have designed. Washington chose the site and he, along with George Mason of Gunston Hall, was on the committee that oversaw its construction between 1769 and 1774. The original walls survive, but the interior of the church was ruined by Union troops, who turned the church into a stable. The interior seen today is the result of a restoration of 1901 to 1916. The sandstone walls still bear the carved initials of soldiers.

GUNSTON HALL

Gunston Hall was the home of George Mason, who had profound influence in the creation of the republic. Mason drafted the 1774 Fairfax Resolves and the Virginia Declaration of Rights, and wrote that "all men are by nature equally free and independent and have certain inherent rights"—a concept that Jefferson made the cornerstone of the Declaration of Independence. As a delegate to the Constitutional Convention, Mason refused to sign the Constitution because it did not include a Bill of Rights. Jefferson referred to him as "one of our really great men, and of the first order of greatness."

Mason began the construction of the house in 1755. He later took as an indentured servant the British master carpenter and joiner William Buckland to design and create the woodwork for several of the rooms. Buckland's Palladian drawing room is his masterpiece; the woodwork in the dining room is probably the first use of Chinese decorative motifs in America (they are definitely the oldest extant examples on this continent). Buckland embellished the exterior with a handsome "Gothick" porch and carved cornices; a second porch was designed by Mason after a Buckland concept. Mason himself was responsible for the design of his gardens, and the house preserves many items of his own furniture. Buckland moved to Annapolis, Maryland, where he designed the superb Hammond-Harwood House.

LOCATION: 'Lorton, Exit 55 off Route 95. HOURS: 9:30–5 Daily. FEE: Yes. TELEPHONE: 703–550–9220.

QUANTICO

A naval center since the Revolutionary War, the Quantico area was leased as a Marine Corps base during World War I. Today, the town of Quantico is entirely surrounded by the 100-acre facility known as the Marine Corps Combat Development Command. The **Marine Corps Air-Ground Museum** on the base (703–784–2606) displays an impressive collection of aircraft, tanks, artillery, small arms, uniforms, and other military items.

FREDERICKSBURG

Located just south of the fall line of the Rappahannock River, Fredericksburg was an important port and center of trade for the region's tobacco and wheat farms in the eighteenth and nineteenth centuries. The Rappahannock, deep enough here for oceangoing ships, carried a flourishing commerce in grain, tobacco, farming equipment, and a variety of luxury items imported from Europe. George Washington spent part of his youth on his family's farm near the town. His sister, mother, and many close friends lived in Fredericksburg. Another distinguished American whose public-service career had its roots here was James Monroe, negotiator of the Louisiana Purchase and, later, minister to France. The **Old Town Hall and Market House,** built around 1816, is one of America's few remaining colonial market houses and the oldest continually used town hall in the South.

In the Civil War the town's advantageous location along the Rappahannock and on the road between Washington and Richmond made it a battleground—the town changed hands seven times. The walls of the **Presbyterian Church** at Princess Anne and George streets still have the marks of cannonballs. **Caroline Street** is a well-preserved district of eighteenth- and nineteenth-century houses. The visitor center is at 706 Caroline Street (540–373–1776).

The **James Monroe Museum** (908 Charles Street, 540–899–4559) preserves the law offices he occupied from 1786 to 1789, including his lawbooks and the elegant Louis XVI furniture he bought in France. The museum is adjacent to a small **Masonic cemetery,** started by the local lodge in 1784.

Rising Sun Tavern

This structure was built about 1760 as a residence by George Washington's brother Charles. George visited the home on a number of occasions. In 1792 the house was converted to a tavern, the Golden Eagle, later renamed the Rising Sun.

LOCATION: 1306 Caroline Street. HOURS: March through November: 9–5 Daily; December through February: 10–4 Daily. FEE: Yes. TELEPHONE: 540–371–1494.

Hugh Mercer Apothecary

Mercer was a Scottish doctor who served in the army of Bonnie Prince Charlie that met defeat at the Battle of Culloden. he fled to America, fought in the French and Indian War, and became a close friend of George Washington. After the war he opened this apothecary, which Washington used as an office when visiting the town. In the Revolutionary War Mercer was a commander at the Battle of Trenton, New Jersey, and lost his life in the fighting at Princeton. A monument to him, erected in 1906, is at Washington Avenue and Faquier Street. His shop has been restored with items typical of the period; the original shelves, drawers, and pigeonholes were uncovered during a renovation. General George S. Patton was a descendant of Mercer.

LOCATION: 1020 Caroline Street. HOURS: March through November: 9–5 Daily; December through February: 10–4 Daily. FEE: Yes. TELEPHONE: 540–373–3362.

The Hugh Mercer Apothecary Shop, Fredericksburg.

Kenmore

Kenmore was built by Fielding Lewis, whose wife, Betty, was the sister of George Washington. Though Lewis never fought in a battle, he built ships, supplied the army with gunpowder, lead, food, and clothing, and operated a gun factory. Betty Lewis, along with many other Fredericksburg women, made powder cartridges. When the public funds authorized for the manufacture of weapons had been used up, Lewis pledged his own money and house to keep the factory in operation. He was never repaid. Fielding Lewis died in 1781 just after the victory at Yorktown; Betty Lewis died in 1797, after which the house was sold.

Kenmore is remarkable for its richly decorated, hand-molded ceilings. The dining room, drawing room, and bedroom ceilings are embellished with superb plaster reliefs done in 1775 by an unknown artisan, the same person who decorated two rooms at Mount Vernon. The drawing room reliefs are mainly floral motifs such as garlands, swags, bouquets, and rosettes, while the bedroom ceiling features seasonal symbols—palms, grapes, acorns, and mistletoe. The plaster overmantel in the drawing room depicts one of Aesop's fables, "The Fox and the Crow." The house, restored and furnished with an excellent collection of period furnishings, is surrounded by a garden in the eighteenth-century style. There is a small museum, with a diorama of colonial Fredericksburg.

> LOCATION: 1201 Washington Avenue. HOURS: March through December: 10–5 Monday–Friday, 12–5 Sunday; January, February: 10–4 Saturday, 12–4 Sunday. FEE: Yes. TELEPHONE: 540–373–3381.

Mary Washington House

George Washington purchased this house, not far from Kenmore, for his mother in 1772. He made frequent visits, despite that his relationship with his mother was a difficult one. She complained he

The drawing room at Kenmore, with its elaborate plasterwork.

Confederate cannon at Hazel Grove, just south of Chancellorsville.

neglected her and left her in poverty. Describing a visit Washington made in 1784, the biographer Elswyth Thane wrote, "Pursuing his always dutiful if reluctant way thither, he listened with his indestructible courtesy to her complaints and what now amounted to hallucinations of fraud and poverty." She had spread such heartbreaking stories about her condition that the Virginia Assembly was about to vote her a pension when Washington was informed of the plan and put a stop to it. The restored house displays some items owned by Mrs. Washington.

> LOCATION: 1200 Charles Street. HOURS: March through November: 9–5 Daily; December through February: 10–4 Daily. FEE: Yes. TELEPHONE: 540–373–1569.

FREDERICKSBURG AND SPOTSYLVANIA NATIONAL MILITARY PARK

The armies of the North and South suffered more than 100,000 casualties in the four battles that took place within the confines of this park—Fredericksburg, Chancellorsville, the Wilderness, and

Trenches of the Confederate Army at Prospect Hill, Fredericksburg.

Spotsylvania Court House. This ground was repeatedly and bitterly fought for because it was located halfway between the opposing capital cities.

The Battle of Fredericksburg

The Battle of Fredericksburg, fought from December 11 to 15, 1862, was an appalling disaster for the North. In November Lincoln had relieved General McClellan of his command of the Army of the Potomac when McClellan once again delayed attacking Lee while the Southerners were retreating from Antietam. Lincoln appointed General Ambrose Burnside, who planned an attack on Richmond by way of Fredericksburg, where he could be supplied by the Richmond, Fredericksburg, and Potomac Railroad. Burnside's 110,000 men reached the shore of the river at Falmouth, just north of Fredericksburg, in mid-November, but organizational confusion caused a week's delay in crossing the river. Lee was thus given time to fortify Marye's Heights west of Fredericksburg and Prospect Hill south of the city.

On December 11 some Northern units crossed the river on pontoon bridges, looting Fredericksburg the next day. On December 13 an attack on Prospect Hill, held by Stonewall Jackson, faltered when General William B. Franklin failed to commit his reserves to exploit a breach in the Confederate line. Meanwhile, a hideous slaughter was underway at Marye's Heights, as Burnside sent wave after wave of men against the virtually impregnable Confederate position. By the end of the day some 13,000 Northerners lay dead or wounded. Burnside retreated on December 15. The defeat touched off a political crisis in Washington, and Lincoln wrote in despair, "If there is a worse place than Hell, I am in it." It was during this battle that Lee said, "It is well that war is so terrible—we should grow too fond of it."

Battle of Chancellorsville

The Battle of Chancellorsville, fought May 1 to 6, 1863, was one of Robert E. Lee's most brilliant victories. That spring Lee had spread twenty-five miles of trenches along the Rappahannock to protect Fredericksburg. Union general Joseph "Fighting Joe" Hooker, now in command of the Army of the Potomac, proposed to send a 40,000-man column against Fredericksburg, but his main attack on Lee's army would fall on the Confederate western flank. To this end 70,000 men crossed the Rappahannock at Chancellorsville, threatening to encircle Lee. His plan now in place, Hooker was suddenly afflicted by the same reluctance to fight that had bedeviled McClellan.

Lee realized that the greater threat lay at Chancellorsville rather than Fredericksburg: He sent the bulk of his army west. On May 1, when the advance guards of the opposing armies encountered each other east of Chancellorsville, on open ground favorable to the Northerners, Hooker ordered a retreat into the woods. That night Lee and Stonewall Jackson hatched a bold and hazardous plan, calculated to take advantage of Hooker's apparent unwillingness to fight. Lee split his forces, keeping only 15,000 men to face Hooker and sending Jackson with 30,000 men in a flanking maneuver to the west. Hooker was informed of the movements but did nothing, believing that Lee was withdrawing.

Lee's gamble paid off handsomely. In the late afternoon of May 2, Jackson's men struck at the right end of Hooker's line and sent it reeling back two miles as Lee attacked Hooker's front. The fighting continued into the night. Riding back to their lines in the dark, Jackson and a group of officers were mistaken for Federals.

Salem Church, Chancellorsville, site of Confederate General Lee's decisive victory over Union General Hooker.

Their own men fired upon them, wounding Jackson in the arm, which had to be amputated. The legendary infantry commander developed pneumonia, and he died on May 10 at a plantation in Guinea, ten miles south of Fredericksburg.

With an advantage of roughly two-to-one in manpower, Hooker still had a chance to win. To distract Lee he ordered the units at Fredericksburg to attack Marye's Heights, the site of Burnside's disaster. But this time, after two assaults were turned back, the Northerners succeeded in taking the hill with a bayonet charge. Lee sent two divisions to the relief of Fredericksburg, but still Hooker refused to press his numerical advantage. Ignoring the advice of his field commanders, Hooker ordered a retreat, and Lee's prestige rose to its greatest height.

The Battle in the Wilderness

The battles in the Wilderness and at Spotsylvania in May 1864 began a yearlong campaign between the Army of the Potomac, now commanded by Ulysses S. Grant, and Lee's Army of Northern Virginia. The armies fought here without any resolution, with both of them leapfrogging south as Grant tried repeatedly to outflank

Confederate casualties in the Sunken Road, Marye's Heights, after the successful Union assault in May 1863.

Lee, only to find Lee's army one step ahead of him. The campaign ended sixty miles to the south with the siege of Petersburg.

In early May the Union army emerged from its winter quarters around Culpeper; Lee's army had passed the winter not far away, on the other side of the Rapidan River in the Mine Run area. Grant's plan was to cross the Rapidan and attempt to position himself between Lee and Richmond, thus drawing Lee into a fight in the open. If possible, Grant hoped to avoid fighting in the Wilderness, a densely tangled region of scrub pine and oak with few cleared fields and few roads. Grant succeeded in crossing the Rapidan without trouble, but his 100,000-man army encountered some of Lee's units, about 60,000 men, in the Wilderness. Two days of terrible fighting at close quarters ensued. Both armies lashed out in confusion, unable to keep good order in the dense brush. A Northerner later wrote, "As for the fighting, it was simply bushwhacking on a grand scale." And a captured Texan yelled at his interrogators: "It ain't no battle . . . our two armies ain't nothing but howlin' mobs!" Both sides lost opportunities to win a clear victory, and dug strong entrenchments. Grant reported to Lincoln: "At present we can claim no victory over the enemy, neither have they gained a single advantage."

Spotsylvania Court House

Instead of battling it out with Lee in the Wilderness, Grant undertook the first of a long series of flanking maneuvers to the southeast. Grant planned to capture the crossroads at Spotsylvania. Lee, with a longer road to Spotsylvania, was saved from disaster by chance: One of his units, unable to occupy its assigned camp because the area was on fire, moved south to Spotsylvania and entrenched there. "By this accident," Grant later wrote, "Lee got possession of Spotsylvania . . . but accident often decides the fate of battle." Union colonel Emory Upton led a heroic assault in which a strong column focused on a single point of the Confederate entrenchments and succeeded in breaking through; but his reinforcements wavered under artillery fire and the attack collapsed.

Impressed by Upton's tactics, Grant ordered a similar assault at dawn on May 12. Once again his men broke through, but Confederate counterattacks forced the Federals to fall back from the captured trenches. Into the night the two armies were locked in hand-to-hand fighting in the trenches at the "Bloody Angle," where the shooting was so fierce that an oak tree was cut down by rifle shots. One of Grant's staff officers recalled that "rank after rank was riddled by shot and shell and bayonet-thrusts, and finally sank, a mass of torn and mutilated corpses; then fresh troops rushed madly forward to replace the dead, and so the murderous work went on." Unable to pierce Lee's lines, Grant moved southeast to outflank Lee, whose units won a race to a rail junction by the North Anna River. Grant leapfrogged yet again to Cold Harbor outside Richmond.

All four battlefields, which are within seventeen miles of Fredericksburg, may be toured. There are museums and visitor centers in Fredericksburg and at Chancellorsville. In Fredericksburg, the stone wall on Marye's Heights that was so bitterly fought over has been partially preserved. Also along the Sunken Road is a monument to Confederate sergeant Richard Kirkland, who risked his life to carry water to wounded Federal troops. Atop Marye's Heights is the Fredericksburg National Cemetery, where more than 15,000 Union soldiers are buried. Five miles of the Confederate entrenchments have been preserved. **Chatham** (120 Chatham Lane, Stafford County, 540–373–4461), an eighteenth-century house which Federal officers, including General Fighting Joe Hooker, used as a command post, is headquarters for the National

Park. Both visitor centers include audiovisual programs, museum exhibits, and information helpful in planning a self-guided tour.

LOCATION: Lafayette Boulevard at Sunken Road. HOURS: April through mid-June: 9–5 Monday–Friday, 9–6 Saturday, Sunday; mid-June through Labor Day: 8:30–6:30 Daily; September, October: 9–5 Monday–Friday, 9–6 Saturday, Sunday; November through March: 9–5 Daily. *Grounds* Dawn–Dusk. FEE: None. TELEPHONE: 540-373-4461.

CULPEPER

At various times during the Civil War this railroad town west of Fredericksburg was a headquarters for both sides. In June 1863 the largest cavalry engagement of the war, the Battle of Brandy Station, was fought five miles north of the town. The **Museum of Culpeper History** (140 East Davis Street, 703–825–1973) looks back at the area's history, from dinosaur tracks through Indian occupation to the Revolutionary and Civil wars.

MONTPELIER

Montpelier, south of Culpeper near Orange, was the farm of President James Madison's family: His grandfather had patented the property in 1723, and his father, James Madison, Sr., built a two-story house which his son enlarged twice—once between 1797 and 1800, then in 1809–1812. After his two terms as president Madison and his wife, Dolley, retired to Montpelier in 1817. According to contemporary accounts Montpelier was beautifully furnished with French carpets, chairs, porcelain, silver, and paintings. His drawing room, entered from the east portico, was something of a portrait gallery, with a half dozen paintings by Gilbert Stuart and busts of people he admired. He enjoyed conversing with guests on the portico, with its view of the Blue Ridge Mountains. "His conversation was a stream of history," one visitor recalled.

After Madison's death in 1836 (he and Mrs. Madison are buried on the property) most of the furniture had to be auctioned: Madison, like Jefferson and Monroe, died on the brink of insolvency. In the twentieth century the house was expanded to fifty-five

OPPOSITE: *Montpelier, family home of President James Madison, is located on 2,700 acres near the Blue Ridge Mountains.*

rooms by William duPont, Sr., who purchased the property in 1901. Today, the house bears little resemblance to the home that Madison knew. Under the auspices of the National Trust for Historic Preservation, it presents changing exhibits about the Madisons, historical subjects, and architecture.

> LOCATION: Route 20, four miles west of Orange. HOURS: March through December: 10–4 Daily; January, February 10–4 Saturday, Sunday. FEE: Yes. TELEPHONE: 540–672–2728.

The **James Madison Museum** in Orange (129 Caroline Street, 540–672–1776) has exhibits about his political career and his agricultural experiments at Montpelier.

   Scotchtown (Route 685 near Beaverdam, 804–227–3500) was the home of Patrick Henry and his family from 1771 to 1777, although he spent much of that time in Williamsburg. His wife, Sarah, was mentally ill, and was confined in a basement room under a doctor's care. She died here in 1775. The house has been restored with period furnishings and family portraits.

The **Stonewall Jackson Shrine** (Route 606 in Guinea, 804–633–6076) is the plantation building where the great Confederate general died on May 10, 1863. He had been wounded in the Battle of Chancellorsville and succumbed to pneumonia with the dying words, "Let us cross over the river and rest under the shade of the trees." The shrine preserves the bed in which he died.

N O R T H E R N   N E C K

East of Fredericksburg is the Northern Neck, a long peninsula bounded by the Potomac on the north and the Rappahannock on the south. In 1669 King Charles II granted five million acres of land, from the tip of the Neck to the northern end of the Shenandoah Valley, to four Cavaliers who had remained loyal to the Crown during Cromwell's interregnum. Thomas, Lord Culpeper, purchased nearly all of it a few years later. In 1689 Lord Fairfax acquired the Culpeper holdings through his marriage to Culpeper's daughter. His son employed the young George Washington to survey his lands and collect rents. Thomas Lee, founder of the Lee dynasty in Virginia, also acted as an agent for Fairfax.

GEORGE WASHINGTON BIRTHPLACE NATIONAL MONUMENT

George Washington was born on this site in 1732. When he was 3½ years old, his family moved to the Mount Vernon property and three years later to Ferry Farm in Fredericksburg. The house in which he was born burned down in 1779. On the site is a 1930 reconstruction of a typical plantation house of that period, called the Memorial House. Washington's father purchased 150 acres at the site on which the house stood in 1718, with the plantation growing to 1,300 acres by the time of George's birth. A family burial ground in the park includes the remains of approximately thirty of Washington's forebears. The National Park Service operates a farm where eighteenth-century agricultural methods are demonstrated and a visitor center, which shows a brief film.

LOCATION: Route 204. HOURS: 9–5 Daily. FEE: Yes. TELEPHONE: 804–224–1732.

STRATFORD HALL

Stratford Hall was the home of the Lees, who, with the possible exceptions of the Adamses of Massachusetts and the Roosevelts of New York, may be the family that has left the deepest mark on the country's history. Thomas Lee built the house in the 1730s. Five of his sons, Thomas Ludwell, Richard Henry, Francis Lightfoot, William, and Arthur, were in the front ranks of the Patriot cause before and during the Revolution. John Adams called them "this band of brothers, intrepid and unchangeable, who like the Greeks at Thermopylae, stood in the gap, in defense of their country." Thomas Ludwell was a member of Virginia's Committee of Safety; Francis Lightfoot was elected to the Continental Congress; to Richard Henry fell the honor of introducing in Congress the resolution calling for independence; he and Francis Lightfoot were the only two brothers to sign the Declaration of Independence. William and Arthur Lee served as diplomats in Europe.

A cousin, General Henry Lee, married into this branch of the family and occupied Stratford Hall in 1782. Better known as Light Horse Harry, this Lee won fame as a cavalry commander in the Revolutionary War, and was later elected governor of Virginia and a member of Congress. Harry Lee gave the eulogy for George

Washington in Congress, praising him with the famous words, "First in war, first in peace, and first in the hearts of his countrymen." After the death of his first wife Lee married Anne Hill Carter of Shirley Plantation, who gave birth at Stratford to Robert E. Lee on January 19, 1807. Four years later Harry Lee's disastrous speculations in land left him virtually penniless, forcing him to move the family to Alexandria.

The house is one of the grandest in Virginia, an H-shaped, fortresslike mansion with imposing chimney clusters. The formal rooms on the second floor include the handsomely panelled Great Hall, which is twenty-nine feet square and seventeen feet high. The southeast bedroom is called the Mother's Room; it is where many of the Lee children, including Robert E. Lee, were born. On the ground floor are additional bedrooms and the estate's counting room. The house is furnished throughout with eighteenth- and early-nineteenth-century antiques and family portraits.

LOCATION: Route 214, Stratford. HOURS: 9–4:30 Daily. FEE: Yes. TELEPHONE: 804–493–8038.

CHRIST CHURCH

Magnificent in its early classicism, yet with a subtle touch of the Gothic at the "crossing," Christ Church (routes 646 and 709, Irvington, 804–438–6855) was erected in 1735 with funds donated by Robert "King" Carter, merchant, planter, and fur-trader, who served as the agent for Lord Fairfax and amassed one of the largest fortunes in the colonies. At his death in 1732 Carter had three hundred thousand acres of land and £10,000 in cash. Members of the Carter family are buried in the church. The bricks for the church, built in the shape of a cross, came from kilns on Carter's property adjacent to the church. The church preserves its original high-back pews and three-tiered pulpit and has in its collection the original communion service made in London. Adjacent to the church is a small museum devoted to the history of Christ Church, along with displays of artifacts unearthed on the site of Carter's mansion on the Corotoman River.

OPPOSITE: *Stratford Hall—birthplace to many generations of Lees—is punctuated by a pair of arcaded quadruple chimneys, top. According to Robert E. Lee, who was born here, an earlier owner "kept a band of musicians to whose airs his daughters danced in the saloon [bottom] or promenaded on the housetop."*

RICHMOND
AND
ENVIRONS

OPPOSITE: *Shirley Plantation, on the shores of the James River.*

Richmond was established in 1737 by William Byrd II of Westover as a mill site and trading center. His landholdings here at the fall line of the James River were, he wrote, "naturally intended for marts, where the traffic of the outer inhabitants must center." Since the 1720s the House of Burgesses had earmarked this spot for a city, but Byrd resisted their efforts, realizing he would have to part with his land at a low price. In 1737 he advertised in newspapers that "on the north side of the James River is lately laid off a town with streets sixty-five feet wide, in a pleasant and healthy situation and well supplied with springs of good water." The town remained a small one through the eighteenth century, with a population well under one thousand, and survived disaster in 1771 when a forty-foot-high wall of water came roaring down the James, sweeping away houses, ships, and tobacco warehouses. In March 1775, just weeks before the outbreak of the Revolution, delegates from the colony gathered at **St. John's Church** (2401 East Broad Street, 804–648–5015) to discuss the political crisis. Patrick Henry astounded the delegates with his inflammatory "Liberty or Death" speech, in which he proclaimed, "We must fight! I repeat it, sir, we must fight!" By a slim margin of five the 125 delegates voted to equip and train local militia units for war with Britain.

During the Revolution Richmond was named the capital of the provisional government, replacing Williamsburg, which was regarded as dangerously vulnerable to British attack. As it turned out, the British raided Richmond twice, burning houses and looting tobacco warehouses. Benedict Arnold, in command of one of the raids, left behind a donation for the poor, which was returned.

From the 1790s through the 1850s Richmond grew and prospered. Railroad lines and a canal that skirted the falls on the James transported tobacco and wheat from western Virginia farms to Richmond's wharves. Tobacco farming was elevated to a thriving industry as Richmond factories processed, flavored, and packed chewing tobacco. Virginia wheat fed Europe and California: Richmond made itself the second largest producer and shipper of flour, after Baltimore. Along Fifth Street newly wealthy merchants, bankers, lawyers, and manufacturers built their brick townhouses. The boom was dampened by tragedy—a theater fire in 1811 killed seventy-two people, many of them from the town's prominent families. (When Edgar Allan Poe was seeking a discharge from the army, he concocted a heartbreaking story about his parents dying in this fire.) As a memorial to the fire victims, **Monumental**

An early nineteenth-century view of plantation life, painted with oil on wood (detail).

Church (1226 East Broad Street, 804–643–7407) was built on the site of the theater in 1814. Robert Mills's design—an octagonal, domed building with a Neoclassical portico—reflects the influence of his mentors, Thomas Jefferson and Benjamin Henry Latrobe.

The city's fortunes sank during depressions that lasted through the 1820s and 1830s, but the 1850s saw a stunning revival. Exports of flour and tobacco soared, and the ships that carried Virginia flour to South America returned with coffee beans. In the decade before the Civil War Richmond was the country's major coffee port. Ironworks and cotton mills sprang up along the James. The block of Greek Revival townhouses known as **Linden Row** (the 100 block of East Franklin Street) reflects this prosperity. Many of Richmond's nineteenth-century houses feature decorative cast-iron fences, gates, and trim produced by local foundries.

On the eve of the Civil War, Richmond, along with most of Virginia, opposed secession. A state convention held at Richmond in April 1861, after seven Southern states had seceded, voted to remain in the Union by a margin of two to one. But when the attack on Fort Sumter prompted Lincoln to call for volunteers to put

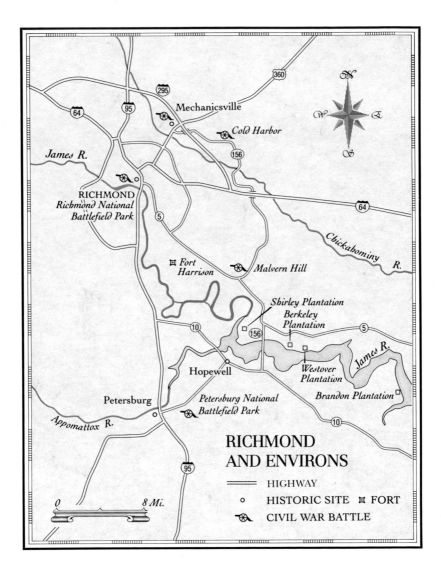

RICHMOND
AND ENVIRONS

══════ HIGHWAY

○ HISTORIC SITE ⌗ FORT

⚔ CIVIL WAR BATTLE

down the rebellion, the convention reversed itself. The Virginians would not bear arms against other Southerners. Governor John Letcher, previously a staunch Unionist, offered the command of Virginia's troops to Robert E. Lee, and the convention invited Jefferson Davis to move the Confederate capital from Montgomery, Alabama, to Richmond. The offer was accepted because Richmond was the major producer of food and iron. The Tredegar Ironworks produced guns, ammunition, rails, and the armor for the ironclad *Virginia*.

To Richmond fell the enormous task of caring for the Confederate wounded brought in from Virginia's battlefields. After just one battle 16,000 wounded, requiring immediate care, were carted into the city. Private homes, offices, churches, schools, and theaters were commandeered for hospitals. Some 76,000 men were tended at Chimborazo Hospital, a huge complex of 250 buildings and tents. The women of the city performed heroic service under the most difficult conditions, cleaning and dressing wounds, feeding the soldiers, and assisting surgeons with amputations. Wagons laden with corpses became a familiar sight.

When Grant's army besieged Petersburg in the fall and winter of 1864–1865, Richmond suffered shortages of food, fuel, and clothing. An officer recalled "people without overcoats . . . their teeth chattering . . . their thin garments buttoned over their chests." When Lee's position became hopeless, he sent a message on April 2, 1865, to Davis, who was attending Palm Sunday services at **St. Paul's Episcopal Church** (815 East Grace Street, 804–643–3589), that the city had to be abandoned. Richmond fell in an atmosphere of apocalypse: The citizens fled carrying whatever they could; tobacco warehouses were put to the torch to deny their revenue to the Yankees, and an acrid stench spread over the area. Flames spread to the business district and explosions shook the city as Confederate officers destroyed their ships on the river and a huge powder magazine was detonated. An arsenal blew up, raining fresh destruction. Mobs of drunken looters prowled the ruins. In order to save the city the mayor formally invited Federal troops to enter. On April 4 President Lincoln toured the fallen capital with his son Tad, protected only by a small contingent of sailors.

From the 1860s to the 1890s Richmond made a slow but steady recovery from the war, hampered by the nationwide financial panics in 1873 and 1893. Flour mills, ironworks, and tobacco factories resumed their work. The city benefited from railroad expansion and from the invention, in the mid-1870s, of the cigarette.

The **Shockoe Slip** commercial district, which had burned down in 1865, was rebuilt in the last half of the century. Much of its fine late-Victorian commercial architecture has been preserved. Memories of the war were stirred in 1890 when the famed equestrian statue of Robert E. Lee was dedicated before a crowd of veterans. The statue was erected on the newly laid out **Monument Avenue,** a broad mall that would become the city's boulevard of honor, with statues of five Southern heroes: Lee, J. E. B. Stuart, Stonewall Jackson, Jefferson Davis, and Matthew Fontaine Maury. **Hollywood Cemetery** (412 South Cherry Street, 804–648–8501), dedicated in 1849, is the burying place of Presidents Monroe and Tyler, Jefferson Davis, J. E. B. Stuart, and 18,000 Confederate soldiers. Its location by the river at first provoked opposition; some said that the roar of the falls would disturb the dead.

In addition to the city itself, this chapter covers the Richmond National Battlefield Park, which administers sites outside the city; Petersburg; and the plantations east of Richmond on the northern bank of the James River. This chapter begins at Capitol Square, then describes sites to the north and west of the square. The Poe Museum and St. John's Church, located in the historic Church Hill district, are southeast of Capitol Square. Farther east is the Chimborazo visitor center of Richmond National Battlefield Park. The city's visitor center (804–358–5511) is at 1700 Robin Hood Road, at exit 14 off Route 95. Tourist information can also be obtained by calling 800–365–7272.

VIRGINIA STATE CAPITOL

Richmond remained the capital of Virginia after the Revolution, providing Thomas Jefferson with an opportunity to design one of the first state capitols erected in the new republic. With the help of Charles-Louis Clérisseau, whom he had met in France, Jefferson designed America's second important temple-form building. (The first was Prince William's Church, near Sheldon, South Carolina.) Jefferson and Clérisseau drew upon the general shape of a Roman temple, the Maison Carrée at Nimes. In a letter to Madison, Jefferson wrote, "We took for our model . . . one of the most beautiful, if not the most beautiful and precious morsel of architecture left us

OPPOSITE: *Robert E. Lee on horseback, framed by the trees of Monument Avenue.*

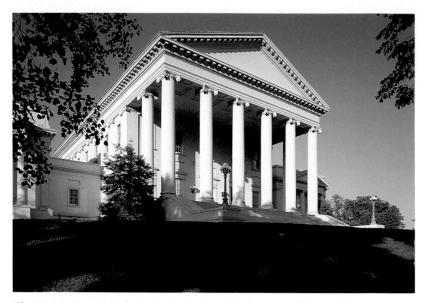

The Virginia State Capitol was the site for Aaron Burr's treason trial as well as sessions of the Congress of the Confederacy. The statue of Washington in its rotunda (opposite) keeps company with busts of Lafayette and the seven U.S. presidents from Virginia.

by antiquity." He called it "very simple" but "noble beyond expression." Jefferson intended the Neoclassical building to announce, architecturally, the absolute break with British authority and culture, symbolized in his mind by Williamsburg's brick buildings.

In the rotunda stands a life-sized statue of Washington by Houdon (the only one executed from life), surrounded by busts of the other seven Virginian presidents. The House of Delegates chamber has a statue of Robert E. Lee, located on the spot where he took command of Virginia's forces.

LOCATION: Capitol Square. HOURS: April through November: 9–5 Daily; December through March: 9–5 Monday–Saturday, 1–5 Sunday. FEE: None. TELEPHONE: 804–786–4344.

CAPITOL SQUARE

At the northwest corner of Capitol Square is the **Washington Monument,** a sixty-foot-high monument, unveiled in 1858, with an equestrian statue of Washington and bronze figures of Thomas Jefferson, George Mason, Patrick Henry, John Marshall, and other famous Virginians. The base of the monument was designed by

Robert Mills; most of the statuary was created by Thomas Craw-
ford. At the square's northeast corner is the **Governor's Mansion**
(804–371–2642), designed by a New Englander, Alexander Parris,
and completed in 1813. The interior has fine carved woodwork
and plaster decoration, and reproductions of Federal furniture.

The **Old City Hall,** located behind the capitol at the corner of
10th and Broad streets, has been converted to offices. Designed by
Elijah Myers and completed in 1894, the building is a virtual
celebration of the Gothic Revival, punctuated by rows of pointed
arches, turrets with conical roofs, and a clock tower with a pyrami-
dical roof. In contrast to the gray exterior, the arcaded stair hall
inside presents an effusion of color on its painted and gilded
columns, entablatures, and arches.

MUSEUM AND WHITE HOUSE OF THE CONFEDERACY

The house that Jefferson Davis lived in during the Civil War was
built in 1818 for Dr. John Brockenbrough. He was a physician and
a banker who served on the jury that tried former vice president
Aaron Burr for treason. When the Confederate government
moved here from Montgomery, the city of Richmond purchased
the house and rented it to the Confederacy. When they moved into
the house the Davises hired a black servant, Mary Elizabeth
Bowser, on the recommendation of a prominent Richmond lady,
Elizabeth Van Lew. Van Lew was the leader of what would become
a highly successful Northern spy ring, and Bowser was one of her
most valuable agents.

Davis was better trained than Lincoln to head a wartime government. A West Point graduate, and a veteran of the Mexican-
American War, he had served as secretary of war. Regarded
among many Confederates as a hero after the war, he was not well
liked during it. The journalist George W. Bagby described him in
his diary with a string of derogatives: "cold, haughty, peevish,
narrow-minded, pig-headed, *malignant.*" His difficult personality
may have resulted from recurrent illness and misfortune—in 1864
his five-year-old son was killed in a fall from the east portico.

Ten rooms on the first and second floors have been restored to
their wartime appearance. This work, completed in 1988, was

OPPOSITE: *The ebullient interior of Old City Hall. It was completed in 1894, twenty years after
its predecessor was demolished for fear it might collapse—as had a floor in the Capitol in 1870.*

aided by an inventory of the house taken in 1870. On the first floor, an oval entrance hall provides access to a central parlor where Davis and his wife, Varina, would have received guests on state occasions. The large dining room was the scene of formal dinners and, occasionally, cabinet meetings. The drawing room and library were semi-private, used mainly for family gatherings.

The second floor holds Davis's office, with furnishings he used during the war; the master bedroom; and the nursery. Two children were born to the Davises in the house.

The adjacent **Museum of the Confederacy** houses the nation's largest collection of Confederate artifacts, including weapons, uniforms, battle flags, letters, diaries, photographs, equipment, and models. Among the displays are Robert E. Lee's field equipment— bed, saddle, clothing, field glasses and other items—a model of the ironclad *Virginia* made by a crewman, the sword Lee wore at the surrender, and the saddle, sword, and plumed hat of the legendary cavalry commander J. E. B. Stuart.

LOCATION: 1202 East Clay Street. HOURS: 10–5 Monday–Saturday, 1–5 Sunday. FEE: Yes. TELEPHONE: 804–649–1861.

VALENTINE MUSEUM AND WICKHAM HOUSE

The history of Richmond is this museum's theme, achieved in a brief narrative film about the city and changing exhibits of clothing, silver, smoking items, antique fabrics, and toys. The museum administers the **Wickham House,** which is a seventeen-room Regency mansion completed in 1812. Alexander Parris was the architect. He arranged the rooms around a circular hall containing a curving staircase. The rooms, with Neoclassical decorative details, display nineteenth-century furniture, clothing, china, and paintings. The walls of the oval parlor are painted with scenes from the *Iliad*. Its original owner, John Wickham, was one of the lawyers who won acquittal for Aaron Burr in his trial for treason. In the garden is the studio of sculptor Edward V. Valentine, whose brother owned the house in the second half of the nineteenth century.

OPPOSITE: *The reception room of the White House of the Confederacy. A portrait of Jefferson Davis, painted while he was in residence there, hangs above the first and second flags of the Confederacy.* OVERLEAF: *The studio of Edward V. Valentine, with casts for his works.*

Valentine, who created statues of many Confederate leaders, is best remembered for his statue of a recumbent Robert E. Lee, which lies over the general's tomb at Washington and Lee University in Lexington, Virginia.

LOCATION: 1015 East Clay Street. HOURS: 10–5 Monday–Saturday, 12–5 Sunday; Guided tours given daily on the hour, 11–4. FEE: Yes. TELEPHONE: 804–649–0711.

JOHN MARSHALL HOUSE

Marshall, the chief justice of the United States from 1801 to 1835, built this brick house in 1791. A cousin of his political opponent, Thomas Jefferson, Marshall was one of the brilliant Virginia lawyers who shaped the federal government in the early years of the republic. His decisions established the precedent giving the federal courts the power to review legislative decisions and uphold or reject them on the basis of the Constitution, and he wrote landmark opinions on contracts and interstate commerce. His restored house displays many original furnishings.

LOCATION: Ninth and Marshall streets. HOURS: 10–5 Tuesday– Saturday. FEE: Yes. TELEPHONE: 804–648–7998.

Located farther north in the historic Jackson Ward, the **Maggie L. Walker House** (110½ East Leigh Street, 804–780–1380) was the home of the daughter of a former slave, who established, in 1903, one of the first black-owned banks in the country, and became the first American woman to be a bank president. Her brick townhouse has been restored and furnished with items of the period.

West of Capitol Square, the **Virginia Museum of Fine Arts** (Grove Avenue and Boulevard, 804–367–0844) is known for its collections of Impressionist paintings and British sporting art, both donated by Mr. and Mrs. Paul Mellon. The museum's American art collection, although small, covers periods from the Colonial era to the present; it includes portraits of two early settlers of Jamestown, as well as twenty-four George Catlin paintings of Indians.

The **Virginia Historical Society,** housed in Battle Abbey (428 North Boulevard, 804–358–4901), has exhibits of Civil War weapons and equipment, including items used by Robert E. Lee and J. E. B. Stuart. The Mural Gallery features four large murals of Civil

OPPOSITE: *A room in the house of Maggie Walker, a woman who founded one of the first black-owned banks in the country.*

E. B. DU BOIS

War scenes painted between 1913 and 1921 by Charles Hoffbauer. The society preserves a large collection of Virginia's historical documents, manuscripts, and art.

MAYMONT

The son of Irish immigrants, James H. Dooley served on the Confederate side in the Civil War and was one of the businessmen who spearheaded the city's resurgence after the war. In so doing he amassed a large fortune in railroads, real estate, and steel. In 1890 he purchased one hundred acres overlooking the James River and built a thirty-three-room mansion, which he called Maymont after his wife's maiden name. The house preserves the Dooleys' collection of furnishings, an eclectic assortment that includes Rococo Revival items and a bedroom set of swan furniture—the bed itself is a massive carved swan. Also in the bedroom is a dressing table and chair with narwhal tusks for legs. After the death of Mrs. Dooley the mansion and its landscaped grounds were given to the city. The park has gardens in the Italian, English, and Japanese styles, a carriage collection, and wildlife exhibits.

LOCATION: Hampton Street and Pennsylvania Avenue. HOURS: April through October: 10–7 Daily; November through March: 10–5 Daily. FEE: Yes. TELEPHONE: 804–358–7166.

Agecroft Hall (4305 Sulgrave Road, 804–353–4241) is a fifteenth-century, half-timbered manor house from Lancashire, England, that when threatened with demolition was taken apart and reassembled in Richmond in the late 1920s. The purchaser was T. C. Williams, Jr., heir to a tobacco fortune. He filled his transplanted residence with a collection of paintings, armor, musical instruments, tapestries, and furniture—including a magnificent multicolored bed—from the Tudor and early Stuart periods. Also on the twenty-three-acre grounds are gardens of the period.

Adjacent to Agecroft Hall is another house imported from England, **Virginia House** (4301 Sulgrave Road, 804–353–4251). This Tudor mansion, brought here in 1925, is furnished with an eclectic and varied collection of English and Spanish pieces, many dating to the sixteenth century.

WILTON

A fine eighteenth-century mansion, Wilton was completed in the 1750s for William Randolph III and moved to its present location

Virginia House, which traces its origins back to an English priory that was rebuilt in the seventeenth century, was transported to Richmond in 1925. OVERLEAF: *The entry hall.*

in the 1930s when threatened with demolition. Wilton's panelling is exceptionally beautiful, particularly in the stair hall and the front parlor. Its superb collection of furnishings has been authentically arranged according to a room-by-room inventory taken in the early 1800s. In 1781 Lafayette briefly used the house as his headquarters.

LOCATION: South Wilton Road. HOURS: March through January: 10–4:30 Tuesday–Saturday, 1:30–4:30 Sunday. FEE: Yes. TELE-PHONE: 804–282–5936.

TUCKAHOE PLANTATION

Located seven miles west of Richmond on a bluff above the James River, Tuckahoe has been altered only slightly since the plantation was started in the early 1700s. The H-shaped mansion retains its original woodwork, including a beautifully carved staircase. Tuckahoe was a property of the Randolph family, who also owned Wilton. Jefferson's mother was a Randolph, and it is said that young Thomas took his lessons in Tuckahoe's schoolhouse.

LOCATION: 12601 River Road. HOURS: By appointment. FEE: Yes. TELEPHONE: 804–784–5736.

EDGAR ALLAN POE MUSEUM

Born in Boston in 1809, Edgar Allan Poe grew up in Richmond
and considered himself a Virginian. None of the Richmond houses
Poe lived in has survived. The Poe Museum displays the few possessions he left at his death: a trunk, walking stick, a pair of boot
hooks, and a mirror and trinket box that belonged to his wife.

Poe's mother, a young, widowed actress, died in Richmond in
1811 when he was not yet 3 years old. The Allan family took him in
as a ward, but they never legally adopted him. Mrs. Allan was kind
to him, but Poe had a poor relationship with his foster father, a
tobacco merchant. Except for five years spent in England with the
Allans, Poe lived in Richmond until 1826, when he left to attend
the University of Virginia. In the summer of 1835 he returned to
edit the *Southern Literary Messenger,* where he gained a national
reputation as a literary critic. He also began to write his longest
prose work, *The Narrative of Arthur Gordon Pym of Nantucket.* On
May 16, 1836, he married 13-year-old Virginia Clemm, his cousin.
He was dismissed from the magazine in January 1837, reputedly
for heavy drinking. In August and September 1849, he returned
for a visit, his last. He died in Baltimore on October 7.

LOCATION: 1914–1916 East Main Street. HOURS: 10–4 Tuesday–Saturday, 1–4 Sunday–Monday. FEE: Yes. TELEPHONE:
804– 648-5523.

RICHMOND NATIONAL BATTLEFIELD PARK

The Richmond Civil War park, with its headquarters in Richmond
itself, preserves ten sites on 768 acres, located in three counties. A
driving tour of the sites would cover about one hundred miles if it
included a visit to Drewry's Bluff on the south side of the James
River. A tour without a stop at Drewry's Bluff covers sixty miles.
The sites under the park's auspices are associated with McClellan's
Peninsula Campaign of 1862 and Grant's campaign of 1864.

The park's main **visitor center** in Richmond (3215 East Broad
Street, 804–226–1981) is located on the site of the Chimborazo
Hospital, the Confederacy's chief medical center, then one of the
largest military hospitals in the world. Several rooms of exhibits tell
the story of the hospital and the defense of the city.

OPPOSITE: *(Above) General Grant, wearing high boots, seated among his officers planning the
attack on Cold Harbor. (Below) The ruins of Richmond, 1865.* OVERLEAF: *White Oak
Swamp, the scene of fighting in June 1862.*

North of Richmond, the heights of **Chickahominy Bluff** (off Route 360) were an important part of the Confederate defenses during the 1862 campaign. From this vantage point Lee observed the first fighting of the Seven Days' Battles.

The 150-acre unit at **Cold Harbor** (off Route 156) has an exhibit shelter with maps outlining the fighting here. In June 1864, having failed to dislodge Lee from Spotsylvania, Grant swung his army south to Cold Harbor in another attempt to outflank Lee. Here he ordered a frontal assault against strong earthworks and suffered a costly defeat—seven thousand Federal troops fell in one day. Grant later said he regretted that attack more than any other. A one-mile road passes Union and Confederate earthworks.

West and south of Cold Harbor, numerous historical markers along Route 156 between Mechanicsville and Seven Pines describe the engagements here. In bitter fighting at **Seven Pines,** on May 31, 1862, General Joseph E. Johnston launched a poorly coordinated attack on McClellan's left wing. Union General Edwin V. "Bull" Sumner, ignoring the warnings of his engineers, led a counterattack over the Chickahominy River across Grapevine Bridge, which was in danger of being swept away by floodwaters, and halted the Confederates. General Johnston, severely wounded by a shell fragment in the chest, had to be relieved of his command and President Davis appointed Robert E. Lee commander of the Army of Northern Virginia the next day.

Engagements at **Gaines' Mill** and **Savage Station,** marked by plaques, were part of the Seven Days' battles, June 25 to July 1, 1862, in which Lee, despite poor coordination, managed to roll back McClellan's numerically superior army.

The sixty-acre site at **Malvern Hill** (off Route 156), still a rural landscape, is marked with explanatory plaques. Federal troops occupied this area on June 30, 1862, as McClellan retreated east. The Confederate attack on July 1 resulted in a slaughter, as waves of men hurled themselves at the massed Federal artillery on the hill. "Brigade after brigade rushed at our batteries," wrote a Union officer, "but the artillery . . . mowed them down with shrapnel, grape, and canister." Confederate General Ambrose P. Hill said that it "was not war—it was murder." Despite the pleas of his officers for a counterattack, McClellan continued his retreat to the river landings at Berkeley Plantation.

The three-hundred-acre **Fort Harrison** (Battlefield Park Road off Route 5) site includes intact earthworks and the remnants of

Confederate Fort Gilmer, which was attacked by black units of Grant's army on September 29, 1864. Of the sixteen Congressional Medals of Honor awarded to blacks in the Civil War, fourteen were won in this battle.

Fort Darling, at Drewry's Bluff, seven miles from Richmond on the southern bank of the James in Chesterfield County (Fort Darling Road off Route 656), was the gun emplacement that repelled the *Monitor* in its attempt to reach Richmond in 1862. The Confederates had also sunk obstructions in the James at this point; but if the *Monitor* had been supported by ground troops it might have been able to run past the fort and shell Richmond. The fort is very well preserved on a high point with a commanding view.

R I C H M O N D   E N V I R O N S

PETERSBURG

The city of Petersburg was laid out in the 1740s by William Byrd II. It had an advantageous position, located about twenty-five miles south of Richmond at the falls of the Appomattox river. There had been a fort and trading post here since the 1640s, and in the eighteenth century it developed into an important tobacco-trading center with a reputation as a gracious town.

In May 1781 General William Phillips descended on the town with an elite two-thousand-man unit, accompanied by Benedict Arnold, leading another one thousand men. They were met by one thousand local militia under the command of General von Steuben and Brigadier General John Peter Gabriel Muhlenberg, who used Blandford Church as the strong point in their defense. The Patriots managed to hold off the attackers for a few hours; but the weight of numbers ensured a British victory. After the initial battle General Phillips contracted typhoid fever. As he lay in his bed, Lafayette began shelling British positions and Phillips, who had fought at Ticonderoga and Saratoga, New York, muttered that the Americans wouldn't even let him die in peace. He was interred at the Blandford Church cemetery, and holds the unfortunate distinction of being the highest ranking British officer of the Revolutionary War buried in the United States. In mid-May Lord Cornwallis arrived in Petersburg, assembled the British troops, and set off in pursuit of Lafayette—a chase that ultimately led him to his defeat at Yorktown.

The first Federal wagon train entering Petersburg, 1865.

In the Civil War, Petersburg was a vital rail junction that supplied Richmond. From June 1864 to April 1865 it was besieged by Grant's Army of the Potomac.

Petersburg National Battlefield

After the indecisive battles at the Wilderness, Spotsylvania, and Cold Harbor, Grant ordered another flanking movement, aimed at Petersburg, on June 15, 1864. Fast-moving columns crossed the James and Appomattox rivers by pontoon bridges and arrived outside the city, which was only lightly defended by General Pierre Beauregard, with about 2,500 men. But the Federal commanders on the scene failed to launch an effective attack. Lee had not realized that Grant was shifting the bulk of his forces to Petersburg, but managed to get into a strong defensive position by June 18. The Northern troops, exhausted by seven weeks of hard fighting and having learned the bitter lesson of Cold Harbor, had little taste for assaults against a well-entrenched enemy. But, after the long chess game that had begun in the Wilderness, Grant had now pinned his opponent: Lee's army could not afford to relinquish

Petersburg, for, without it, Richmond would surely fall. Grant was determined to keep his grip on the Army of Northern Virginia if it took all summer. Lee had failed to break up Grant's army before it could reach the James River, and he realized the consequences. Lee had confided to one of his generals, "If he gets there [the James] it will become a siege, and then it will be a mere question of time."

By mid-June, a long siege of Petersburg did seem inevitable. Then Henry Pleasants, a Pennsylvania colonel who had been a mining and railroad engineer, realized he could tunnel under the Confederate defenses, pack the end of the shaft with explosives, and blast a gap in the Southern line. The Union high command was skeptical, but Pleasants set to work with his regiment, some of whom had been coal miners, once General Burnside gave his assent. To the amazement of army engineers, Pleasants's men were able to dig a well-ventilated five-hundred-foot shaft from the Union position to a spot directly under the Confederate line. In lateral galleries, they placed about eight thousand pounds of gunpowder. Early on the morning of July 30, Pleasants detonated the explosives: With a roar the earth exploded, tearing a 170-foot-long hole in the Confederate entrenchments, with a crater thirty feet deep, and killing 278 Southerners in the initial blast.

What could have been the coup that broke the siege became a fiasco. Northern troops poured into the crater instead of skirting it and attacking the exposed positions on its sides. The black division originally designated to lead the attack had been replaced with a white division a few days before by staff officers who feared the army would be accused of using black troops as cannon fodder. This change in the assault plans combined with lack of leadership created confusion among the attacking Union troops. At one point there were 15,000 men in and around the hole. The Confederates trained their artillery on the crater and mounted a counterattack that cost the Federals 4,000 killed, wounded, and captured; the Southern casualties numbered 1,500. Grant, discouraged over the lost opportunity, called the event "the saddest affair I have witnessed in the war."

In the fall, Grant's lines continued to encircle Petersburg as he attempted to cut the remaining supply lines into the city, but he could not break through the tough Confederate defenders, spread out on a line thirty-five miles long. Lee held on through the winter of 1864–1865, but by March realized his position was becoming untenable. A last gamble—an attack on Fort Stedman spearheaded by men posing as deserters—failed in late March. A powerful Northern counterattack convinced Lee that Petersburg and Richmond had to be abandoned. His exhausted men withdrew west along the rail line to Danville, preceded by President Davis.

The national battlefield preserves miles of the original entrenchments, the gaping crater, and the entrance to the tunnel dug by the Pennsylvanians. In summer months there are artillery demonstrations and a reconstructed Federal siege encampment with a field hospital. On display is a huge mortar, a muzzle-loading cannon of the same type as the one called the Dictator, which threw two-hundred-pound shells into Petersburg. The visitor center features a large, three-dimensional map of the battlefield, describing troop movements during the nine-and-one-half-month siege.

LOCATION: Route 36, two miles east of Petersburg off I-95. HOURS: *Visitor center:* 8–5 Daily; *Grounds:* 8–dusk. FEE: Yes. TELEPHONE: 804–732–3531.

The **U.S. Army Quartermaster Museum** (804–734–4203), located on the grounds of Fort Lee near the battlefield park, displays a variety of military items related to the quartermaster corps, such as uniforms, flags, rations, and various kinds of equipment. The museum has a jeep used by General George Patton in 1944, one of General Eisenhower's uniforms, and equipment from a bomber that disappeared in the Sahara in 1943 and was found in 1960. In Petersburg itself there is a **visitor center** at 19 Bollingbrook Street (804–733–2400). The **Siege Museum** (15 West Bank Street, 804–733–2402) exhibits weapons, clothing, household items, and a film that tells of life in the city during the ten-month siege. **Trapezium House** (244 North Market Street, 804–733–2402) is so named for its odd, trapezium shape. The story goes that the man who built it in the early 1800s was fearful of spirits. Told by his West Indian servant that right angles were the hiding places of ghosts, he built his house without any such angles. (Similar stories are told of similar houses in several other towns; the West Indian servant apparently got around.) The house has been restored and furnished with early-nineteenth-century pieces. **Centre Hill Mansion** (Centre Hill Court, 804–733–2401), built in 1823, is the headquarters of the state chapter of the Victorian Society, which has restored and furnished it with fine antiques of the Victorian period.

Tiffany windows at Blandford Church, Petersburg. The church has been a Confederate memorial since 1901.

Blandford Church

This church, important in Petersburg's Revolutionary War battle, was converted into a Confederate memorial in 1901. Its fifteen stained-glass windows were designed by Louis Comfort Tiffany and executed in his studios. There is a reception center adjacent to the church and a cemetery in which 30,000 veterans are buried. The observance of Memorial Day had its origin at this cemetery in 1866, when Mary Cunningham Logan noticed girls placing flowers on the soldiers' graves. She suggested to her husband, General John A. Logan, that a national observance of this sort would be appropriate—Congress established the holiday in 1868.

LOCATION: 3195 Crater Road. HOURS: 10–5 Daily. FEE: Yes. TELE-PHONE: 800–368–3595.

HOPEWELL

The present-day City Point National Historic District of Hopewell was the command and supply center for General Grant's campaign against Petersburg and Richmond from June 1864 until the end of the war. **Appomattox Manor Plantation** is now the City Point Unit of the Petersburg National Battlefield (800–863–TOUR). Grant's headquarters on the lawn of Appomattox, where tents or cabins occupied nearly every available square foot of ground, became a nerve center for the Northern war effort. Grant's restored headquarters cabin stands on the lawn. President Lincoln visited City Point on two occasions, and was here for two of the last three weeks of his life. Remnants of **Union breastworks** are still visible on Appomattox Street. **Weston Manor** (21st Avenue and Weston Lane, 804–458–4682), a restored three-story late Georgian plantation house built in 1735, was quarters of General Philip Sheridan. In **City Point National Cemetery** (Memorial Avenue) several thousand soldiers from both sides are buried.

The **Flowerdew Hundred Foundation Museum** (1617 Flowerdew Hundred Road, 804–541–8897) is one of the nation's most important and active archaeological sites. Researchers have unearthed artifacts showing that the area was occupied by Indians as early as 9000 BC. In 1618 Governor George Yeardley built a house here, which has not survived. An eighteenth-century windmill has been reconstructed on the grounds. A museum displays the site's archaeological finds and presents a film about the windmill.

Brandon Plantation (Spring Grove, off Route 10, 757–866–8416) is a country villa in one of the Anglo-Palladian styles—in this case, of the extended variety. Thomas Jefferson may have advised its builder, Benjamin Harrison, on the design. The house is privately owned but may be visited by appointment.

J A M E S   R I V E R

Three mansions along the James River southeast of Richmond, Shirley, Berkeley, and Westover, give the modern visitor a good sense of eighteenth-century plantation atmosphere. Like most Virginia houses of that period, these were designed by their owners, who consulted English builders' guides such as James Gibbs's *A Book of Architecture*, published in 1728, Batty Langley's *The City and Country Builder's and Workman's Treasury of Designs* (1739), Abraham

Swan's *The British Architect* (1745), and Thomas Chippendale's *The Gentleman and Cabinetmaker's Director* (1754). These handbooks included floor plans, facades, and patterns for doorways, windows, and interior woodwork. After 1720 or so, major plantation houses became symmetrical. Most were severe, with unadorned brick facades, but Westover achieves an exuberance with its tall chimneys, slightly arched window frames, and boldly baroque doorway.

SHIRLEY PLANTATION

Shirley Plantation is an exceptionally well-preserved working farm centering upon a mansion, occupied by the ninth and tenth generations of the Hill and Carter families. The graceful, three-story brick house on the James River shore was started in 1723 by Edward Hill III as a wedding present to his daughter, Elizabeth, and her new husband, John Carter. The eldest son of Robert "King" Carter, John held the post of secretary of Virginia and sat on the Governor's Council. The house was subsequently remodeled several times in the eighteenth century. Light Horse Harry Lee, the governor of Virginia and a widower, married Charles Carter's daughter Anne at Shirley in June 1793. The Lees resided at Stratford Hall until Light Horse Harry's financial reverses prompted Anne to move into Alexandria and spend extended periods at Shirley with her children, including Robert E. Lee.

The conservative Carters kept the interior of the house as it had been in the early eighteenth century. When former president John Tyler and his wife, Julia, visited in 1854, they were taken aback to see that "everything should remain so old fashioned."

During the Civil War, wounded Federal troops were brought to the lawn around the house after the Battle of Malvern Hill. Louise Carter wrote that "they lay all about on this lawn and all up and down the river bank. Nurses went about with buckets of water and ladles for them to drink and bathe their faces. . . . Mama had to tear up sheets and pillow cases to bind their wounds, and we made them soup and bread every day until they died or were carried away." General McClellan sent a letter, "with the highest respect," thanking the Carters for their aid to men "whom you probably regard as bitter foes."

OVERLEAF: *The pigeon house, Shirley Plantation, hid young Beverly Carter in 1864 as he crossed Union lines to visit his aging mother.*

The house is distinguished by its panelling and the "flying" or "hanging" staircase, which rises from the ground floor to the attic without any visible means of support. The seventeenth- to nineteenth-century furniture, silver, china, glassware and portraits are, remarkably, all original family pieces.

LOCATION: Off Route 5, between Richmond and Williamsburg. HOURS: 9–5 Daily. FEE: Yes. TELEPHONE: 804–829–5121.

Edgewood (Route 5, Charles City, 804–829–2962) is a Gothic Revival anomaly in this Georgian district. It was built in the 1850s for Richard S. Rowland, a New Jerseyite who came here to operate the mill that still stands on the property. Rowland became a Southern sympathizer and opened Edgewood to the parish of Westover Church for five years while the church was used as a stable by the Union Army. The third floor of the home also became the Confederate lookout to Berkeley to spy on McClellan's troops. J. E. B. Stuart made his last stop here, for coffee, before going on to Richmond to warn General Lee of the strength of the Union army.

Built in 1725 by Benjamin Harrison IV, the mill is an early example of labor-saving automation.

BERKELEY PLANTATION

Berkeley was the plantation of the Harrisons, the prominent Virginia family that included a signer of the Declaration of Independence and two presidents, William Henry and Benjamin Harrison. The land was part of a large 1619 grant—called Berkeley Hundred—to Sir George Yeardley and Richard Berkeley. The leader of the settlers wrote that the day of their landing, December 4, 1619, "shall be yearly and perpetually kept holy as a day of Thanksgiving." Thus Virginia claims to have celebrated a Thanksgiving a year before the Plymouth Pilgrims did; however, no description of an actual observance at Berkeley survives.

The two-story brick plantation house was built by Benjamin Harrison III in 1726. A decade later he and two of his children were killed when a lightning bolt struck a window. His grandson, William Henry Harrison—born in the house in 1773—emigrated to the Northwest Territories, where he served as the governor, gaining a reputation as an Indian fighter and the nickname "Tippecanoe," after the site of one of his victories. He was elected

OPPOSITE: *A downstairs bedroom at Shirley Plantation, home to ten generations of the Hill and Carter families.*

the ninth president in 1841 with the slogan "Tippecanoe and Tyler Too," the "Tyler" being a reference to his vice president, John Tyler, of nearby Sherwood Forest. Harrison died just thirty days after his inauguration. His grandson Benjamin Harrison was elected the twenty-third president. In the Civil War, General McClellan used the house as his headquarters and main point of embarkation in the 1862 Peninsula Campaign. General Daniel Butterfield composed the bugle call "Taps" when he was staying here.

In 1907 the property was purchased by John Jamieson, who had been a drummer boy with the Federal forces that camped at the plantation. The house has been restored and furnished with eighteenth- and nineteenth-century pieces. The extensive garden between the house and the river has also been restored.

LOCATION: Route 5, Charles City County. HOURS: 8–5 Daily. FEE: Yes. TELEPHONE: 804–829–6018.

WESTOVER

Westover recalls the "Queen Anne," or first phase of Virginia "Georgian," with a steeply pitched roof, tall chimney stacks, and a baroque doorway made of imported stone. The house was built about 1730 by William Byrd II, who had been sent to England for his education by his father, a prosperous fur trader and planter. There, the younger Byrd studied law, but also pursued scientific studies that won him election to the Royal Society at 22 years old. After his father's death in 1704, Byrd returned to Virginia and took up the life of a gentleman planter, merchant, and trader. For much of his life he kept diaries, written in a coded shorthand, which were not discovered until the 1930s. He wrote a number of works that vividly portray Virginia society, politics, and private life in a highly polished prose. He also left a valuable account of political events in Williamsburg, where he served as burgess and member of the Governor's Council. In the 1730s he established Richmond and Petersburg at the sites of his father's trading posts.

Westover is privately owned, and the interior of the house is not open to visitors, though the grounds may be toured. Adjacent to the house is Byrd's garden, where he is buried.

LOCATION: 25 miles east of Richmond, just off the Route 5 Scenic Byway. HOURS: 9–5 Daily. FEE: Yes. TELEPHONE: 804–829–2882.

Westover, the elegant James River house built about 1730 by William Byrd II. The sophistication of the architecture mirrors that of its builder, who was one of the adornments of pre-Revolutionary Virginia society.

Two miles east of the house is **Westover Church** (Route 5, 804–829–2488), built in the 1730s. **Sherwood Forest** (Route 5, 35 miles east of Richmond, 804–829–5377) was owned by Presidents John Tyler and William Henry Harrison. The house, open daily, is 301 feet long, possibly the nation's longest frame house. Several miles to the north, on Route 249 in New Kent County, **St. Peter's Parish Church** (804–932–4846) is a picturesque country church notable for its embellishments. It was built between 1701 and 1703; its squat tower, with arches at the base, was added in 1741. George and Martha Washington were married in this church, which she had attended as a child. The interior was restored in the 1960s.

WILLIAMSBURG
AND THE
HISTORIC
TRIANGLE

OPPOSITE: *North wing of the Governor's Palace, Williamsburg.*

Williamsburg, Jamestown, and Yorktown form what is called the Historic Triangle, comprising respectively the second colonial capital of Virginia, the first permanent English settlement in America, and the site of a great Revolutionary War victory. This chapter also encompasses Norfolk and the southern bank of the James River.

Williamsburg was founded in 1699 to replace Jamestown as the colonial capital of Virginia, a move instigated by Governor Francis Nicholson. He had just finished his term as royal governor of Maryland, where he had designed the town of Annapolis, and he had similar urban ambitions for Virginia. The increasingly wealthy planters also felt the need for a sophisticated gathering place, although none of them considered living in town the entire year. The College of William and Mary had been founded here in 1693, and Nicholson believed that locating the capital near the college would lend a much-needed polish to the colony's society and government. The landowners in Jamestown, of course, did not agree, and when the college building burned down in 1705 there were whispers that Jamestowners had set the fire.

Nicholson laid out the town along French lines, centering it on Duke of Gloucester Street, nearly a mile long and ninety-nine feet wide. The street is bounded at its western end by the Wren Building of William and Mary College, at its eastern end by the capitol. At the head of a broad mall in the center of the town, Nicholson sited the Governor's Palace. He envisioned a Baroque capital city, with open spaces and long vistas, in which the three great public buildings—capitol, palace, and college—would be the brick jewels in a setting of greenery. Private houses would stand on half-acre lots: He wanted no cheek-by-jowl townhouses in his capital.

Williamsburg was a ceremonial city, with little manufacturing—its industries were those of government and the entertainment of the planters who came to conduct official business. The town bustled during the last three weeks of April and October, the "Public Times" when the House of Burgesses and the Governor's Council were in session. One traveler wrote in 1758: "At the time of the assemblies, and general courts, it is crowded with the gentry of the country. On those occasions there are balls and other amusements; but as soon as business is finished, they return to their plantations and the town is in a manner deserted." Hugh Jones, a professor at William and Mary, wrote that the town was "delightful, healthful, and thriving," and that the inhabitants "behave them-

Map of Eastern North America: Florida to Chesapeake Bay, by John White. The arms and crest of Sir Walter Raleigh appear on the Virginia mainland.

selves exactly as the gentry in London." Thomas Jefferson lived in Williamsburg in the early 1760s, when he was a student at William and Mary, and returned in 1769 as a burgess. He recalled in his autobiography that "I have heard [in Williamsburg] more good sense, more rational and philosophical conversations, than in all my life besides." He called the town "the finest school of manners and morals that ever existed in America," though he disliked its brick architecture, which he associated with British colonialism.

In the 1760s and 1770s, the capitol, the taverns, and Williamsburg's private homes were forums for such colonial leaders as Jefferson, Patrick Henry, George Mason, George Washington, and Richard Henry Lee. In 1769, Governor Botetourt dissolved the House of Burgesses as it was about to vote on a resolution to boycott British goods. The representatives simply reconvened at the Raleigh Tavern and voted there. In May 1774, Governor Dunmore dissolved the same body after it voted for a day of fasting and prayer "to implore divine interposition" in the crisis over the closing of the port of Boston. The delegates met at Raleigh Tavern once again and approved Richard Henry Lee's resolution "to consider means of stopping exports and of securing the constitutional rights of America." The resolution signaled Virginia's determination to make common cause with the Bostonians who had lately dumped British tea into Boston Harbor. During the Revolutionary War, the town played a small role in the battle of Yorktown: Lafayette made it his headquarters as he awaited the arrival of George Washington and the troops that would besiege Cornwallis.

COLONIAL WILLIAMSBURG

When Richmond was designated the capital during the Revolution, Williamsburg began a long decline. It was the scene of a sharp battle in 1862 when Confederate troops made a stand here to stop the Federal column pursuing them from Yorktown. By the early twentieth century the town was dilapidated. Convinced that Wil-

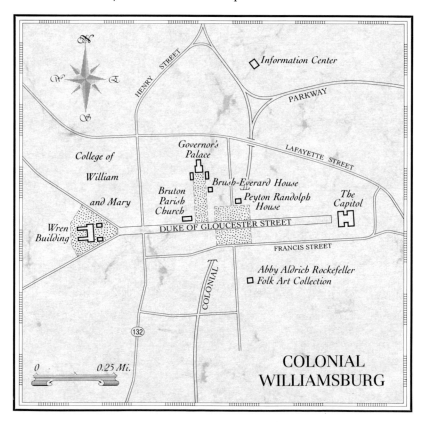

liamsburg had great historical and architectural importance, the rector of Bruton Parish Church, W. A. R. Goodwin, persuaded John D. Rockefeller, Jr., to purchase the town and restore it. Beginning in the late 1920s, Goodwin acquired houses one by one as Rockefeller's agent. In 1934 a partially restored Colonial Williamsburg was opened to the public. This was the first restoration in the country to employ costumed guides to interpret colonial life. **Bassett Hall,** (800–447–8679), the eighteenth-century house in which the Rockefellers resided during their visits to Williamsburg, is open to the public and displays selections from the family's collections of furniture, needlework, and folk art.

Colonial Williamsburg represents the country's most ambitious attempt to re-create the past. On 173 acres, some 100 original buildings have been restored and another 400 reconstructed to form a showcase of eighteenth-century architecture and town planning, furniture, and decorative arts. The result provides a setting

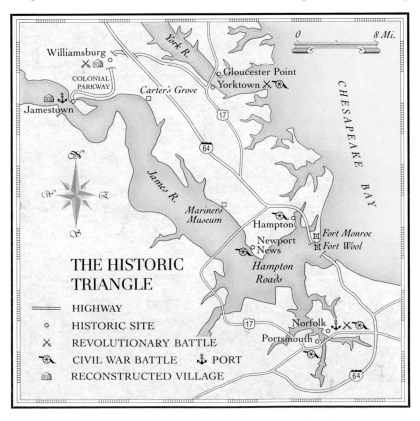

Colonial Williamsburg's Capitol, a reconstruction of the 1705 building.

for the re-creation of social life and political events in eighteenth-century Virginia. Costumed interpreters enact the official and mundane routines typical of the old colonial capital while eighteenth-century crafts and trades are demonstrated in reconstructed shops. In recent years, as scholars uncovered new information about eighteenth-century behavior and taste, the restoration itself has been restored. In a continuing pursuit of historical accuracy, Colonial Williamsburg has supported research concerning the ways of life of slaves, servants, and the less prosperous.

The **Colonial Williamsburg Visitor Center** sells the tickets and passes needed for admission to the restored buildings. It also presents a film about the pre-Revolutionary events in Williamsburg and has a large bookstore.

LOCATION: Colonial Parkway. HOURS: Open every day of the year, generally 8:30–6, but hours vary by season. FEE: Yes. TELEPHONE: 800–447–8679.

This tour of Williamsburg begins at the capitol and follows route markers, proceeding west along Duke of Gloucester Street. The two streets parallel to Duke of Gloucester are Nicholson and Francis streets, both named for the town's designer.

The Capitol

A handsome brick building in the shape of an H, the capitol contains chambers for the Governor's Council, the House of Burgesses, and the General Court. The original building, finished in 1705, burned down in 1747 and its replacement met a similar end in 1832. The present capitol is a reconstruction of the first.

Elected by popular vote, the burgesses gave voice to the growing sentiment for independence in the 1760s and 1770s. The **Hall of the House of Burgesses** is an austere room lit by round windows. The Governor's Council, on the other hand, met in the more elegant surroundings of the **Council Chamber.** The Council, whose members were appointed from the colony's planter aristocracy, advised the governor. The **General Court,** where thirteen of Blackbeard's pirates were tried and condemned, has also been reconstructed and features handsome marble paneling.

The restored **Public Gaol,** north of the capitol, on Nicholson Street, was built in 1704 and was in use until 1910. On Duke of Gloucester Street, the **Pasteur and Galt Apothecary Shop,** built in 1760, displays eighteenth-century medicines, druggists' equipment, and surgical instruments.

Raleigh Tavern was the informal capitol of the colony—the exchange for news and gossip—and the burgesses even convened in its Apollo Room on the two occasions when the governor dissolved the assembly. The billiard room features a table made in England in 1738. Gambling was among the favorite amusements of

OVERLEAF: *Inside the Capitol, the General Court was home to a supreme tribunal that consisted of royal appointees.*

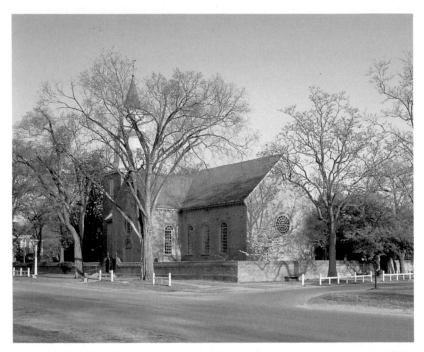

Bruton Parish Church, designed by Governor Alexander Spotswood, was consecrated in 1715.

the gentry when they visited Williamsburg; huge sums were wagered at cards and dice. A New Yorker who visited in the 1770s wrote that "Gaming is amazingly prevalent in Williamsburg."

The **Magazine** is an octagonal brick building that was erected in 1715. On the night of April 20, 1775, Governor Dunmore removed the powder stored here in order to keep it out of the hands of rebels, which spurred Patrick Henry to lead a detachment of militia to demand its return. They accepted payment instead. Dunmore claimed that he needed the powder to suppress a rumored uprising of slaves; in fact, it was the governor himself who was about to arm slaves to put down the rebellion. The restored Magazine today has displays of eighteenth-century weapons.

At the **James Geddy House Foundry and Silversmith Shop** eighteenth-century methods of silversmithing are demonstrated. The restored building also displays household furnishings and a collection of children's toys, puzzles, and doll's furniture.

Bruton Parish Church, at the foot of Palace Green, has been in continuous use since its construction in 1715. Governor Spotswood designed the building in the shape of a cross and included an enclosed, canopied pew for himself and future governors.

The **Brush-Everard House,** facing the Green, was built in 1717 by John Brush, a gunsmith of modest means. Its furnishings reflect the income and the tastes of an up-and-coming craftsman. The table settings, for example, are earthenware rather than fine china or silver. The fine quality of the stairway and panelling in the stair hall suggest that they were added by a later owner. In the 1770s, the house was owned by Thomas Everard, the mayor and county clerk. The library displays books Thomas Jefferson said should be the core of an educated gentleman's collection.

Located east of the Green on Nicholson Street, the **Peyton Randolph House,** with its spacious stair hall, handsome library, and seven panelled rooms, may have been the most elegant private residence in Williamsburg. Its owner, a cousin of Thomas Jefferson, was one of the most respected political figures in the colony. He served as speaker of the House of Burgesses from 1766 to 1775, and was elected president of the First Continental Congress by acclamation. During the Yorktown campaign, Lafayette and Rochambeau lived at the house.

The church's interior, with the canopied Governor's Pew at left.

Governor's Palace

Begun in 1708 and completed twelve years later, the Governor's Palace was home to seven royal governors and lieutenant governors. During his student days in the 1760s, Thomas Jefferson spent many pleasant evenings as a guest of Governor Fauquier. He would later live there, as would Patrick Henry, during their terms as the commonwealth's first governors.

The palace has been restored to its appearance during the 1768–1770 tenancy of Governor Botetourt. An affable, conciliatory official who entertained lavishly in the hope of ingratiating himself with the colony's influential political and social leaders, Botetourt sometimes hosted fifty or more dinner guests at the palace. His sudden death in 1770 was sincerely mourned. Jefferson later wrote that Botetourt was such a respected governor that he may have forestalled the independence movement; "His death was, therefore, a fortunate event for the cause of the Revolution," Jefferson concluded. The last Crown appointee to live here was the Earl of Dunmore, whose high-handedness inflamed the Patriots.

The restoration of the palace was based on an inventory, taken upon the death of Botetourt, in which some 16,000 items were tallied in its room-by-room survey of the governor's possessions. The governor's butler had also kept detailed account books to which the curators referred. The entrance hall displays elaborate arrangements of muskets, pistols, and swords, which were intended to impress colonial visitors with the Crown's military power. Flanking the entrance to the ballroom are large portraits of King George III and Queen Charlotte.

The **George Wythe House,** built in the 1750s, has the plain, well-ordered brick facade that appealed to many conservative Virginians. The doorway has no pediment, and the only embellishment on the facade are rubbed bricks around the windows and door. The house was designed by Richard Taliaferro, a planter and talented amateur architect, whose daughter married George Wythe. A signer of the Declaration of Independence and a member of the faculty of William and Mary, Wythe was the first professor of law in an American college; Jefferson, James Monroe, Henry Clay, and John Marshall, the future chief justice, were among his

OPPOSITE: *Upon arriving at the Governor's Palace, visitors were greeted by an array of glistening glass and armaments, suggesting the English king's and colonial governor's power.*

pupils. It was here that George Washington stayed before the Battle of Yorktown. Today, the room where Wythe tutored pupils displays astronomical instruments.

The **Public Hospital,** which burned down in the 1880s and has now been reconstructed, was the first hospital in the country to care exclusively for the mentally ill. It opened in 1773, in an era when treatment of people with mental disorders meant little more than confinement. A reconstructed cell reveals the harshness of life here, however: Violent patients were held in wire cages or were manacled to a wall, for example. Exhibits that illuminate changes dating to the middle of the nineteenth century show the improvements in treatment at that time. As therapy, patients were encouraged to participate in sports and to play musical instruments.

Next to (and entered from) the hospital, the **DeWitt Wallace Gallery** displays an outstanding collection of American and English furniture, paintings, silver, glass, ceramics, textiles, and prints. Among the more notable exhibits are a chest by the Philadelphia cabinetmaker Thomas Affleck, Charles Willson Peale's portrait of George Washington painted after the Battle of Princeton (paired with a portrait of King George III), and a tall case clock made for King William III in 1699. The collection of prints and maps includes a copy of the 1755 Mitchell map of the colonies that was used by the Treaty of Paris negotiators in setting the boundaries of the new United States. The gallery also displays the Blagojevich Collection of seventeenth- and early eighteenth-century furniture.

The **Abby Aldrich Rockefeller Folk Art Center** houses the world's most significant collection of eighteenth- to twentieth-century American folk art. Items include toys, painted furniture, weathervanes, whirligigs, carvings, signs, and household items, as well as paintings and sculptures.

The **Wren Building** of William and Mary, the oldest college building in English America, has been restored to its appearance of 1716. Although its name is due to a resemblance to works by the British architect Christopher Wren, there is little evidence that he actually designed it. The U-shaped, three-story brick building was originally intended to surround a courtyard, but the fourth side was never built. The restored chapel in the south wing is the burial place for several colonial officials.

OPPOSITE: *The Wren Building of the College of William and Mary, an early example of the English Renaissance style of architecture that would translate into Virginia's Georgian style.*

Carter's Grove

Carter Burwell, a grandson of Robert "King" Carter, began work on this mansion in 1750. Although the roof was raised in the twentieth century to create a third story, the facade remains one of the most handsome in the state. The most distinctive feature of the house is the beautifully panelled entrance hall, with a broad elliptical arch serving as a monumental gateway to a long flight of stairs. Slash marks on the rail are said to have been made by Banastre Tarleton as he spurred his horse up the stairs, swinging his saber. Another legend is associated with the "Refusal Room," in which the marriage proposals of George Washington and Thomas Jefferson were turned down. The interior has not been restored to its eighteenth-century appearance; rather, it is furnished in the 1920s Colonial Revival style. Some of the furnishings are those of the McCrea family, who purchased the house in 1928. It was left to Colonial Williamsburg upon Mrs. McCrea's death in 1960. Behind the house, archaeologists have excavated the site of **Wolstenholme Towne,** an English settlement wiped out by Indian attacks in 1622. The remains of the settlement were discovered accidentally during the construction of new outbuildings for Carter's Grove.

JAMESTOWN

In May 1607, the first permanent English settlement in the New World was established when three ships arrived on the James River carrying 104 colonists, all men and boys. The settlers were not religious or political refugees coming to these shores for freedom but the employees and indentured servants of the Virginia Company of London, which had been formed by a group of investors. Impressed by the wealth Spain had squeezed out of its New World adventures, England was eager to search North America for gold and any other commodities of value. The settlers had also been assigned to look for the "northwest passage" to the "South Seas."

The loss of life in the first two decades was appalling: Of the nearly 7,300 settlers sent by the London company, over 6,000 died. The hot summer months were called "the sickly season" because "people who have lately arrived from England die during these

OPPOSITE: *Two superb artistic works from the DeWitt Wallace Gallery: A hand-tinted engraving, the "Mock-Bird," top, one of Mark Catesby's eighteenth-century natural history prints; a detail from a 1693 sampler, bottom, showing Britain's heraldic beasts at sport in the Garden of Eden.*

months like cats and dogs." In one year, four out of five newcomers were dead after twelve months. Women fared better than men in resisting disease, to the extent that there arose a saying: "Hogs and women thrive well amongst them." During the winter of 1609–1610, known as the "starving time," the Jamestown settlement came as close as it would ever come to complete obliteration; just sixty out of the five hundred settlers were able to survive into the spring.

The history of U.S. slavery began in Tidewater Virginia. The first blacks (about twenty) were brought there in 1619, probably from the West Indies. Strictly speaking, they were indentured servants rather than slaves, but by the 1640s the institution of slavery was taking shape. Most white settlers also came as indentured servants (the Virginia Company, which paid for their passage and supplies, owned the indentures). At landfall the ship captains auctioned the white servants to plantation owners. The whites were bound to work for several years to pay off their indentures and then became free.

Despite the harshness of the indenture system, Jamestown is justly remembered as the place where English law and the rights of the common man gained a toehold in the New World. The settlement's original charter, granted by the Virginia Company, promised that settlers would enjoy "all the liberties, franchises and immunities . . . as if they had been abiding and born within this realm of England." From the start, the colonists had a right to trial by jury. The first legislative assembly in America met at Jamestown in 1619. Jamestown also established Virginia's economic base for centuries to come when John Rolfe began to cultivate tobacco and ship the leaves back to England.

The company's insistence that the settlers concentrate on raising cash crops for export meant that they had to get their food from the Indians by trade—or by theft. The Indians of the region—the Powhatan—lived quite well until the arrival of the English. Their diet of corn and meat was better than that of many people in England and they were often taller and stronger than the settlers as a result. Pocahontas, the daughter of the Powhatan chief, repeatedly interceded with her father on the Englishmen's behalf. After the settlers took her hostage to ensure peace, she converted to Christianity and married John Rolfe. Their son, Thomas, initiated several famous Virginia families. She died on shipboard

OPPOSITE: *The ruins of the seventeenth-century Jamestown Church Tower.*

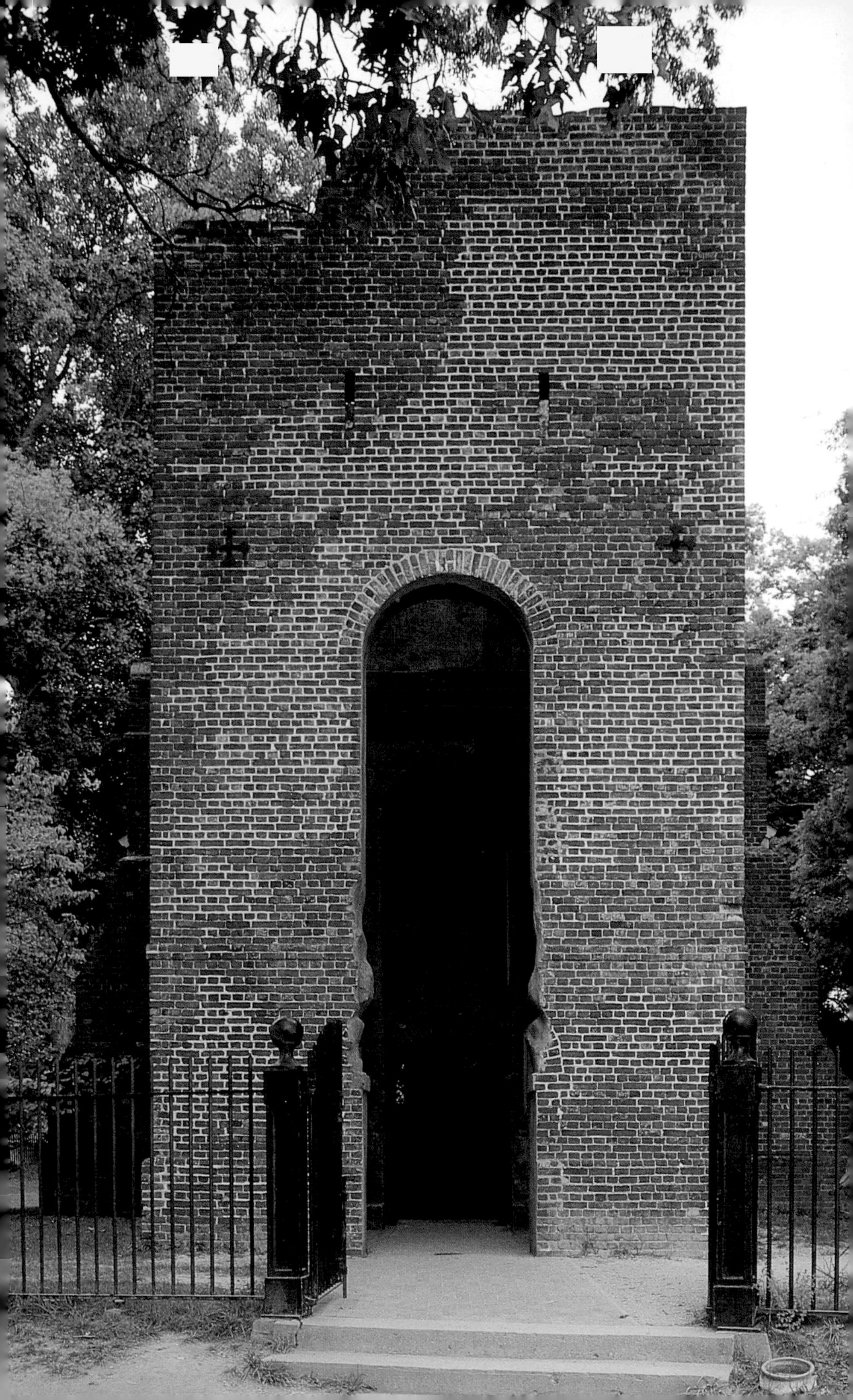

after a visit to England. The provocations of the English brought down on them two Indian attacks, in 1622 and 1644. Jamestown was not directly attacked by Indians, however, but by whites during Bacon's Rebellion in 1676, when Bacon burned the town while skirmishing with Governor Berkeley. Though rebuilt, the town never fully recovered and became the site of a plantation after the capital was moved to Williamsburg in 1699.

COLONIAL HISTORICAL PARK

Two agencies administer sites at Jamestown, the site of the original settlement being part of Colonial National Historical Park. The park maintains a visitor center as well as a glass house where seventeenth-century glassmaking is demonstrated. On the site itself, lines of bricks mark the foundations of the settlement's buildings. The only original remains are the ruins of the church burned by Bacon's rebels. Two roads loop through Jamestown Island, whose landscape remains much as it was in the 1600s.

LOCATION: Colonial Parkway. HOURS: *Entrance gate* 8:30–4:30 Daily, *Visitor Center* 9–5 Daily. FEE: Yes. TELEPHONE: 757–898–3400.

Jamestown Settlement

Administered by the Jamestown–Yorktown Foundation, Jamestown Settlement includes re-creations of a Powhatan Indian village, the original English palisaded settlement, and the three ships that brought the settlers from England. Exhibit galleries explore Jamestown's beginnings in the Old World, the culture of its original Native American inhabitants, and the first century of the colony. The re-created fort contains eighteen buildings with wattle-and-daub walls and thatched roofs, including a church, storehouse, guardhouse, and homes. The settlement reflects the period 1610 – 1614, when a few women had arrived. Costumed interpreters in the fort, aboard the ships, and in the Indian village carry out typical daily tasks using seventeenth-century tools and techniques.

Visitors may board the *Susan Constant,* a full-size, 110-foot replica of a square-rigger. The ships were severely overcrowded because the Virginia Company wanted to maximize profits by packing on as many people as possible. One passenger wrote that "betwixt the decks there can hardlie a man fetch his breath by

OPPOSITE: *A replica of the* Discovery, *one of the three ships that brought the first settlers to Jamestown.*

One battery of McClellan's 44 Federal mortars deployed—but not fired—at Yorktown. Had they been used, they could have delivered 400 tons of shells a day, more than enough to destroy the Confederate defenses. McClellan was notorious for being indecisive. OPPOSITE: *A cross-section of a Federal ordnance build-up at Yorktown.* OVERLEAF: *An aerial view of the Yorktown battlefield.*

reason there arises such a Funke in the night that it causes putrefaction of the bloud and breeds a disease much like the plague." The terrible conditions on the voyages from England contributed to the colony's high death rate.

LOCATION: Route 31 South. HOURS: 9–5 Daily. FEE: Yes. TELE-PHONE: 757–229–1607.

Yorktown

The Revolutionary War was brought closer to its end by the victory of a combined French and American force at Yorktown in October 1781. In the spring and summer of that year, Washington grappled with the problems of dwindling manpower, supplies, and money. Strategically, his situation was muddled. The well-trained French troops at his disposal were languishing at Newport, Rhode

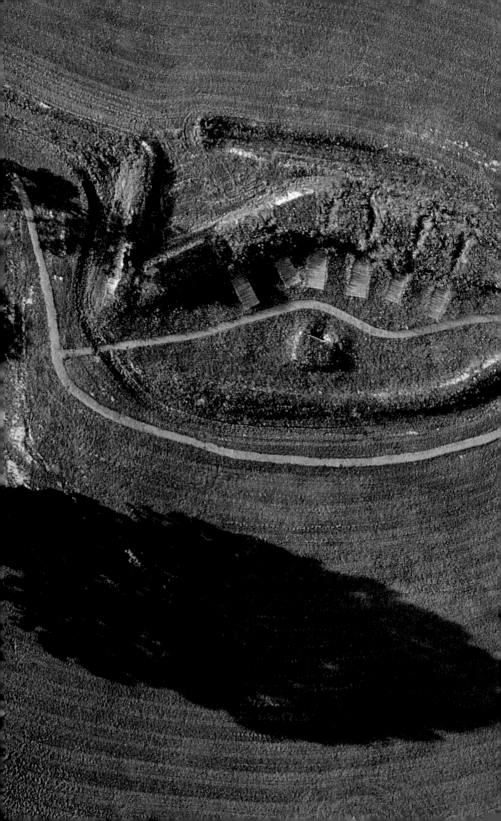

Island, blockaded by the Royal Navy. He was eager to drive Sir Henry Clinton from New York City but did not have enough troops for the task; meanwhile, Lord Cornwallis and Benedict Arnold were loose in Virginia, chasing Lafayette and laying waste where they could. In May, Washington noted in his diary: "Instead of having everything in readiness to take the field, we have nothing; and instead of having the prospect of a glorious offensive campaign before us, we have a bewildered and gloomy defensive one."

In August, Washington was given two pieces of news that changed the situation entirely. Lafayette reported that Cornwallis had apparently given up his attempts to provoke a battle and had moved east to Yorktown, along the York River seven miles from Chesapeake Bay, where he had been ordered by Clinton to establish and fortify a naval depot. As he withdrew toward Yorktown, Cornwallis tried to draw Lafayette and General Anthony Wayne into a trap at Green Spring. The Americans pulled back, narrowly escaping disaster. (The battle site is not accessible to the public.)

The information from Lafayette was followed by the news that the French fleet under Admiral de Grasse was on its way from the West Indies to the Chesapeake. Washington quickly assembled some seven thousand American and French troops in Connecticut and New York and ordered a fast march that on September 20 brought the army to Williamsburg, where Lafayette was waiting. The previous week, de Grasse had driven off a British fleet and landed more French troops; another French fleet, under Admiral de Barras, joined de Grasse in blockading Yorktown. In the words of historian Mark Boatner, "the cork was in the bottle Cornwallis had picked for himself."

On October 6, Washington had earthworks dug from which to launch an attack, then began the bombardment of Yorktown. On October 14, French and American detachments, the latter commanded by Alexander Hamilton, took two British redoubts by storm. Penned in and seriously short of ammunition, Cornwallis ordered his drummer to beat out the signal for a parley. After some negotiation he agreed to surrender. On October 19, the defeated British and Hessian troops, some of them in tears, marched past the silent victors and surrendered their arms as a

OPPOSITE: *Detail from the* Surrender of Lord Cornwallis *at Yorktown, as depicted by John Trumbull.*

band played British or German tunes. The war was not yet officially over, but Cornwallis's defeat exhausted the patience of British officialdom, and King George III, the staunchest proponent of the war, was ultimately persuaded that the cause was lost.

During the Civil War, General McClellan dallied for a month preparing to besiege Yorktown in April and May 1862, at the opening of his Peninsular Campaign. A weak Confederate force led by General John Bankhead Magruder had dug in among the old Revolutionary earthworks. General Joseph E. Johnston, who felt the position was weak, also knew his adversary: "No one but McClellan could have hesitated to attack." McClellan spent two weeks getting his guns in position, by which time the Confederates slipped away.

The Yorktown battlefield, along with historic Jamestown, is administered by the Colonial National Historical Park. The **Yorktown Victory Center** (Route 238, 757–887–1776), an exceptionally good museum, has exhibits about the Revolution and a narrative film. Complementing the center's indoor exhibits are an outdoor Continental Army encampment, comprising some 20 tents, and an eighteenth-century tobacco farm.

The National Park Service **Visitor Center** (Colonial Parkway, 757–898–3400) also has exhibits and a film about the battle. This visitor center is on a high point within the boundaries of the British earthworks, offering a panoramic view of strategic points of the battlefield, which has been well preserved. Some of the American and French earthworks, as well as British redoubts stormed on October 14, 1781, have been reconstructed. A self-guided auto tour begins at the visitor center and leads to various points of interest, including **Surrender Field** and the **Moore House,** where the terms of the British surrender were negotiated. The Moore House has been restored to its eighteenth-century appearance. Fifty French soldiers who died in the siege are buried in a cemetery in the park. Thirty British ships, which Cornwallis ordered scuttled to forestall a French amphibious assault, still lie at the bottom of the York River.

In Yorktown, the **Nelson House** (Main Street, 757–398–3400) is a restoration of a house shelled by the Americans during the battle. The bombardment was ordered by the owner, Thomas Nelson, Jr., commander of the Virginia militia units in Washington's army and a signer of the Declaration of Independence. When he arrived at Yorktown he feared his home could be behind enemy lines and assumed that Cornwallis was using it as his headquarters.

The grandeur of Rosewell is apparent even in a state of ruin.

Afterwards, as tradition has it, the British held their councils in a grotto, out of artillery range. At the house, interpretive programs about daily life and historical events are presented during the summer months. Nearby is the **Yorktown Victory Monument,** erected in 1884, at which bronze plaques list the names of the American and French soldiers who died in the battle.

In **Gloucester,** across the York River, about ten miles from Yorktown, are the ruins of **Rosewell,** once the largest mansion in Virginia and one of the finest in the colonies. The country seat of the Page family, it was begun in the 1720s by Mann Page, who married the daughter of Robert "King" Carter. It was completed in the 1740s. Page's grandson, John, was a close friend of Thomas Jefferson, who frequently visited the house for evenings of philosophical discussion. They made astronomical observations from the roof. The house burned in 1916. Portions of the walls and four chimneys survive. The house is open Sundays 2–5, April through October, or by appointment (804–693–2585).

H A M P T O N   R O A D S

Hampton Roads, where the James River empties into Chesapeake Bay, has been an important naval center since the Revolution. Today the navy maintains one of its largest bases at Norfolk. Four cities overlook Hampton Roads: Hampton and Newport News on the northern shore, Norfolk and Portsmouth on the southern.

The first confrontation of ironclads in history took place in Hampton Roads. On March 8, 1862, the heavily armed Confederate ironclad *Virginia,* a refitted northern vessel that had been named *Merrimack,* attacked the Federal fleet blockading Hampton Roads. She rammed the Federal ship *Cumberland,* sank her, and then destroyed the *Congress.* By a stroke of luck, the Union's own ironclad, *Monitor,* was already on its way to Hampton Roads. Navy officials had learned in 1861 of the Confederate plan to build an ironclad and had authorized engineer John Ericsson to begin work on the *Monitor,* which appeared off Norfolk on March 9, looking like "an immense shingle floating in the water with a gigantic cheese box rising from its center." The faster, more maneuverable *Monitor* battled the better-armed *Virginia* for four hours. Both ships were battered, but the fight ended in a draw. The *Virginia* remained a threat to the Union fleet, preventing it from sailing up

The battle of the ironclads Monitor *and* Virginia *at Hampton Roads, as depicted by Henry Bill in 1862 (detail).*

Two ca. 1870 pieces from the Mariners' Museum: The figurehead for the Benmore, *left, and a paddlebox plaque, right, carved with the state seal of Massachusetts.*

the James to attack Richmond. In May the Confederates, having to abandon Norfolk to an advancing Union army, scuttled the *Virginia*. The *Monitor* sank in a storm off Cape Hatteras in December 1862; its wreck was discovered in 1974.

MARINERS' MUSEUM

This museum, ranked among the top maritime museums in the country, houses an impressive collection of figureheads, including a one-and-a-half-ton gilded eagle with a wingspan of over eighteen feet. Sixteen ship models by August F. Crabtree trace the development of boats from prehistoric times to the nineteenth century: They include an Egyptian warship, a Roman merchant vessel, two of Columbus's vessels, and a luxury liner. The museum's comprehensive collection of small boats, gathered from all over the world, includes fishing boats, yachts, dugouts, rafts, a sampan, and a gondola. Among the other maritime items on display are weapons, uniforms, scrimshaw, photographs, and porcelain.

LOCATION: 100 Museum Drive, Newport News. HOURS: 9–5 Daily. FEE: Yes. TELEPHONE: 757–596–2222.

HAMPTON

St. John's Church (100 West Queen's Way, 757–722–2567) was built about 1728 to serve an Anglican parish. Its Victorian interior is the result of the church's unfortunate wartime history—it was bombarded during the Revolution, looted and turned into a barracks by the British in the War of 1812, and burned by retreating Confederates in the Civil War. **Hampton University** (757–727–5253) was founded in 1868 to educate freed slaves. The university's **museum** (757–727–5308) has a fine collection of African and Indian art, the majority gathered in the early 1900s.

FORT MONROE

Massive, star-shaped Fort Monroe was built between 1819 and 1834 by the French engineer Simon Bernard, who had served with Napoleon and who designed many of the fortresses built from Maine to Key West after 1815. The largest stone fort constructed in the United States, it was known as the "Gibraltar of Chesapeake Bay." Robert E. Lee was stationed here in the 1830s when he was an army engineer, and Union forces held it throughout the Civil War. The fort is still an active military base, but portions are open to the public. The **Casemate Museum** (757–727–3391) includes the cell where Jefferson Davis was confined after the collapse of the Confederacy; it also contains exhibits about Edgar Allan Poe, who spent four months at Fort Monroe during his two-year stint in the army. Sergeant Major Poe was discharged from the army at this fort in April 1829, the year before he entered West Point. The fort preserves the Lincoln Gun, a 15-inch Rodman gun, named for the president, which was used to bombard Confederate positions in Norfolk. During World War II the fort was headquarters for the defense of the Chesapeake Bay.

FORT WOOL

Fort Wool, also designed by Bernard, stands on an artificial island constructed to protect Hampton Roads. The fort was begun in 1819 and was not abandoned by the Army until 1967. It proved to be an engineering nightmare, partly because the stone slabs used as the foundation for the island kept settling. The fort was first named for John C. Calhoun (who had served as secretary of war), and renamed during the Civil War for a Federal commander, Major General John E. Wool. A federal stronghold throughout the war, Fort Wool provided artillery support to the Union fleet as the *Monitor* battled the *Virginia* in March 1862. It was from Fort Wool that Abraham Lincoln observed the Federal invasion of Norfolk. Today, the island can be reached by tour boats (757–727–6000).

NORFOLK

Norfolk has been an important seaport since its founding in the 1680s. In the colonial period it was a center of trade between Virginia, the West Indies, and England. With a population of six thousand at the outbreak of the Revolution, it was the colony's largest, most prosperous town and a Loyalist stronghold. Late in 1775, Lord Dunmore, the royal governor who had been chased out of the capital at Williamsburg, took refuge off Norfolk in a British warship—one of four anchored at Hampton Roads—crowded with Tory refugees. The town itself was in the hands of Patriot militia. Refused permission to land and take on supplies, Dunmore ordered the ships to bombard the town. The Patriots, for their part, put Tory houses to the torch and the town was virtually leveled.

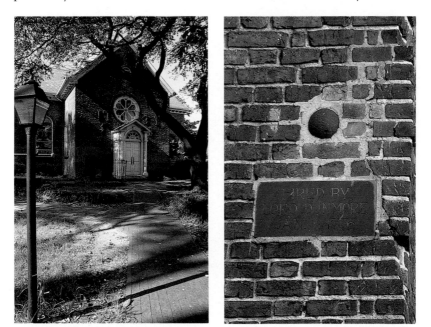

St. Paul's, built in 1739, is the only building in Norfolk to survive the 1776 bombardment by Lord Dunmore and the Patriots' burning of the town. The cannonball embedded in its south wall attests to the Tory onslaught.

Only **St. Paul's Episcopal Church** (201 St. Paul's Boulevard, 757–627–4353) survived the fires, although it was heavily damaged. A British cannonball is embedded in one wall, and Revolutionary War veterans are buried in the churchyard.

During the Revolution, Norfolk's shipyard built the forty-four-gun *Chesapeake*. The Navy Yard here was the site of the country's first drydock, which was built in the early 1830s. At the outbreak of the Civil War, Federal naval officers hastily set fire to the installation and abandoned it. Confederate units rushed in, put out the flames, and salvaged a great deal of equipment and weapons as well as the scuttled vessel *Merrimack*, which was later refitted as the ironclad *Virginia*.

The Chrysler Museum

Founded in 1933 as the Norfolk Museum of Arts and Sciences, the museum was renamed in 1971 when it received the art collection of Walter P. Chrysler, Jr. The museum's holdings include ancient works of art from Greek, Roman, Asian, and pre-Columbian cul-

Eugéne Louis Boudin's Beached Boats at Berck, *part of the collection of the Chrysler Museum (detail).*

tures as well as an excellent collection of nineteenth-century French paintings. Its renowned glass collection, with eight thousand items, ranges from Roman glass to nineteenth-century Sandwich glass and twentieth-century Tiffany pieces. Among the American painters in the collections are Benjamin West, Thomas Cole, Asher B. Durand, Winslow Homer, and John Singer Sargent. The museum also displays folk art collected by Edgar William and Bernice Chrysler Garbisch, and it administers the Moses Myers, Willoughby-Baylor, and Adam Thoroughgood houses.

> LOCATION: Olney Road and Mowbray Arch. HOURS: 10–4 Tuesday–Saturday, 1–5 Sunday. FEE: None. TELEPHONE: 757–664–6200.

Two historic houses on East Freemason Street reflect Norfolk's renewed prosperity in the years after the Revolution. The **Moses Myers House** (323 East Freemason Street, 757–627–2737) was built in 1792 and expanded a few years later by Myers, who came to Norfolk from New York. Myers ran a successful export business and also served as both president of the city council and U.S. consul to France, Denmark, and the Netherlands. His fifteen-room house remained in the Myers family until 1931 and contains many original family furnishings, including portraits of Myers and his wife by Gilbert Stuart. The nearby **Willoughby-Baylor House** (601 East Freemason Street, 757–627–2737) dates to 1794. It has been restored and furnished with eighteenth-century items. The 1840 **Norfolk Academy** (1585 Wesleyan Drive, private) was designed in the Greek Revival style by Thomas U. Walter, who later designed the expansion of the U.S. Capitol.

Douglas MacArthur Memorial

A four-building complex commemorates the general who led U.S. ground forces to victory in the Pacific in World War II. He also commanded United Nations forces in the Korean War until President Truman relieved him of his post due to a dispute over MacArthur's request for permission to bomb military installations within China. The city of Norfolk offered its former city hall as a memorial site because MacArthur's mother was a native of the city. (MacArthur was born in Little Rock, Arkansas, in 1880; he died in 1964.) The hall had been built in 1850 by Thomas U. Walter but was extensively altered in the early 1960s to accommodate MacArthur's tomb in the rotunda, as well as eleven exhibition galleries. The memorial complex includes a theater, where a film about the

The garden and box-hedging at the Adam Thoroughgood House, built in the 1680s, are
representative of seventeenth-century design.

general's career is shown, and his library and archives. The galleries
in the main hall display uniforms, weapons, and memorabilia.

LOCATION: Bank Street and City Hall Avenue. HOURS: 10–5 Monday–Saturday, 11–5 Sunday. FEE: None. TELEPHONE: 757–441– 2965.

ADAM THOROUGHGOOD HOUSE

This small brick farmhouse was erected in the 1680s by a descen-
dent of Captain Adam Thoroughgood, who came to the colony in
his teens as an indentured servant and died at the age of 36 in
1640. The brick house, with chimneys on the sides, was built in a
style typical of late medieval England. It has been restored with
furnishings of the seventeenth and eighteenth centuries.

LOCATION: 1636 Parrish Road, Virginia Beach. HOURS: April
through December: 10–5 Tuesday–Saturday, 12–5 Sunday; January
through March: 10–5 Tuesday–Saturday. FEE: Yes. TELEPHONE:
757–627–2737.

Another important architectural monument in the area is **St. Luke's Church** (Route 10, two miles south of Smithfield in Isle of Wight County, 757–357–3367). Dating to 1632, St. Luke's is the most complete Gothic church in Virginia and the oldest place of worship built by English settlers to survive largely unaltered. The communion table, baptismal font, and organ all date to the mid-1600s; the stained-glass windows are from the nineteenth century.

BACON'S CASTLE

Bacon's Castle became known by that name after a group of Nathaniel Bacon's followers (but not Bacon himself) barricaded themselves in the house for three months during Bacon's Rebellion in 1676. Built about 1665 by an English settler named Arthur Allen, it is a fascinating survivor that reveals the architectural taste of the colony's well-to-do class in the seventeenth century. The stairway enclosed in its own tower is a medieval characteristic, while the curved gables are a Flemish fashion then popular in England. The three towerlike chimneys are a declaration of status: Until the 1500s, chimneys were rare in England, and to make a display of them proclaimed that the householder was a person of substance.

LOCATION: Route 617, just off Route 10. HOURS: 10–4 Tuesday–Saturday, 12–4 Sunday. FEE: Yes. TELEPHONE: 757–357–5976.

Chippokes Plantation State Park (Route 634, 3.5 miles east of Surry, 757–294–3625), a working farm operated by the state, demonstrates eighteenth- and nineteenth-century agricultural methods. The land has been tilled since the 1600s, but all the farm buildings date to the 1800s.

Smith's Fort Plantation (Route 31, Surry, 757–294–3872) is a small, restored mid-eighteenth-century farmhouse typical of its period. It derives its name from **Smith's Fort,** an intriguing, but entirely undramatic, landmark nearby. The fort is literally a hole in the ground with the barely visible remains of an earthwork running along it. This hole was ordered dug by Captain John Smith in 1608 to be a fortified refuge for the Jamestown colony in case of Indian attack. The colonists gave up building the fort when rats destroyed their supplies. This forlorn would-be stronghold is the oldest surviving work of English hands in Virginia.

THE SHENANDOAH VALLEY AND JEFFERSON'S VIRGINIA

The Shenandoah Valley, a fertile region of farms and or-
chards, is 135 miles long, lying between two ranges of the
Appalachian Mountains. During the Civil War, the valley
supplied much of the food to Lee's army. Its control assured not
only an ample food supply but also an invasion route to the North
or South. As a result, more than one hundred battles were fought
in the valley; Winchester changed hands seventy-two times.

In May and June 1862 the valley was the scene of Stonewall
Jackson's most celebrated exploits—a thirty-five day cat-and-mouse
campaign in which Jackson befuddled Federal commanders who
had twice as many troops at their disposal, disrupting General
McClellan's carefully laid strategy for an assault on Richmond as
well as General Fremont's plans for the conquest of eastern Tennessee. In 1864 the genius was on the other side: General Philip
Sheridan's leadership at Cedar Creek turned a defeat into a stunning Union victory.

This chapter covers the Shenandoah Valley, sites in southwestern
and southern Virginia along the North Carolina border, and then
turns north to Charlottesville, the heart of Thomas Jefferson's
Virginia. A traveler touring the Shenandoah Valley could also turn
east at Staunton to see Charlottesville. **Shenandoah National Park**
(540–999–2243) preserves a 105-mile stretch of the Blue Ridge
Mountains, traversed by the Skyline Drive along the eastern edge
of the valley. The park has four entrance stations at Front Royal,
Thornton Gap (Route 211), Swift Run Gap (Route 33, near Harrisonburg), and Rock Fish Gap (near Waynesboro).

THE   SHENANDOAH   VALLEY
WINCHESTER

Once the site of Shawnee Indian camping grounds, Frederick
County and the town of Winchester were settled by Pennsylvania
Quakers in 1732. Winchester was the center of the area's defense
during the French and Indian wars, when George Washington was
a young colonel commanding the Virginia troops here.

During the Civil War there were several battles in the area, two
battles fought in and near Winchester during General Stonewall
Jackson's campaign in 1862. **Plaques** on Valley Avenue mark their
sites. On March 23, Jackson attacked a Federal force under General Nathaniel P. Banks at nearby **Kernstown.** Jackson had miscalcu-

Portrait of a statesman and scholar, Thomas Jefferson, by Charles Willson Peale (detail).

lated his enemy's strength and was badly defeated, but the attack unnerved President Lincoln, who believed that it indicated a Confederate move upon Washington, DC was imminent. He ordered General McDowell's army, which had been promised to McClellan for his attack on Richmond, to be kept in northern Virginia for the defense of the capital. The absence of McDowell's army severely hampered McClellan's plans and contributed to the failure of his campaign. On May 25, after attacking Front Royal, Jackson's men caught up with Banks's troops at Winchester and routed them in a short battle, the First Battle of Winchester.

Two other battles were fought nearby in 1863 and 1864. In the Second Battle of Winchester, on June 14, 1863, Confederate General Richard B. Ewell defeated General Robert H. Milroy to secure Winchester and the Lower Valley as a line of communication between Virginia and Lee's army in Pennsylvania. On September 19, 1864, Sheridan's Federal cavalry routed Jubal Early's 15,000 men

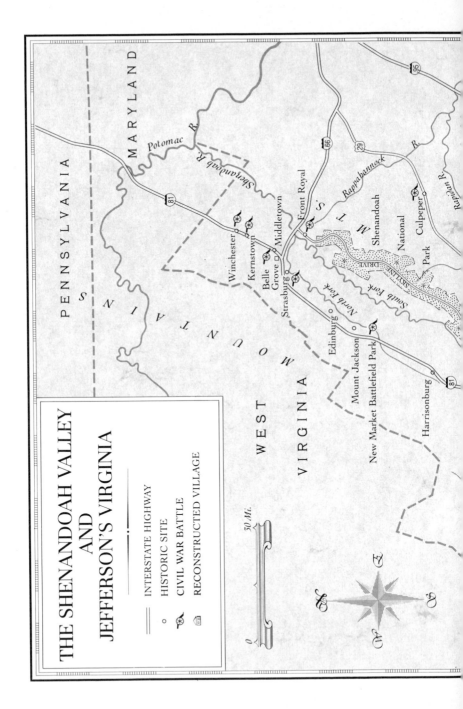

THE SHENANDOAH VALLEY
AND
JEFFERSON'S VIRGINIA

INTERSTATE HIGHWAY

HISTORIC SITE

CIVIL WAR BATTLE

RECONSTRUCTED VILLAGE

50 Mi.

0

PENNSYLVANIA

MARYLAND

Potomac R.

Shenandoah R.

Winchester

Kernstown

Belle
Grove

Middletown

Strasburg

Front Royal

Rappahannock R.

Rapidan R.

Shenandoah

National

Culpeper

Park

SKYLINE DRIVE

South Fork

North Fork

Edinburg

Mount Jackson

New Market Battlefield Park

Harrisburg

WEST

VIRGINIA

MOUNTAINS

B L U E   R I D G E

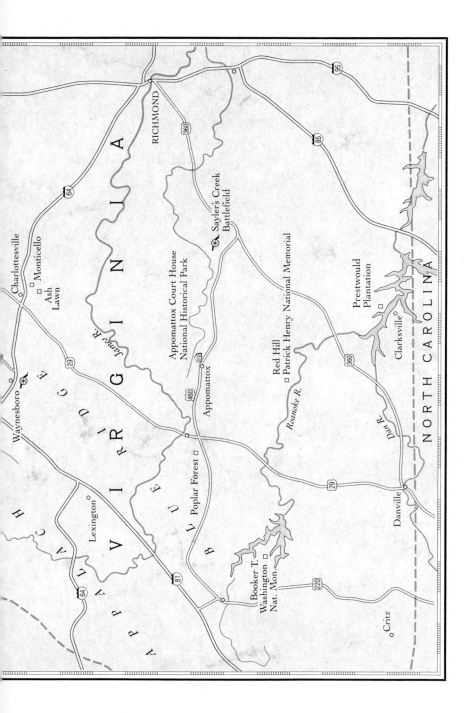

RICHMOND

VIRGINIA

NORTH CAROLINA

APPALACH

BLUE RIDGE

James R.

Roanoke R.

Dan R.

Charlottesville
□ Monticello
Ash Lawn

Waynesboro

Lexington

Appomattox Court House
National Historical Park

Poplar Forest □

Appomattox

Sayler's Creek
Battlefield

Red Hill
□ Patrick Henry National Memorial

Prestwould
Plantation

Clarksville°

Booker T.
Washington □
Nat. Mon.

Danville

Critz

64

29

81

460

360

360

95

85

29

220

with a saber charge, taking 2,000 prisoners. **Markers** for the engagement, known as the Third Battle of Winchester, or Opequon Creek, are north of the town on Route 11.

The **Stonewall Jackson Headquarters Museum** (415 North Braddock Street, 540-667–3242) preserves furniture, personal items, and photographs from Jackson's winter encampment here in 1861–1862. General Sheridan had his headquarters in a building (private) at the southwest corner of Braddock and Piccadilly streets.

A relic of earlier warfare is **George Washington's Office Museum** (Braddock and Cork streets, 540–662–4412). Washington used this office from September 1755 to December 1756, while a colonel in the Virginia Regiment. The museum displays a reproduction of Fort Loudoun, which Washington built to protect Winchester from possible French attacks after Braddock's defeat in Pennsylvania.

Winchester was also the home of the legendary rifleman Daniel Morgan, hero of the battle of Cowpens, South Carolina. He is buried, along with five of his comrades from the Revolutionary War, at **Mount Hebron Cemetery** (East Boscawen Street), near the ruins of the **Old Lutheran Church,** built in 1764.

Just east of downtown Winchester 2,576 Confederate and 6,786 Union soldiers are buried at **Stonewall Cemetery** (within Mount Hebron Cemetery) and **National Cemetery** (National Avenue). Stonewall Cemetery has a memorial obelisk to 829 Confederate unknowns; both cemeteries were dedicated in 1866.

Winchester's oldest house, **Abram's Delight** (1340 South Pleasant Valley Road, 540–662–6519), also known as the Hollingsworth House, was built in 1754 of native limestone by a Quaker family. It has been restored and furnished by the Winchester-Frederick County Historical Society. Next door, in the stone Hollingsworth Mill House, is the area's visitor center (540–662–4118).

MIDDLETOWN

The Battle of Cedar Creek, marked with signs along Route 11 south of Middletown, was one of the most dramatic episodes of the Civil War. At dawn on October 19, 1864, Confederate General Jubal Early launched a surprise attack on General Sheridan's headquarters encampment at Belle Grove Plantation while the com-

OPPOSITE: *A minor setback in the Shenandoah Valley campaign: Sheridan and his army retreat in the Charlestown fire. This drawing, by newspaper artist James E. Taylor, is based on field sketches done at the scene.*

*Opposing forces: Union General Philip Sheridan, left, and Confederate General Stonewall
Jackson, right.* OPPOSITE: *The parlor at Belle Grove Plantation.*

mander was away in Washington. The Federals were routed, and
their confused retreat threatened to lay open Sheridan's entire
corps to attack. But at the moment of Early's triumph, Sheridan
returned. Amazed to see a retreat in progress, he rode among the
men shouting, "If you love your country, come up to the front!"
With Sheridan in command the Federals swept down on the un-
suspecting Confederates and pushed them back across Cedar Creek.
Early's victory turned into a full-scale rout in a matter of hours.

Belle Grove Plantation

Belle Grove was built in 1794 by Isaac Hite, who had married the
sister of James Madison. At Madison's request, Thomas Jefferson
offered Hite advice on the design of the house. It bears many scars
of its use by Sheridan's men—names and initials scratched into
the woodwork, and the words "U.S.A. Signal Corps 1864" decorating the attic ceiling. The corps had set up a signal tower on the
roof. The grounds are now occupied by a working farm.

LOCATION: Route 11, south of Middletown. HOURS: Mid-March
through mid-November: 10–4 Monday–Saturday, 1–5 Sunday. FEE:
Yes. TELEPHONE: 540–869–2028.

FRONT ROYAL

On May 23, 1862, Stonewall Jackson's men surprised a small Federal garrison here, took 750 prisoners, and set off to engage General Banks's force, retreating toward Winchester. Front Royal was the home of the Confederate spy Belle Boyd, who gathered information for Jackson about Union troop movements. The **Warren Rifles Confederate Museum** (95 Chester Street, 540–636–1446) has exhibits about Jackson, Boyd, and others in the 1862 campaign.

STRASBURG

On September 22, 1864, two miles south of Strasburg (Route 11), at a place marked by a **plaque,** Sheridan caught up with Jubal Early's force, in retreat after the Third Battle of Winchester. Early had taken refuge in entrenchments on rugged Fisher's Hill, but Sheridan's men picked their way through the forest to attack Early's left flank and propelled the Confederates farther south.

EDINBURG

This town preserves an 1848 grain mill (Route 11) that was set afire by Federal soldiers in 1864. General Sheridan ordered the fire put out at the plea of the townspeople, who said they would starve without the mill. It is now a restaurant. In **Mount Jackson** there is an obelisk at the graves of 112 Confederate soldiers.

NEW MARKET BATTLEFIELD PARK

On May 15, 1864, Confederate General John C. Breckinridge, leading 5,000 hastily assembled troops, including 257 teenaged cadets called up from the Virginia Military Institute, met a superior Union force on its way to plunder the supply depot at Staunton. Breckinridge skillfully out-generaled the Union commander, but the outcome of the battle was uncertain until, in desperation, Breckinridge ordered the cadets into battle. The boys bravely charged the Federal line and helped secure the Southern victory. The **Hall of Valor** in the park presents superb exhibits tracing the events of the whole war, as well as films about the VMI heroes and Stonewall Jackson's 1862 campaign.

LOCATION: Route 305, Collins Parkway. HOURS: 9–5 Daily. FEE: Yes. TELEPHONE: 540–740–3101.

The **Virginia Quilt Museum** in Harrisonburg (301 South Maple Street, 540–433–3818) is open for the study of quilting in the cultural life of American society. Roadside markers in **Cross Keys** (Route 276) and **Port Republic** (Route 340) describe the last battles, June 8–9, 1862, of Jackson's Shenandoah Valley campaign. Sheridan's 1865 valley campaign concluded at **Waynesboro,** where he scattered the remnants of Jubal Early's army.

LEXINGTON

One of the most beautiful towns in the Shenandoah Valley, Lexington was the prewar home of Stonewall Jackson and the postwar home of Robert E. Lee. There is a **visitor center** at 102 East Washington Street (703–463–3777). General Jackson's simple brick **townhouse** (8 East Washington Street, 540–463–2552) has been preserved with some of his furniture and personal items. On South Main Street, the **Stonewall Jackson Memorial Cemetery** is where the great Confederate general is buried along with hundreds of his compatriots. A statue of the general, sculpted by Edward V. Valentine and dedicated in 1891, faces south.

The interior of the Stonewall Jackson Headquarters Museum in Winchester.

In the 1850s Jackson taught physics and artillery tactics at the **Virginia Military Institute** (540–464–7000), which had been founded in 1839. In 1864, 257 cadets fought in the Battle of New Market: 10 of them were killed. The **VMI Museum** (540–464–7334) on the campus displays a small collection of military items, including the raincoat Jackson was wearing when he was fatally shot at Chancellorsville. The bullet hole is clearly visible. The institute's most famous graduate was General George C. Marshall, chief of staff of the army during World War II and the architect of the postwar Marshall Plan that helped to restore the European economy. The **George C. Marshall Museum and Library** (VMI Parade, 540–463–7103), on the VMI grounds, has exhibits about his life and his activities in both World Wars.

Washington and Lee University (540–463–8400) was founded in 1749, making it the sixth oldest college in the country. It was named the College of Washington in Virginia in 1796 after George Washington donated James River Canal stock to the Liberty Hall Academy. Robert E. Lee was president of the college from 1865 to 1870. He is buried in Lee Chapel, which he helped to design. His office in the chapel has been preserved, and there is a museum with memorabilia of both Washington and Lee.

NATURAL BRIDGE

This limestone arch over Cedar Creek, 215 feet high and 90 feet long, has been one of the region's most admired natural wonders since the eighteenth century. George Washington surveyed the bridge and (we regret to say) cut his initials into it. Thomas Jefferson was so enthralled by the arch that he purchased it from the British Crown in 1774. He called it "the most sublime of nature's works . . . so elevated, so light, and springing as it were up to heaven! the rapture of the spectator is really indescribable!" He dreamed of building a cottage there.

LOCATION: Routes 11 and 130. HOURS: 8–Dusk Daily; night drama presented after dark, phone for information. FEE: Yes. TELEPHONE: 540–291–2121.

OPPOSITE: *Long before Jefferson purchased the Natural Bridge, or before it earned inclusion in the "seven wonders of the world," it was worshipped by the Monocan Indians as "the Bridge of God."*

SOUTHERN VIRGINIA

BOOKER T. WASHINGTON
NATIONAL MONUMENT

The black educator and civil rights leader who founded Tuskegee Institute in 1881 was born a slave on this farm in 1856, forbidden by law to go to school. The farm, where Washington's mother was a cook, was owned by the Burroughs family. After the Civil War the family moved to West Virginia, but Washington returned at age sixteen to attend the Hampton Institute, founded in 1868 to educate former slaves; he taught there after his graduation. He described his experiences in his 1901 autobiography, *Up From Slavery*.

On the reconstructed 207-acre farm, nineteenth-century farming methods are demonstrated. The Burroughs's main cash crop was tobacco, but they also raised corn, wheat, oats, flax, and livestock. The one-room log cabin where Washington lived has been reconstructed. It doubled as the farm's kitchen. He, his mother, and his two siblings slept on a bare dirt floor.

LOCATION: Routes 116-S and 122-N, twenty miles southeast of Roanoke. HOURS: 9–4:30 Daily. FEE: No. TELEPHONE: 540–721–2094.

CRITZ

Tobacco magnate R. J. Reynolds was born at the **Reynolds Homestead** (Route 1, 540–694–7181) in 1850. The house operates as a museum of Virginia plantation life. The 1843 farmhouse has been restored and contains many original furnishings including a rosewood grand piano and the Empire mahogany four-poster bed in which Reynolds' mother gave birth to her sixteen children. The house is surrounded by well-preserved outbuildings; a family graveyard and a slave cemetary are also on the grounds. The homestead is situated at the foot of No Business Mountain, the first rise of the Blue Ridge Mountains and a popular hiding place for moonshiners and their stills. A person would have "no business" up there unless he or she were up to no good.

DANVILLE

Sutherlin House (975 Main Street, 804–793–5644) was one of the places to which Jefferson Davis fled as the Confederacy collapsed in April 1865. Known locally as the last Confederate White House, it displays some artifacts and furnishings of the period.

CLARKSVILLE

Prestwould Plantation (two miles north of Clarksville on Route 15, 804–374–8672) was completed in 1795 by Sir Peyton Skipwith, the only baronet born in the state. Sir Peyton built his stone country seat, graced by scenic wallpaper from France, handsome furniture, and an excellent library, in this remote part of Virginia because the land came to him for nothing. He won its ten thousand acres gambling with the unfortunate William Byrd III of Westover, who took the losing side in the Revolutionary War and lost Westover to his creditors. Lady Jean Skipwith's pastime was her garden, which has been restored, and her records are the earliest listings of native American plantings yet found.

RED HILL SHRINE—THE PATRICK HENRY NATIONAL MEMORIAL

Patrick Henry retired from public life to this plantation in 1793 and died here in 1799. His modest five-room frame house, the headquarters of a three-thousand-acre plantation, has been reconstructed. The original burned down in 1919. Also on the grounds are the kitchen, cook's house, carriage house, his simply furnished law office, and a museum that displays items owned by Henry. He is buried on the property under a stone slab with the inscription: "His fame his best epitaph."

Born in 1736, Henry was a self-taught lawyer and an orator without peer. George Mason called him "by far the most powerful speaker I ever heard . . . your passions are no longer your own when he addresses them." As a delegate to the House of Burgesses from 1765 to 1774 he led the campaign against the Stamp Act. He served in the Continental Congress and as the first governor of Virginia. At the Richmond convention in March 1775 he electrified the assembled Virginians with his "Give me Liberty or give me Death" speech, in which he correctly predicted that "the next gale that sweeps from the North will bring to our ears the clash of resounding arms!" His fiery speech prodded the reluctant delegates into placing the colony in "a posture of defence."

LOCATION: Red Hill, Brookneal. HOURS: March through October: 9–5 Daily; November through February: 9–4 Daily. FEE: Yes. TELEPHONE: 804–376–2044.

Sayler's Creek Battlefield Historical State Park (Route 617, east of Farmville, 804–392–3435) is the site of the last major battle of the

Civil War in the state. Federal cavalry chased down the rear guard of Lee's army, in retreat from Richmond. Over eight thousand Confederates were captured. The **Hillsman House** served as a Federal field hospital; bloodstains still remain on the floors.

APPOMATTOX COURT HOUSE NATIONAL HISTORICAL PARK

In this village on April 9, 1865, General Robert E. Lee surrendered the Army of Northern Virginia to General Ulysses S. Grant. Lee's exhausted army was trying to make its way to Danville pursued by two Federal armies and Sheridan's cavalry. The last Confederate attack against Sheridan, whose men blocked the road south, came to nothing, and Lee realized that he had no alternative but surrender, "and I would rather die a thousand deaths." Lee and Grant met at the home of Wilmer McLean. Grant's terms were generous, helping to bring about a reconciliation and reunification of the divided nation. At Lee's request his men were allowed to keep their sidearms and baggage and take their horses to plow their fields. Grant sent food to Lee's army, and when his men began firing cannon to celebrate, Grant halted them, saying, "the rebels are our countrymen again, and the best sign of rejoicing . . . will be to abstain from all demonstrations." As Lee's infantry marched past Union ranks at **Surrender Triangle** on April 12, piling up their arms and battle flags, the Northerners saluted them.

In 1893 an entrepreneur bought and dismantled the McLean house with the idea of reconstructing it in Washington, DC as a museum. But the piles of brick and wood remained where they lay until the reconstruction of the village was begun in the 1940s. McLean's house and twenty-six other buildings have been restored or reconstructed so that the village now looks as it did in 1865.

LOCATION: Route 24, north of Appomattox. HOURS: June through August: 9–5:30 Daily; September through May: 8:30–5 Daily. FEE: Yes. TELEPHONE: 804–352–8987.

POPLAR FOREST

Poplar Forest was built by Thomas Jefferson as a refuge from the visitors who streamed to Monticello. He began constructing it, one of the first octagonal houses in America, in 1806, but work on the

OPPOSITE: *The reconstructed McLean House, where General Robert E. Lee surrendered the Army of Northern Virginia to General Ulysses S. Grant, April 9, 1865.*

Created as a place where he could "enjoy the solitude of a hermit," Poplar Forest, Jefferson wrote, was "the best dwelling house in the state, except. . . Monticello." OVERLEAF: *Another Jefferson design, the campus of the University of Virginia.*

interior continued until 1823. In 1781 he had fled to the plantation on this property, which had belonged to his late wife's family, when Tarleton's cavalry raided Monticello. While here he started to write his only book, *Notes on the State of Virginia.* He was in the habit of making the eighty-mile trip from Monticello to Poplar Forest three or four times a year for stays of two to three weeks.

The octagonal shape reflects Jefferson's fascination with putting abstract geometrical forms to practical use. The house has six rooms in its single story, over a raised basement. In the center is a square dining room, which Jefferson designed to be illuminated by skylights. Three rooms are octagons; the other two, semi-, or bisected, octagons. On the exterior, he flanked his octagon with two pavilions holding stairwells and placed Neoclassical porticoes in the front and back. In private hands until 1984, Poplar Forest was being restored in the late 1990s while open to the public.

LOCATION: Route 661 southwest of Lynchburg. HOURS: April through November: 10–4 Wednesday–Sunday; open for group tours by appointment. FEE: Yes. TELEPHONE: 804–525–1806.

JEFFERSON'S VIRGINIA

Charlottesville and the region around it were Thomas Jefferson's home ground. He was born here at his father's farm, Shadwell, in 1743. From his father he inherited the land southwest of Charlottesville where he built his house, Monticello. The town stood on the edge of the wilderness in Jefferson's time and was not touched by the events of the Revolution, except for an unsuccessful British attempt to arrest Jefferson and other Revolutionary leaders. After the Revolution Jefferson persuaded the Virginia legislature to establish a university in Charlottesville. Southeast of Charlottesville, the town of **Palmyra** preserves an unaltered Greek Revival building, the 1830 temple-form **Fluvanna County Courthouse.** Nearby is the **Old Stone Jail** (Courthouse Green, Palmyra), designed by John Hartwell Cocke of nearby Bremo, possibly as a replica of an old English prison.

THE UNIVERSITY OF VIRGINIA

The University of Virginia opened its doors in March 1825 with sixty-eight students and a faculty of ten. It had been founded through the efforts of Thomas Jefferson, who planned it as the first secular college in America. Since the founding of Harvard two centuries earlier, American colleges had been started to train ministers. The university was an important part of Jefferson's campaign to bring the Enlightenment to American education. As early as 1786 he had written, "the diffusion of knowledge among the people [is the] sure foundation . . . for the preservation of freedom and happiness." The cost of public education, he thought, would be small compared to that of an uneducated populace. "The tax which will be paid for this purpose is not more than the thousandth part of what will be paid to kings, priests, and nobles who will rise up among us if we leave the people in ignorance."

Jefferson had a revolutionary's attitude toward education—"Science is progressive. What was useful two centuries ago is now become useless, e.g., one-half the professorships at William and Mary"—and drew up the curriculum to include history, law, political economy, physics, ancient and modern languages, mathematics, botany, zoology, anatomy, medicine, and government.

He also designed the campus itself. He conceived it as an "academical village," with ten pavilions—one for each professor's residence and a hall below it for his class—facing a long lawn in two

An elevation of the University of Virginia's rotunda and its flanking wings, attributed to Thomas Jefferson's granddaughter, Cornelia Jefferson Randolph.

rows or "ranges," each a different example of classical forms from British and French derivations of Italian Renaissance prototypes. He expected that the students would learn about "taste and good architecture" by living and working in an architectural museum. At the suggestion of Benjamin Henry Latrobe, Jefferson added the rotunda at one end of the lawn to serve as the focal point for the campus. Ultimately derived from the Pantheon in Rome, the rotunda housed the library, lecture halls, and a laboratory. He wanted to install a planetarium in the dome, but it was never built. Within the rotunda he designed an elegant suite of oval rooms, inspired by a building he had seen in France, the Desert de Retz. The rotunda was gutted by fire in 1895, and redesigned by Stanford White, but Jefferson's original design was restored in the 1970s. Although Jefferson planned for the campus to serve as a real-life textbook of architecture, he was also deeply concerned with practicalities, such as "fire, infection, and tumult." "This village form," he wrote, "is preferable to a single great building for many reasons. . . . Instead of a large and common den of noise, of filth and of fetid air [the village plan] would afford the quiet retirement so friendly to study."

One of the first students was Edgar Allan Poe, whose room in the West Range has been restored. When he was enrolled from February to December 1826 he earned good grades in classical and modern languages and wrote many of the poems published in his first collection, *Tamerlane and Other Poems,* in 1827.

LOCATION: University Avenue, Charlottesville. TELEPHONE: 804–924–7969.

In the eighteenth and nineteenth centuries **Michie Tavern** (Route 53, 804–977–1234) was frequented by many weary Virginians. The land was owned by Patrick Henry's father, and sold to John Michie in 1746. His descendants operated a tavern in the house from 1784 until 1910. Still a functioning restaurant, it was moved to its current location on the road to Monticello in 1927. Some original woodwork and furnishings have been preserved. Adjacent is the **Meadow Run Grist Mill,** in operation for over 150 years.

ASH LAWN—HIGHLAND

A 3,500-acre farm, Highland was the home of President James Monroe and his family from 1799 to 1823. The simple farmhouse contains a collection of Monroe furnishings, many of which were purchased while Monroe served as President Jefferson's minister to France. The Monroes moved to Highland to be near Jefferson, whose Monticello is visible on the mountaintop two miles away. Although Monroe had hoped to retire to Highland, financial difficulties forced its sale in 1826. His primary residence in his mature years was at Oak Hill in Loudoun County; he died in New York City, where he was living with his daughter and son-in-law. Later owners changed Highland's name to Ash Lawn and built a Victorian house adjoining the Monroe residence.

LOCATION: Route 795, 2.5 miles southeast of Monticello. HOURS: March through October: 9–6 Daily; November through February: 10–5 Daily. FEE: Yes. TELEPHONE: 804–293–9539.

MONTICELLO

Monticello, the home of Thomas Jefferson, is one of the nation's most important architectural landmarks. In its design, Monticello was as revolutionary as the political ideas of its builder. Jefferson despised the early-eighteenth-century brick architecture of Williamsburg ("the most wretched style I ever saw") as a reminder of

Monticello inspired the Marquis de Chastellux to name Jefferson "the first American who has

British colonial rule. He said if the houses did not have roofs they could be mistaken for brick kilns. In 1789, after spending five years in France, he returned to Virginia with fresh ideas about domestic architecture and undertook a complete redesign of the first house he had built on this site. Although he used many classical elements, Jefferson was not advocating academic, antiquarian architecture. As he wrote in a letter to John Adams, "I like the dreams of the future better than the history of the past."

In the second Monticello, finished in 1809, he used a single classical portico, not the double loggia of his first design. Atop the house he placed a dome, the first one in Virginia—his carpenter had never heard of such a thing. The finished form is partly French, partly British, partly Italian, and mostly Jefferson.

The house has three stories but seems from the outside to have only one because Jefferson arranged the small upper windows to appear as extensions of the first-floor windows. This creates an effect of unity without bulk and makes the house look much smaller than it is. The symmetrical exterior belies the irregular interior, with rooms of different shapes, sizes, and heights. Tall windows

consulted the fine arts to know how he should shelter himself from the weather."

and skylights bathe the interior with sunlight. The ingenious mechanical devices of Jefferson's own design that fill the house prompted Dr. William Thornton's wife to remark, "Everything has a whimsical and droll appearance." Restored with many furnishings original to the house, Monticello looks much as it did between 1809 and 1826, when Jefferson died here. Only the first floor is open to the public.

The **entrance hall** was Jefferson's private museum. He exhibited many Indian artifacts, such as clothing, weapons, and paintings; mastodon bones; a model of the Great Pyramid of Egypt; a statue of the mythical Greek heroine Ariadne; antlers; and a collection of minerals. Some items were collected by the Lewis and Clark expedition, which Jefferson ordered during his presidency.

Over the door is a large, seven-day calendar clock designed by Jefferson and built for him in Philadelphia in the 1790s. Weights suspended from a pulley indicate the day of the week against marks on the wall. To accommodate the length of the rope, Jefferson cut a hole in the floor. By Friday afternoon the weights sink out of sight, not to reappear until the clock is rewound on Sunday

The south side of Monticello. OPPOSITE: *The entrance hall served as Jefferson's museum of art and natural sciences.*

morning. The double glass doors to the parlor are semiautomatic. They are connected to a loop of chain under the floor; when one of the doors is pushed the other one also moves.

The **parlor** is an elegant, semi-octagonal room with a magnificent view of the mountains. Here Jefferson displayed about fifty portraits and copies of paintings by European masters whom he admired, such as Raphael and Guido Reni. The cherry and beechwood floor is one of the country's earliest parquet floors, and the French furnishings include two pier mirrors that have never left the house. The **dining room,** lit by a skylight, features two of Jefferson's "whimsical" devices—a concealed dumbwaiter by which fresh bottles of wine were brought up from the cellar and empty bottles sent down, and revolving shelves on which the servants could deliver food without entering the room. In the adjoining semi-octagonal **tea room** Jefferson displayed busts of Washington, Benjamin Franklin, John Paul Jones, and Lafayette, in the company of Roman emperors.

The southern wing of Monticello contains Jefferson's **private suite,** consisting of his bedroom, study, and library. Even something as apparently simple as the bed was the object of Jeffersonian cleverness: He placed it in an alcove open on both sides so that he could get out of bed on the dressing room side if he wished to

dress, or on the study side if he wished to write down a midnight thought. The **study,** which he called his cabinet, has the chaise longue and writing table where he wrote, using a dual-pen "polygraph" that automatically made a copy of a document as it was being written. Also in this room are his telescope and surveying instruments. The study is connected to the library, as is the glassed-in **piazza** where Jefferson carried out horticultural experiments.

The **library,** like all of the rooms in the suite, is far neater today than it was in Jefferson's time, when his enormous collection of almost seven thousand books overflowed the shelves into piles on the floors. He sold his holdings to the Library of Congress in 1815, to replace the books burned by the British in the War of 1812. The collection on display duplicates a portion of Jefferson's original library. The **south square room** next to the library was used as a family sitting room.

The second floor, not open to the public, holds small bedrooms. It is reached by two very narrow staircases hidden from sight in passageways. In the eighteenth century, staircases were often regarded as the decorative centerpiece of a house; Jefferson considered them a waste of space. On the third floor are three bedrooms and the mysterious room under the dome. It is not known how Jefferson used this octagonal room, lit by round windows; he may have written letters there to his friend Maria Cosway, whom he met in Paris under a similarly constructed dome.

Jefferson took full advantage of his mountaintop site: He placed the service buildings in the hillside below the level of the house, so that his views would not be obscured. "Where has Nature spread so rich a mantle under the eye?" he wrote, describing his view from Monticello. "How sublime to look down into the work-house of nature, to see her clouds, hails, snow, rain, thunder, all fabricated at our feet!" Around the lawn on the western side of the house he laid out a serpentine path and flower beds. Gardening was one of his passions: "No occupation is so delightful to me as the culture of the earth & no culture comparable to that of the garden," he wrote in 1811 to the painter Charles Willson Peale.

The mountaintop on which the house stands (Monticello means "little mountain" in Italian) was part of Jefferson's inheritance from his father. He built the first version of Monticello between 1769 and 1782. During the Revolution the British raided Charlottesville in search of Jefferson, then serving as governor, and other members of the revolutionary government. On the night of June 3, 1781, a Virginia militia captain, Jack Jouett, saw 250

Just off Jefferson's bedroom is his cabinet, where he wrote most of his correspondence.

British horsemen, led by Colonel Banastre Tarleton, riding through the town of Louisa toward Charlottesville. He guessed, correctly, that they were on their way to Monticello to arrest Jefferson. Jouett galloped forty miles through thick forests—the British were using the only road—arriving at Monticello at 4:30 AM. Jefferson took the time to have breakfast and gather up some papers before leaving, just as Tarleton's men were closing in on the house.

Jefferson died in his bed at Monticello on July 4, 1826, the fiftieth anniversary of the Declaration of Independence. He is buried on the grounds under an obelisk he designed himself. The stone is inscribed with three achievements, "because by these, as testimonials that I have lived, I wish most to be remembered":

Author of the Declaration of American Independence
Of the Statute of Virginia for religious freedom
And Father of the University of Virginia.

LOCATION: Route 53, 3 miles southeast of Charlottesville. HOURS: March through October: 8–5 Daily; November through February: 9–4:30 Daily. FEE: Yes. TELEPHONE: 804–977–1783.

ANNAPOLIS
AND THE
EASTERN
SHORE

In March 1634, two small ships, the *Ark* and the *Dove*, arrived on St. Clements Island at the mouth of the Potomac. They carried Leonard Calvert, the Jesuit missionary Father Andrew White, and some 140 settlers to colonize what John Smith had described as a "fruitful and delightsome land." From the chief of the Piscataway Indians, Calvert obtained a thirty-square-mile site along a river he named St. Mary's, and here he founded a small settlement of the same name, the fourth permanent English settlement in America. Calvert's brother Cecil, Lord Baltimore, had received a royal charter to some seven million acres. The Calverts were Roman Catholics, and their colony, named Maryland, was to be a haven for members of their faith and, no less important, a source of rental income. The elder Calvert's notion was to establish a manorial system in which gentlemen who brought a certain number of laborers to Maryland would be given two-thousand-acre manors. The manor lords would collect rents from their tenant farmers and turn a portion of their income over to Lord Baltimore. Labor would be provided by indentured servants and slaves.

The region was, indeed, a fertile and fruitful one. The English acquired a taste for crabs and oysters, found deer plentiful, and had no trouble raising corn, wheat, oats, apples, and other food on this rich soil. In 1680 there were so many ducks a Dutchman noted that the water was black with them and the sound of their flight was like thunder—"a great storm coming through the trees." A single musket blast into a flock would bring down a dozen. Forests of oak, cypress, tulip, hickory, chestnut, and pine provided ample materials for houses and farms. The Piscataway Indians, whose land this was, had welcomed the Englishmen peacefully, hoping that the newcomers would protect them from the attacks of the Susquehannock. As it turned out, the Piscataway fell victim to European diseases and the continuing raids of their traditional enemies.

The majority of Maryland's settlers, about 70 percent, arrived as indentured servants. They worked off their indentures to masters who had paid their passage, and then struck out to establish their own farms. From the start Maryland's most important crop was tobacco; by the late 1630s the colony was annually shipping more than 100,000 pounds of tobacco back to England. That figure rose to the millions of pounds by the 1660s. Most of the tobacco farms in the colony were small, covering 100 to 150 acres,

OPPOSITE: *Cecil Calvert, the second Lord Baltimore. His grandson points to a map of Maryland.*

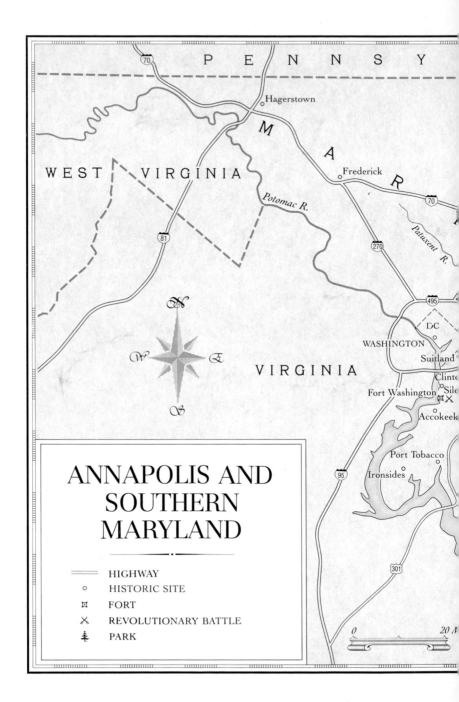

P E N N S Y

70

Hagerstown

M A R

WEST VIRGINIA

Frederick

70

Potomac R.

81

270

Patuxent R.

495

DC

WASHINGTON

Suitland

VIRGINIA

Clint

Fort Washington Sile

Accokeek

Port Tobacco

95   Ironsides

301

0   20 M

ANNAPOLIS AND
SOUTHERN
MARYLAND

———— HIGHWAY
○ HISTORIC SITE
Ⱨ FORT
✕ REVOLUTIONARY BATTLE
♣ PARK

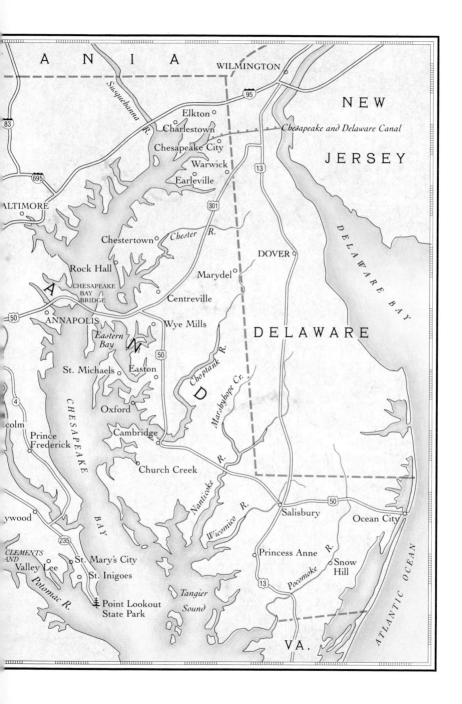

Annapolis seen from the air. OPPOSITE: *The Chinese Chippendale stairway at Sotterley Plantation, the work of master carpenter Richard Boulton, an indentured servant.*

not unlike the Spray Plantation reconstructed at Historic St. Mary's City. They were spread out along the Chesapeake, its rivers, and its inlets, all of which provided easy transportation by water.

The Calverts had proclaimed freedom of religion to all who recognized the Trinity. This included Catholics and Protestants, but not Jews. Within a few decades, Protestants in the colony outnumbered Catholics. At the time of England's "Glorious Revolution," when Protestant William and Mary unseated the Romeward-leaning King James, Maryland's Protestants staged a religious and political coup, ousting Lord Baltimore's governor at St. Mary's City and denying Catholics the right to vote—a right that was not restored until after the American Revolution. (Charles Carroll, a Catholic, signed the Declaration of Independence for Maryland, but he could not vote.) The colony was removed from the hands of Lord Baltimore and placed under a royal governor. Francis Nicholson, arriving in 1694, transplanted the capital from its Catholic stronghold at St. Mary's to Protestant Annapolis.

"All the Country lives upon Credit," wrote one man in the 1690s, "and talk not of payments but in the Tobacco Season." A few families, such as the Carrolls, Lloyds, and Dulaneys, owned large amounts of land, traded tobacco, wheat, corn, timber, and other commodities, lent money, and invested in ironworks and

shipping. But the 1700s brought the "Tobacco Coast" to full flower, aided by easy credit from London merchants—and a slave-labor
population that amounted to 20 percent of the total in 1700.
Sotterley Plantation provides an example of this growing success
and its impact on the upper middle class of the colony: The house
was enlarged several times in the 1700s, and in the 1760s was
graced by a handsome carved stairway and carved woodwork.

Prosperity at the top created a thriving class of artisans and
shopkeepers; but at the very bottom, tenant farmers scratched out
a miserable living. In the 1770s an oversupply of tobacco sent the
price plummeting and London merchants scurrying to collect their
debts. The credit crisis coincided with the political one, perhaps
contributing to the willingness of Marylanders on the Tobacco
Coast to cut ties with the motherland. Maryland sent supplies and
some of America's bravest men to the Revolution, but neither the
war itself nor, completely, its benefits descended on these shores.
Benjamin Banneker, a free black engineer of many accomplish-
ments, quoted the Declaration of Independence in a letter to its
author, Thomas Jefferson, and forcefully pointed out to him that
in 1791 blacks in Maryland still labored "under that State of tyran-
nical thraldom, and inhuman captivity."

The Revolution marked the economic and political high tide
of the Tobacco Coast. Up rose Baltimore in the nineteenth century,
its trade based on the wheat fields of Pennsylvania and Maryland.
The center of roads and rail lines, Baltimore seized the lion's share
of the shipping business. The Eastern and Western shores of the
Chesapeake saw their prosperity and influence wane as the far-
western counties of the Piedmont boomed. Little has changed in
two hundred years—the region remains agricultural except for the
suburbs of Washington and Baltimore and the resort communities
of the Eastern Shore. It was not until 1952 that the construction of
the Bay Bridge from Annapolis brought the Eastern Shore within
easy reach of Baltimore and Washington. Routes 301 and 50, the
area's main arteries, run through farmlands where one might see,
half-hidden in a stand of trees, an eighteenth-century brick farmhouse. The more substantial mansions of the landholding families
are still there, too, tucked away on back roads at the end of long
drives. Towns like Oxford and Chestertown, where seagoing ships
called in the 1700s, are now harbors for pleasure craft.

This chapter covers the Chesapeake region in two sections: first
Annapolis and Southern Maryland, then the Eastern Shore.

A N N A P O L I S

In 1694 Governor Francis Nicholson moved the colonial capital from St. Mary's City to this place on the Severn River, then called Arundel Towne, which had been settled in 1649 by Puritans from Virginia. It was renamed Annapolis in honor of Queen Anne. As he would later do in Williamsburg, Virginia, Nicholson designed the new town himself. Basing his plan on Baroque principles then popular in England, Nicholson set down two large circles, one for the capitol and one for a church, with the major streets radiating from them through a grid of lesser streets. The oblique intersections and the vistas to the major buildings and the waterfront created a pleasing townscape with a sense of charming irregularity and vest-pocket grandeur. The State House occupies the highest point, making its cupola visible from much of the town.

Throughout the eighteenth century, Annapolis was Maryland's premier port, handling much of the colony's exports of tobacco and iron, and imports of rum, coffee, tea, sugar, manufactured goods, and slaves. By the middle of the century, Annapolis had become both the social and political center of the colony. The wealthy planters of Maryland—who had a greater taste for urban life than did their peers in Virginia—built brick mansions here that rank among the finest American houses of the century. The architect William Buckland came from Virginia and created the elegant Hammond-Harwood House and the gracious interior of the Chase-Lloyd House. Writing in 1770, Reverend Jonathan Boucher called Annapolis "the genteelest town in North America. . . . I hardly know a town in England as desirable to live in." William Eddis, a Crown official, commented on its "polished society" and large number of "fashionable women." George Washington enjoyed taking his family to the horse races held here each September. He attended plays and balls, lost money at cards and the racetrack, and spent jovial evenings among the Maryland gentry at the Homony Club, which had been founded "to promote innocent mirth and ingenious humor."

Annapolitans joined the independence movement with fervor: In 1765 they chased the tax collector out of town; in 1774 they burned the *Peggy Stewart* because its owner, an Annapolis man, had paid the hated tax on the tea in her hold; and three men from this town, William Paca, Samuel Chase, and Charles Carroll, signed the Declaration of Independence. "I hear strange language every day," wrote William Eddis in puzzlement. "The colonists are ripe for any

measures that will tend to the preservation of what they call their natural liberty. . . . Where will these matters end?"

After the war, Congress sat at the State House for a few months, and Annapolis was one of the places under consideration for the site of the permanent U.S. capital. But the westward migration that elevated the fortunes of Baltimore left Annapolis to molder. In 1845, George Bancroft was able to locate his naval academy in the harbor's Fort Severn because the fort no longer protected anything of strategic importance. The business of state government and of educating the naval officer corps kept the town's economy alive. One of the finest eighteenth-century houses, the Paca House, was converted into a hotel catering to the academy's visitors, and its extensive garden was sold off in parcels; the nineteenth-century occupants of the Hammond-Harwood House also had to sell off land to maintain the house.

Much of eighteenth-century Annapolis survives, however, and today's stroller on Duke of Gloucester Street, Prince George Street, and Maryland Avenue sees the town much as it was two centuries ago. Three beautiful mansions of that era have been restored, the Old State House still stands atop its hill, and the brawny Beaux-Arts campus of the Naval Academy overlooks a harbor filled with the boats of a new leisure class.

This tour of Annapolis begins with the State House and the sites near it, then proceeds to the houses on Maryland Avenue, to the waterfront, and finally to the academy.

MARYLAND STATE HOUSE

Dominating the city from its position atop the area's highest hill is the Maryland State House. Begun in 1772 and occupied by the legislature in 1780, it is the oldest state capitol still in use. Today the state senate and house of delegates meet in an addition built in 1905, but the historic chambers of the old portion have been preserved and restored. The two-story brick building has an octagonal dome and cupola added in 1788. The dome, fashioned of cypress beams held together with pegs, is the largest wooden dome in the country. Running the length of the first floor is an arcaded central hall decorated with plaster ornamentation. The ornamentation beneath the dome was done by an artisan named Thomas Dance, who died after falling to the floor from his scaffolding.

OPPOSITE: *The Maryland State House is the only state house ever to have served as the nation's capitol.*

The U.S. Congress met in the **Old Senate Chamber** from November 1783 to August 1784. Here George Washington resigned his commission as commander-in-chief on December 23, 1783, and here the Treaty of Paris, officially ending the Revolution, was ratified on January 14, 1784. A life-size figure of Washington stands where he resigned. Eight pieces of original furniture remain, and the room preserves its decorative details of carved woodwork and molded plaster. William Buckland may have done some of the woodwork, including the ladies' balcony, which is finely decorated with carved tobacco leaves. On display is Charles Willson Peale's 1784 painting *Washington at the Battle of Yorktown*, which the legislature commissioned "in grateful Remembrance of that most illustrious character." One of the figures in the painting is Colonel Tench Tilghman of Maryland, who brought the news of the Yorktown victory to Congress in Philadelphia.

The adjacent **Old Senate Committee Room** has exhibits about Washington's resignation and a large portrait of the British statesman William Pitt in the garb of a Roman senator, by Charles Willson Peale. The **Constitution Room** displays an ornate forty-eight-piece sterling silver service, presented to the cruiser *Maryland* in 1906. Some pieces are decorated with scenes from the state's history. The room also displays nineteenth-century paintings depicting events in Maryland's history, including Frank Mayer's 1896 painting, *The Burning of the Peggy Stewart*. Exhibits concerning the architecture and construction of the building are in the **Archives Room,** which has its original fire-proof brick floor.

LOCATION: State Circle. HOURS: 9–5 Daily. FEE: None. TELEPHONE: 410–974–3400.

On the grounds of the State House is the **Old Treasury Building,** a small brick building erected in 1737. It is the tour office of Historic Annapolis Foundation (410–267–7619).

ST. ANNE'S CHURCH

A fire in 1858 destroyed the second church that had been built on this site in the 1780s; but portions of its tower and front wall survived and were incorporated in the present church, completed in 1859. The octagonal steeple is an addition of 1866. The church possesses a silver communion service, made in London in the 1690s and donated by King William III. The oldest burial in the graveyard around the church is that of the first mayor of Annapolis,

Amos Garrett, who died in 1727. The other graves with seventeenth-century markers were moved to this site from surrounding burying grounds. Also interred here is Sir Robert Eden, the last colonial governor of Maryland.

LOCATION: Church Circle. HOURS: 8–6 Daily. FEE: None. TELEPHONE: 410–267–9333.

BANNEKER-DOUGLASS MUSEUM OF AFRICAN-AMERICAN HISTORY AND CULTURE

The museum, which presents changing exhibits about the history and culture of blacks in America, is named after both the civil rights leader Frederick Douglass and Benjamin Banneker, a Maryland farmer, engineer, mathematician, and surveyor who assisted in the design of Washington, DC. In 1791, Banneker sent a copy of an almanac he had compiled to Thomas Jefferson with a letter reminding Jefferson that the freedoms described in the Declaration of Independence had not been extended to blacks. Jefferson responded with a letter praising the almanac but said nothing about slavery. The museum is housed in the former Old Mount Moriah African Methodist Episcopal Church, a Gothic building built in 1874. The congregation was founded by free blacks in 1799.

LOCATION: 84 Franklin Street. HOURS: 10–3 Tuesday–Friday, 12–4 Saturday. FEE: None. TELEPHONE: 410–974–2893.

St. John's College (College Avenue, 410–263–2371) originated in 1696 as King William's School. The oldest building on the campus, the **Carroll House,** dates to 1722. Birthplace of Charles Carroll, who wrote Maryland's Bill of Rights, the house was moved here from Main Street in 1955. **McDowell Hall** was begun in 1742 as the governor's mansion, but the legislature halted the construction when costs overran the budget. It was completed in 1792 when the legislature gave it to the college. It was here that Francis Scott Key, who graduated as class valedictorian, attended classes. In 1824 its great hall was the site for two dinners and a ball in honor of General Lafayette. During the Civil War the hall was used as a prison. St. John's College campus has another landmark, a tulip poplar "Liberty Tree," which stands nearly one hundred feet tall and, in four centuries, has seen much of Annapolis's history.

HAMMOND-HARWOOD HOUSE

One of the finest Colonial houses in America, Hammond-Harwood vies with Virginia's Gunston Hall for the honor of being the masterpiece of architect and joiner William Buckland. At Gunston Hall, Buckland was responsible for only the interior; here he was able to design the entire house and to oversee the creation of much of the woodwork. Its five-part plan, consisting of the main house connected to two wings by one-story passageways, was derived from Italian villas designed by Andrea Palladio and from English country estates based on Palladio's work. Hammond-Harwood was built from 1774 to 1776.

Buckland's skill as a designer is immediately evident in the doorway, with its arched fanlight, engaged columns, and beautifully carved floral and leaf decoration. Inside, Buckland placed the stairway in a side hall, thereby leaving space for a larger dining room at the rear of the house. The carved woodwork and plaster ornamentation of the dining room's cornice, doorways, windows, and fireplace are the mansion's finest. The windows and interior shutters, for example, feature carved hexagons, arabesques, and flowers. The room also reveals Buckland's concern with symmetry. The door to the right of the fireplace is a false one, that balances the door to the left. One of the windows is a "jib" door, with a hinged wainscot below the window that opens out. Thus Buckland provided access to the garden without spoiling the symmetrical arrangement of windows with the imposition of a door.

The early history of the house was not a happy one. Mathias Hammond, the young plantation owner and lawyer who commissioned Buckland, never lived in it, but left Annapolis for his country house. The story has been told that he wanted to build the finest house he could for his bride-to-be, but became so obsessed with its design and construction that he neglected the young lady, who left him. It is also said that he vowed not to inhabit it, and the house may have stood empty for several years. He died in 1786 at age 38.

Buckland himself never saw the completed house. As work was in progress, he received a commission to build a courthouse for Caroline County on the Eastern Shore, where he died in late 1774 under unknown circumstances. Even his burial place is unknown. The only documentary evidence of the talented architect's death is

OPPOSITE: *A view through the magnificent entryway at the Hammond-Harwood House reveals the "jib" door in the dining room beyond: It was designed to incorporate a window, which, its sash raised and hinged wainscot open, becomes a door onto the garden.*

a newspaper advertisement of December 1774 that offers his house for sale, referring to him as "deceased." Oddly enough, one of Buckland's descendants became the proprietor of the house. His great-grandson William Harwood married Hester Ann Loockerman, whose grandfather had purchased it. Harwood's income as a schoolteacher was insufficient to maintain so grand a property, but their daughter Hester Ann Harwood managed to hold it until her death in 1924. St. John's College purchased the house intending to maintain it as a museum. In 1940 it was acquired by the Hammond-Harwood House Association.

The house is furnished with a splendid collection dating from 1760 to 1800. There are some Harwood family items (including portraits by Charles Willson Peale), although most were sold at auction in 1924. Several pieces on display in the dining room and elsewhere were made by the Annapolis cabinetmaker John Shaw. The dining room also holds a copy of Peale's portrait of Buckland, in which he is seen with the plans for this house spread before him.

LOCATION: 19 Maryland Avenue. HOURS: Guided tours on the hour, 10–4 Monday–Saturday, 12–4 Sunday; closed January 1, Thanksgiving Day, and December 25. FEE: Yes. TELEPHONE: 410–269–1714.

CHASE-LLOYD HOUSE

This three-story brick house across Maryland Avenue from the Hammond-Harwood House was begun in 1769 by Samuel Chase, an attorney who later sat on the Supreme Court. Chase did not have the funds to complete this unusually large house and sold it in 1771 with just the exterior walls completed. The purchaser, the wealthy Eastern Shore planter Edward Lloyd IV, hired William Buckland to complete the interior. In the stair hall a pair of Ionic columns rise to a beam decorated with a classical pattern of wave crests. The cantilevered stairway in the center of the hall divides at the first landing beneath a handsome Venetian window. Exceptionally fine woodwork and delicate plaster ornamentation, in the Adam style, can be seen on the doorframes, windows, and ceilings of the first-floor rooms.

LOCATION: 22 Maryland Avenue. HOURS: 2–4 Tuesday–Saturday. FEE: Yes. TELEPHONE: 410–263–2723.

OPPOSITE: *The gaming room at the Hammond-Harwood House features an English Chippendale gaming table and chairs, designed ca. 1760.*

WILLIAM PACA HOUSE

This house, built between 1763 and 1765, was the home of one of Annapolis's most active Patriots, the lawyer William Paca. He served on the Committee of Correspondence (which kept Maryland's Patriots in touch with events in other colonies), the Council of Safety, and in the Continental Congress. He was also a signer of the Declaration of Independence. Paca occupied this thirty-seven-room house until 1780. In the nineteenth century it was used as a boardinghouse, and in 1900 additional hotel rooms were built behind it. Slated for demolition when the hotel closed, it was saved by preservationists and underwent extensive restoration in the 1960s and 1970s. Today many of the rooms have been furnished to reflect the period of Paca's residence.

Paca's two-acre formal garden, which was described by one eighteenth-century visitor as the most elegant in Annapolis, has also been restored. Archaeological investigations revealed the remains of a garden wall, five terraces, a canal, a pond, and a Chinese Chippendale bridge. A portrait of Paca by Charles Willson Peale shows the pond, the bridge (with a Chinese trellis pattern that was also used in balustrades within the house), and a two-story pavilion.

LOCATION: Prince George Street. HOURS: March through December: 10–4 Monday–Saturday, 12–4 Sunday; January, February: 10–4 Friday–Saturday, 12–4 Sunday. FEE: Yes. TELE-PHONE: 410–263–5553.

The **Brice House** (42 East Street, private), a substantial, five-part house, was built between 1766 and 1774, possibly to designs by William Buckland, by James Brice, another of the town's ardent Patriots. George Washington, Lafayette, Nathanael Greene, and James Madison were among the Revolutionary leaders who visited Brice at the house. Today it is owned by the International Masonry Institute. The house is said to be haunted by Brice, a nursemaid, and a woman who visits the parlor at midnight.

U.S. NAVAL ACADEMY

The academy occupies a beautiful three-hundred-acre campus on the Severn River. As early as 1777 John Paul Jones had suggested that a training school for naval officers be established. Between

OPPOSITE: *The parlor at the William Paca House.*

1800 and 1845 twenty attempts had been made to persuade Congress to do so; but all of them failed. One senator declared that such an academy would produce "trifling or effeminate leaders" who would be held in contempt by sailors; another feared that graduates would get into mischief without a war to fight, and thus they would provoke wars. Finally George Bancroft, a historian appointed by President Polk to be secretary of the navy, took the matter into his own hands and ordered a committee of officers to draw up a curriculum without congressional approval or funding. One contributing cause to his impatience was the 1842 mutiny on the warship *Somers*, which ended with the hanging at sea of two sailors and a midshipman who was the son of the secretary of war. Many in the navy felt that the political appointment of midshipmen created the discipline problems exemplified by the *Somers* incident.

Bancroft persuaded the War Department to cede Fort Severn in Annapolis for the school. At first, the curriculum called for three years of seagoing training and two in the classroom; in 1851 the current calendar of four years of study, with cruises in the summer, was adopted, and the school got its official approval as the U.S.

An aerial view of the U.S. Naval Academy, on the Severn River.

Naval Academy. During the Civil War the academy was transferred to Newport, Rhode Island, and the campus was used as a hospital and supply depot. The man who had been the academy's first superintendent, Franklin Buchanan, served as an admiral in the Confederate navy and commanded the ironclad *Virginia* (formerly the *Merrimack*) in its historic clash with the *Monitor*. Oddly enough, the commander of the *Monitor*, John L. Worden, later became superintendent of the academy.

President Theodore Roosevelt, an ardent believer in the navy as the mighty arm of American imperialism, expanded the size of the academy classes to meet the need for officers aboard new steel battleships. A rebuilding of the campus had already been ordered in 1899, spurred by the important role the navy had played in the Spanish-American War. The nineteenth-century buildings were demolished, and an impressive complex of Beaux-Arts buildings designed by Ernest Flagg went up—Bancroft Hall, a new chapel, superintendent's house, administrative building, and classroom buildings, all arranged around a quadrangle and all on a heroic scale in keeping with the self-assurance of the era. Also to be seen are many memorials of various kinds to important figures in naval history. Guided tours of the academy leave from the visitor center in Ricketts Hall (410–293–3363).

The U.S. Naval Academy Museum (410–293–2108), located in Preble Hall, displays a large collection of paintings, ship models, weapons, medals, and naval memorabilia, such as a sword captured by Stephen Decatur in the Barbary Wars; the sea anchor of the USS *Constitution,* which Isaac Hull used to escape from British pursuers in July 1812; a model of an early self-propelled torpedo from the 1870s; mementoes of the ill-fated 1879–1881 Arctic voyage of the USS *Jeannette,* during which many of the crew perished; artifacts from the USS *Maine,* which blew up in Havana Harbor; and a sled used by Admiral Byrd during his 1928–1930 Antarctic expedition. In 1935 the museum received the Henry Huddleston Rogers Collection of 108 sailing-ship models depicting vessels from 1650 to 1850. Some of the models had been made for the official use of the British Admiralty. The painting collection includes works by Robert Salmon, Edward Moran, Thomas Sully, Gilbert Stuart, and John Wesley Jarvis. The museum also has a collection of personal items owned by George Washington.

Down the street is the **Macedonian Monument,** the original wooden figurehead of a British ship captured by Stephen Decatur in 1812. He brought the *Macedonian* to New London, where it was

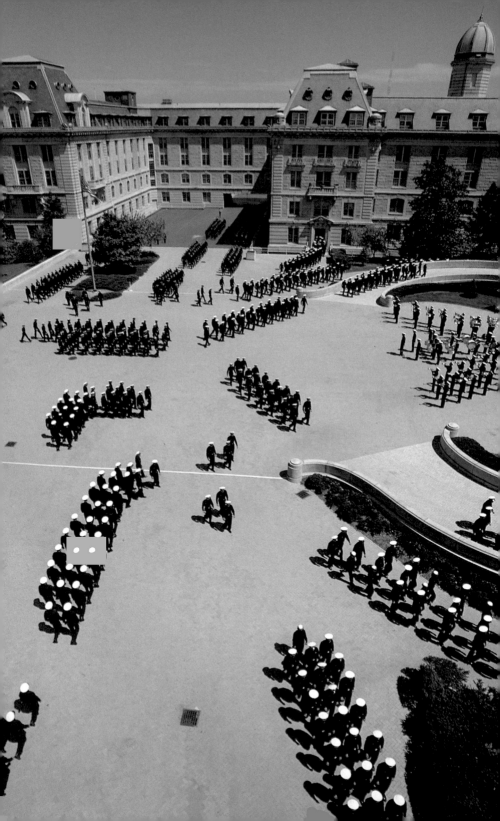

refitted for the U.S. Navy. Behind the museum is the **Tripoli Monument,** a marble rostral column topped by an eagle that commemorates five officers killed during the Barbary Wars in 1804. The monument was made in Italy and carried to the U.S. on the USS *Constitution*, which played an important role in the Barbary Wars.

Mahan Hall was named for Admiral Alfred Thayer Mahan, the author of the 1890 book *The Influence of Sea Power upon History, 1660–1783,* which had a tremendous impact on strategic thinking all over the world. By arguing the critical importance of foreign trade and the equally critical role of navies in protecting that trade, Mahan spurred the development of large navies at the turn of the century. Kaiser Wilhelm of Germany said that he was trying to learn it by heart, and had copies placed on all his navy's ships. The hall displays flags, including the only British Royal Standard ever captured in battle.

The **Naval Academy Chapel** was begun in June 1904, when the cornerstone was laid by Admiral of the Navy George Dewey, the victor at Manila Bay ("You may fire when you are ready, Gridley"). The anchors at the main entrance were made for the armored cruiser *New York,* which saw action during the Spanish-American War. Suspended from the ceiling over the choir loft is a votive ship model, donated in 1941, intended to remind the congregation to pray for those at sea. The chapel dome is two hundred feet above the floor. Stained glass windows by Tiffany commemorate naval heroes. Beneath the chapel is a **crypt** containing the remains of the great naval leader of the American Revolution, John Paul Jones, in an elaborate marble sarcophagus within a circular colonnade. A Marine guard is constantly on duty here, in recognition of Jones's signal achievements. His request to American agents in Paris for a vessel—"I wish to have no Connection with any Ship that does not sail *fast,* for I intend *to go in harm's way*"—has become a navy slogan. Commanding the *Ranger* he received the first salute to the American flag given by a foreign warship, from the French, in 1778, and captured HMS *Drake.* In September 1779, watched from the shore by Englishmen, Jones's *Bonhomme Richard* battled the British *Serapis* in a fierce night engagement in which over two hundred men were killed or wounded. At a point when the battle seemed lost, his men urged Jones to strike his colors and

OPPOSITE: *Fronting the U.S. Naval Academy's enormous Bancroft Hall—home to all 4,000 midshipmen—is Tecumseh Court, scene of Noon Formation in spring and fall.*

The Chapel of the U.S. Naval Academy, opposite, a Beaux-Arts masterpiece designed by Ernest Flagg in 1904. The interior, above, is graced by Tiffany windows depicting naval heroes.

surrender, but Jones replied, "I have not yet begun to fight!" For his victory over the *Serapis,* King Louis XVI awarded Jones the Order of Military Merit and a gold-hilted sword.

When he died of natural causes in Paris in 1792, his friends buried him in a lead coffin filled with alcohol to preserve his body. In the nineteenth century the graveyard was built upon, and the exact location of Jones's tomb was forgotten. When designing the new chapel, Flagg, who admired Jones, set aside space for a crypt in case Jones's grave was ever found. A search was begun in 1899, and in 1905 the remains were brought to Annapolis and eventually placed in the crypt with pomp and circumstance. Set into the floor of the crypt are the names of Jones's ships; his medals, swords, and other items are displayed in wall cases.

Near the chapel is a granite **obelisk** erected in tribute to Commander William Lewis Herndon, who, after ensuring the safety of his passengers, went down with his ship during a hurricane in 1857. Near the academy's dormitory is *Tecumseh,* a bronze copy of a wooden figurehead representing Tamanend, chief of the Delaware Indians, and used to decorate the bow of the USS *Delaware.*

The monumental dormitory, **Bancroft Hall,** is entered through a domed rotunda with an inlaid marble floor. A grand staircase ascends to **Memorial Hall,** where one of the navy's most prized relics is displayed, the blue battle flag bearing the dying words of Captain James Lawrence to his officers, "Don't give up the ship!" He was killed in battle off Boston in June 1813. Commodore Oliver Hazard Perry had the flag sewn with that motto and flew it during his victory over the British on Lake Erie the following September. Ironically, Perry was forced to give up his own ship in the middle of the battle, but he clutched the battle flag to his chest as he was rowed through heavy fire to another vessel, on which he directed his fleet to victory. Perry's post-battle dispatch became another famous naval quotation: "We have met the enemy; and they are ours." The hall also displays portraits, murals, captured flags, and in an alcove, dioramas of the Vietnam War.

LOCATION: Entrance at Gate 3, Maryland Avenue. HOURS: *Yard* 9 AM–sunset; *crypt* 9–4:30; *museum* 9–5 Daily. FEE: None. TELEPHONE: None.

There are several historic buildings in the vicinity of the waterfront. At 18 Pinckney Street the **Shiplap House,** built in 1713, was the home of the nineteenth-century painter Frank Mayer. At the small **Tobacco Warehouse** (4 Pinckney Street) guides (in the summer) explain the shipping and weighing of tobacco. The **Market House,** facing the harbor, was built as a market in 1858 and now contains food shops. The city's plan to demolish it to make a parking lot was thwarted by preservationists who pointed out that the land had been deeded to the city late in the eighteenth century with the proviso that it be used in perpetuity as a marketplace. If the building were to be torn down, the land would have to be returned to the heirs of the donors. The city opted for renovation. The **Historic Annapolis Foundation Museum Store** (77 Main Street, 410–268–5576) has an excellent diorama of eighteenth-century Annapolis as well as exhibits about the history of the port.

West of the dock area is **St. Mary's Church** (109 Duke of Gloucester Street, 410–263–2397), a Gothic building dedicated in 1860. Its steeple is clearly visible from the harbor. On the grounds is the **Charles Carroll House,** birthplace of Charles Carroll of Carrollton, one of the wealthiest men in the colonies and the only Roman Catholic to sign the Declaration of Independence.

OPPOSITE: *Old Trinity Church, St. Mary's City. The church was built in 1829 with bricks salvaged from the ruins of the colony's original State House.*

SOUTHERN MARYLAND

PAUL E. GARBER FACILITY

Ninety aircraft and spacecraft, engines, and other aviation items are displayed at this storage and restoration facility operated by the National Air and Space Museum. The collection includes fighter planes from World Wars I and II, the engine of a Saturn rocket, and the nose cone that carried monkeys into space in 1959 on an early experimental flight. The workshops where restoration work is done may also be toured.

LOCATION: Silver Hill Road in Suitland. HOURS: Tours by reservation only. FEE: None. TELEPHONE: 202–357–1400.

SURRATT HOUSE

John Surratt, one of John Wilkes Booth's coconspirators in the assassination of Abraham Lincoln, hid weapons in this house, a tavern and post office operated by his mother, Mary. Although she almost certainly did not know of the plot, a military court found her guilty of aiding the conspirators, and she was hanged. The jury failed to agree on the guilt of John Surratt; charges against him were dismissed. Booth stopped here after the assassination.

LOCATION: Brandywine Road in Clinton. HOURS: March through mid-December: 11–3 Thursday–Friday, 12–4 Saturday–Sunday. FEE: Yes. TELEPHONE: 301–868–1121.

FORT WASHINGTON PARK

Fort Washington was completed in 1824 to guard the Potomac River approach to the capital. In 1795, George Washington personally chose this site, on a bluff commanding the river, for a fortification. During the War of 1812 the British frightened off the garrison of an earlier fortification without firing a shot. It is surrounded by a dry moat and entered by a drawbridge and a large archway with a portcullis. Interpreters demonstrate the firing of weapons and re-create the daily life of a nineteenth-century soldier.

LOCATION: Fort Washington Road, off Route 210 south of Washington, DC. HOURS: *Park:* 8:30–Dusk Daily; *visitor center and fort:* 9–5 Daily. FEE: Yes. TELEPHONE: 301–763–4600.

OPPOSITE: *The Roman-arch entrance to Fort Washington, the oldest fortification designed specifically to protect the nation's capital.*

The **National Colonial Farm Museum** (Bryan Point Road in Accokeek, 301–283–2113) demonstrates farming methods typical of eighteenth-century Maryland.

DR. SAMUEL A. MUDD HOUSE

On his escape from Washington, DC, Lincoln's assassin, John Wilkes Booth, came to Dr. Mudd's home to have his broken leg tended. (He had injured it in leaping to the stage of Ford's Theater after shooting the president.) Although Dr. Mudd had no part in the conspiracy, he was convicted of helping and harboring a fugitive, and sentenced to life in prison. He was pardoned by President Johnson in 1869. Mudd's two-story frame house has been preserved.

LOCATION: Route 232, Waldorf. HOURS: Late March through late November: 11–3 Wednesday, 12–4 Saturday–Sunday. FEE: Yes. TELEPHONE: 301–934–8464.

SMALLWOOD STATE PARK

The park is the location of **Smallwood's Retreat,** a small brick house of one and one-half stories with a steeply pitched roof that was the plantation house of William Smallwood. During the Revolution, Smallwood commanded the Maryland Line of the Continental Army, which performed heroically throughout the war. The greatest, and most tragic, battle for Smallwood's men was the Battle of Long Island, which took place in 1776 in Brooklyn, New York. There the Maryland men held off a superior British force until the rest of Washington's army could escape, at a cost of the lives of 250 men. After the war Smallwood was elected governor. His grave is marked by an obelisk put up in 1898. The 1732 **Old Durham Church** in Ironsides was restored in 1932 as a memorial to him.

LOCATION: Off State Highway 224, just south of Marbury. HOURS: Dawn–Dusk Daily. FEE: Yes, on weekends and for boat ramp. TELEPHONE: 301–743–7613.

PORT TOBACCO

Like St. Mary's City, the village of Port Tobacco had virtually disappeared when preservationists began to restore and reconstruct the settlement in the 1930s. Two houses on the town square, the 1732 **Stagg Hall** and the 1765 **Chimney House,** are private, but the reconstructed **Port Tobacco Courthouse** (off Route 6, 301–934–4313) has exhibits about the history of the town and the cultivation of tobacco. This spot was a thriving Indian community—perhaps one of the oldest settled sites in Maryland—when the English arrived. In 1642, Jesuit missionary Father Andrew White converted the Indians here to Catholicism. The town declined as a tobacco port by the end of the eighteenth century.

Two houses of architectural interest are found in this region. **Bachelor's Hope** (Manor Road off Route 238 in Chaptico, private) was built in the late eighteenth century and has a front portico and a hipped gable roof. **Ocean Hall** (private), at Bushwood Wharf in Bushwood, dates to the late 1600s. The "upper-cruck" roof was constructed by a medieval English technique rarely found in America.

Bachelor's Hope was built in the early eighteenth century, probably for use as a hunting lodge.

ST. CLEMENTS ISLAND

A forty-foot cross on this island, in the Potomac River off Colton's Point, marks the place where Leonard Calvert and the voyagers on the *Ark* and the *Dove* landed on March 25, 1634. The island may be visited by boat. The **St. Clements Island — Potomac River Museum** (Bay View Road in Colton's Point, 301–769–2222) has exhibits about the early history of the colony.

SOTTERLEY

Begun sometime after 1710, when James Bowles purchased the property, Sotterley is a large, rambling country house on the Patuxent River that was the home of moderately affluent farmers, lawyers, and government officials in the eighteenth century. The house was enlarged several times, and during the 1760s a fretwork stairway in the Chippendale style was added. The drawing room has a finely carved chimneypiece and a pair of shell alcoves flanking it. The property preserves some outbuildings, including a slave cabin. One owner, George Plater V, is reputed to have lost the house to a relative in a dice game in 1822.

LOCATION: East of Hollywood on Route 245. HOURS: June through September: 11–4 Tuesday–Sunday. FEE: Yes. TELEPHONE: 301–373–2280.

CALVERT MARINE MUSEUM

Located where the Patuxent River flows into the Chesapeake, this museum focuses on the biology, paleontology, and maritime history of the Bay. The museum exhibits fossils, a re-creation of the offshore seabed, a model of an extinct pelican, and an "estuarium" containing the fish, crab, shrimp, and other creatures that inhabit the Bay. There are also exhibits about the history of commercial fishing and naval warfare in the region, including one that deals with the War of 1812. Also of interest are the restored 1883 Drum Point Lighthouse, a restored seafood-packing house, and an oyster buy-boat dating to 1899. One-hour harbor tours are available on an 1899 vessel.

LOCATION: Route 2, Solomons. HOURS: 10–5 Daily. FEE: Yes. TELEPHONE: 410–326–2042.

OPPOSITE: *One slave cabin remains of the row that lined the road to Sotterley's wharf. It provides a grim picture of slave life in the eighteenth century.*

HISTORIC ST. MARY'S CITY

St. Mary's City was the capital of the colony from 1634 to 1695, when Governor Nicholson moved the seat of government to Annapolis. Although it never became a grand city on the European model, the village of St. Mary's City contained numerous ordinaries or inns, lawyer's offices, a mill, and houses. An imposing State House, the "great brick" Chapel of the 1660s, and St. Peter's, home of Chancellor Philip Calvert, were structures of extraordinary size and quality on the Chesapeake frontier. After 1695, St. Mary's City declined, until by the time of the American Revolution, little of the former capital was left but memories of its importance. Today, several buildings have been reconstructed as a living museum of early Maryland history, with costumed interpreters reenacting the daily life of the settlement in the 1600s.

The brick, cruciform **State House** seen today is a 1930s reproduction based on measurements taken from the original foundation and on the detailed instructions that the assembly had given to the builders. The original, built in 1676 on a different site, stood into the nineteenth century despite poor construction. The building has a hanging staircase that ascends three floors and a large, first-floor Assembly Room where delegates met and judges held court. The second floor holds committee rooms, and the third floor is a re-creation of the arsenal, where weapons and powder were stored. In 1689, while Lord Baltimore was in England, hundreds of "Protestant Associators" captured the State House and ousted the government. The Calverts lost control of the colony and Catholics were disenfranchised until after the Revolution.

The **Godiah Spray Tobacco Plantation** reconstructs the appearance and daily activities of a successful plantation. The structures have all been built using methods and materials typical of the 1600s. The Dwelling House, though the home of a relatively prosperous family, consists of one room where the family cooked, ate, and slept. The great majority of settlers in the 1600s lived in houses with fewer than three rooms. In such a house, privacy was nonexistent: Older children and servants may have slept in a loft, but it was common for two to four people to sleep in the same bed. Other structures include tobacco sheds, animal pens, and a tenant house.

The *Maryland Dove* is a reconstruction of one of the two vessels that brought Leonard Calvert, his 140 settlers, and their supplies from England; as the smaller of the two, the *Dove* carried the

The reconstructed State House in St. Mary's City was built in 1934 to mark Maryland's Tercentenary. It is the result of meticulous archaelogical and historical research.

supplies. This tiny ship has a deck only fifty-six feet long. The original ships made a storm-tossed, three-month-long crossing. In 1634 the captain of the *Dove* abandoned the ship at Point Comfort, Virginia, her hull having been eaten by sea worms. Calvert retrieved the vessel and repaired it, but it vanished at sea on a voyage to England, bearing the colony's shipment of timber and furs.

Old Trinity Church was built in 1829 with bricks salvaged from the ruins of the State House, the original site of which is now the church graveyard. The **Chancellor's Point Natural History Area** preserves sixty acres of woodland, marshes, and beaches along the St. Mary's River. Chancellor's Point is a center for the study of the culture of the Woodland Indians. An Indian Longhouse has been reconstructed using stone and bone tools, deerhide lashings, and other natural materials. The **Leonard Calvert Monument** has been placed at the spot where he signed a treaty with the king of the Yaocomico Indians.

LOCATION: Off Route 5, about 6 miles south of Lexington Park. HOURS: April through last Friday in November: 10–5 Wednesday–Sunday. FEE: Yes. TELEPHONE: 301–862–0960.

St. Ignatius Roman Catholic Church (Villa Road in St. Inigoes, 301–872–5173) was built in 1785 at a Jesuit mission established in 1662. It was the first Catholic mission in the English colonies.

During the Civil War there was a camp for Confederate prisoners on the site of **Point Lookout State Park** (301–872–5688). Polluted water, poor-quality food, and freezing winters all led to the deaths of four thousand prisoners and seven hundred guards. A monument marks the nearby cemetery. One of the earthworks that guarded the prison is being restored.

E A S T E R N   S H O R E

C H E S A P E A K E   C I T Y

When the Chesapeake and Delaware Canal was completed in 1829, the town of Chesapeake City grew up at its Maryland terminus. The canal, linking the Chesapeake Bay and the Delaware River, reduced the water route between Baltimore and Philadelphia by almost three hundred miles. The waterway was of importance during World War II, providing an inland shipping route that was safe from German submarines. The **C&D Canal Museum** (Route 213, 410–885–5621) features an 1837 pump house with a huge waterwheel (thirty-eight feet in diameter).

MOUNT HARMON PLANTATION

Mount Harmon, overlooking the Sassafras River, preserves three buildings from a typical medium-sized tobacco plantation of the eighteenth century. The main house, a two-story brick residence built in 1730, has been restored and furnished to the period 1760 to 1810. On the grounds are a kitchen and a "prize house" where tobacco was shipped. Tobacco was last grown here in 1806. Visitors may explore the 300-acre grounds.

LOCATION: Grove Neck Road, Earleville. HOURS: By appointment. FEE: Yes. TELEPHONE: 410–275–8819.

CHESTERTOWN

In the eighteenth century, Chestertown, on the Chester River, was a busy port serving the surrounding agricultural region. Several brick houses (private) along **Water Street** and **High Street** were built by well-to-do shippers and merchants of that period. The most impressive is **Widehall** (101 Water Street), built in the 1760s. In May 1774 the residents staged their own Tea Party, in emulation of Boston's, when the *Geddes* arrived carrying a small cargo of tea. The Chestertown tea-dumping is reenacted each May.

Washington College, founded in 1782, was named for the general who had just led the successful forces of revolution. He visited the college in 1784, and received an honorary degree.

The **Geddes-Piper House** (Church Alley, 410–778–3499), a restored townhouse, is the headquarters of the Kent County Historical Society. Some rooms have been furnished with eighteenth- and nineteenth-century items, and exhibit rooms on the third floor have undergone renovation. The house was built by William Geddes, the customs collector, who sold it to James Piper.

Two houses in **Centreville** display eighteenth- and nineteenth-century furnishings and household items: **Tucker House** (124 South Commerce Street, 410–758–3010) and **Wright's Chance** (119 South Commerce Street, 410–758–3010). The 1792 **Queen Anne's County Courthouse** is at 122 North Commerce Street.

A portion of Chestertown as seen from the Chester River. OVERLEAF: *When seen from the air, the Chesapeake Bay reveals its series of intricate inlets and coves.*

WYE MILLS

This tiny rural crossroads is the location of the beautiful **Old Wye Church** (Route 662, 410–827–8484), built in 1721. Restored, it preserves a slave gallery, hanging pulpit, and box pews. Nearby is the **Wye Oak,** four centuries old and one of the largest white oaks in the country. The town was named for its sawmills and gristmills, including the **Wye Mill** (Route 662, 410–827–6909), built sometime in the early 1700s. During the Revolution this mill provided flour to Washington's troops at Valley Forge. In operation until 1953, the mill is now undergoing restoration.

EASTON

The seat of Talbot County, the town of Easton sprang up in the early 1700s after the county courthouse was built here. In the late eighteenth and the nineteenth century, it was the largest and most important center of commerce and government on the Eastern Shore. The **Historical Society of Talbot County Museum** (25 South Washington Street, 410–822–0773) is a fine local museum that features changing exhibits about the history of the town and the region. Easton's most notable historic site is the **Third Haven Friends Meetinghouse** (South Washington Street), a simple frame building erected in the early 1680s, before the town was established. Its name is derived from the nearby Tred Avon River, formerly called the Thread Haven and Third Haven River. Quakers came up the river by boat from all over the Eastern Shore, and William Penn was among the well-known Quakers who worshiped here. Sliding screens at the center divided the male and female seating sections. The meetinghouse is still used in warm weather and may be visited on Sundays. The adjacent brick meetinghouse, for winter use, was put up in 1880.

ST. MICHAELS

Situated on a narrow peninsula between the Miles River and Broad Creek, St. Michaels was a famed shipbuilding village from the late 1600s to the early 1800s. Many of the sloops and schooners that carried Maryland's commerce, and the shallow-draft "bugeyes" used for oystering, were made here. During the War of 1812 the British raided the town one night but were driven off by cannon fire. A local legend says that the villagers fooled British gunners by

The Chesapeake Bay Maritime Museum complex provides an opportunity to view each of the twenty-eight different types of Bay craft.

putting out all the lights in the town and hanging lanterns in trees beyond it, so that British shells overshot the area. **St. Mary's Square Museum** (410–745–9561), on the original town green, has exhibits on local history. The **Chesapeake Bay Maritime Museum** (Mill Street, 410–745–2916) has an excellent floating collection of Bay craft, ship models, bird decoys, and other nautical items.

OXFORD

In the middle of the eighteenth century, this small fishing village was one of the colony's important ports, with an international commerce arriving at its wharves. By the waterfront is a replica of the tiny, one-room **Custom House.** The father of Robert Morris, the "financier of the Revolution," lived in a nearby house that was incorporated in the construction of the **Robert Morris Inn.** Morris was accidentally killed by a ball fired from a signal cannon in the harbor. The small **Oxford Museum** (Market and Morris streets, 410–226–0191) displays a collection of ship models, engines, tools, and other maritime items.

CAMBRIDGE

This industrial town on the Choptank River, the seat of Dorchester County, was one of Maryland's earliest settlements, dating to the 1680s. No vestige of that era survives here, but there is a group of late-eighteenth- and early-nineteenth-century houses (private) along **High Street,** in the block leading down to the river. On the other side of town, the county historical society maintains the **Meredith House & Neild Museum** (La Grange Avenue, 410–228– 7953), displaying Indian artifacts, a doll collection, and other items of local history. The Meredith House was built in the 1760s.

Southwest of Cambridge is another of the Eastern Shore's handsome country churches, **Old Trinity Episcopal Church** (Route 16, 410–228–2940). Built about 1675 on the shore of Church Creek, this small brick church is surrounded by a grave- yard, both still in use. The church was restored in the 1950s.

SALISBURY

This industrial and commercial town on the Wicomico River pre- serves a small district of Victorian houses along **Elizabeth Street** and **Poplar Hill Avenue** called the **Newton Historic District. Pop- lar Hill Mansion** (117 Elizabeth Street, 410–749–1776), a planta- tion house built in the early 1800s, has fine interior woodwork.

West of Salisbury on the other side of the Wicomico River is **Pemberton Hall** (Pemberton Drive off Route 349, 410–742– 1741), a small, gambrel-roofed brick house built in 1741. It was the plantation house of Colonel Isaac Handy and his wife, Ann. The house is part of 210-acre park with five miles of trails.

PRINCESS ANNE

Founded on the Manokin River in the 1730s, Princess Anne is the seat of Somerset County and a commercial center. The river silted up early in the twentieth century, cutting off seagoing commerce. The substantial brick **Teackle Mansion** (Prince William Street, private), dating to the early 1800s, is evidence of the town's prosperity in that era. The finest house in the area is **Beckford** (Route 13, private), built in the 1760s by a successful merchant. The town's oldest building, **Tunstall Cottage** (Church and Broad streets, private), dates to the 1730s. Nearby, on North Somerset Avenue, is the 1744 **Washington Hotel.**

The five-part late-Georgian Teackle Mansion was built in 1801 by Littleton Dennis Teackle.

SNOW HILL

Snow Hill, on the Pocomoke River, was chartered in 1686 and found early prosperity in trade with the West Indies. The early history of the town is documented at the **Julia A. Purnell Museum** (208 West Market Street, 410–632–0515), which has exhibits of farm tools, spinning wheels, kitchen equipment, clothing, uniforms, and Indian artifacts. The museum also provides information about local walking tours. Although two fires in the nineteenth century destroyed much of the town, a row of handsome houses survived along **Federal Street,** including the Greek Revival house called **Chanceford,** now a bed and breakfast.

Four miles north of Snow Hill is **Furnace Town** (off Route 12, 410–632–2032), the remains of an industrial village that was active from 1829 to 1837. The **Nassawango Iron Furnace** on the grounds processed low-quality bog iron ore. Along with several other buildings in the village complex, the furnace has been restored.

BALTIMORE AND NORTHERN MARYLAND

OPPOSITE: *One of the prized steam locomotives on exhibit at the B & O Railroad Museum.*

Although the area was settled as early as the 1660s, Baltimore's official origin dates to 1729, when Governor Calvert signed a bill establishing a town at Jones Falls on the Patapsco River. It was named after the Irish proprietors of the colony, the Lords Baltimore. There had been a gristmill at the falls in the 1720s, and in 1750 an Irish immigrant shipped a load of flour back to his homeland, built a wharf to enlarge his business, and launched Baltimore's commerce. By the Revolution it was the most populous town in Maryland, with about fifty-seven hundred inhabitants, more than three times the population of Annapolis. While Annapolis displayed the architectural and social fruits of the colony's eighteenth-century tobacco wealth, Baltimore amassed its riches later when it became the transportation center for the grain trade of southern Pennsylvania and northern and western Maryland. In addition to its agricultural exports of wheat, bread, and flour, the city shipped lumber and hides. Iron producing, which began here as early as 1731, was fast becoming a major local industry. After the Revolution Annapolis went into its long sleep, while Baltimore entered a boom that lasted, with some interruptions, into the twentieth century.

In the late 1700s and early 1800s the town's shipbuilders produced a generation of fast topsail schooners known as Baltimore Clippers. Designed for speed rather than carrying capacity, the Baltimore Clippers were ideally suited to long voyages carrying precious metals and for semilegal activities. Privateering was a Baltimore specialty; during the War of 1812 the city was home port for 126 privateers. In British eyes it was simply "a nest of pirates." In September 1814 General Ross's British army, having just burned Washington, DC, turned its attention to Baltimore. When the ground forces were stalled outside the city, an invasion fleet stood in the harbor and pounded Fort McHenry for twenty-five hours. The fort and its men held firm, saving Baltimore from destruction. A lawyer named Francis Scott Key watched the bombardment and paid tribute to the defenders and their flag by writing the four verses of "The Star-Spangled Banner." Earlier, events in Baltimore had taken an uglier turn. Many Federalists opposed "Mr. Madison's War"; a mob attacked the office of a Federalist newspaper, killing one man and leaving the Revolutionary War hero Light-Horse Harry Lee crippled and disfigured. Lee left the country in disgust.

This 1814 aquatint, A View of the Bombardment of Fort McHenry, *depicts the battle during which the national anthem was written (detail).*

Baltimore was an early gateway to the West. From the late 1700s into the first three decades of the nineteenth century, private turnpike companies built toll roads from Baltimore to York, Pennsylvania, and to Harper's Ferry via Frederick. One was also constructed to Cumberland via Frederick, which was of particular importance to the state's development since, in 1805, Congress authorized funds for the construction of a road from Cumberland to the Ohio River at Wheeling. West of Cumberland it was known as the National Road (today it is Route 40). In the first half of the nineteenth century this was a major supply and immigration route from the Eastern seaboard to the burgeoning West—by 1850 it reached Illinois—but the road was tremendously expensive to maintain, and tolls were accordingly high.

The search for cheap, reliable transportation led to the development of two huge engineering projects in the 1820s—a canal and a railroad. In 1828 the Chesapeake and Ohio Canal was begun to link Washington (and, by a spur canal, Baltimore) with Pittsburgh. It took twenty-two years to complete the 184 miles from

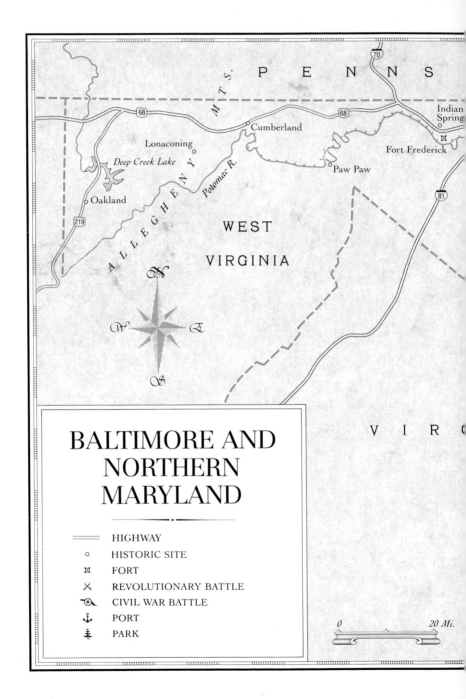

P E N N S

70

68

Indian
Spring

68

Cumberland

Fort Frederick

Lonaconing

Deep Creek Lake

Potomac R.

Paw Paw

81

Oakland

219

WEST

VIRGINIA

N

W

E

S

V I R G

BALTIMORE AND
NORTHERN
MARYLAND

HIGHWAY

○ HISTORIC SITE

⊟ FORT

✕ REVOLUTIONARY BATTLE

CIVIL WAR BATTLE

⚓ PORT

⚘ PARK

0   20 Mi.

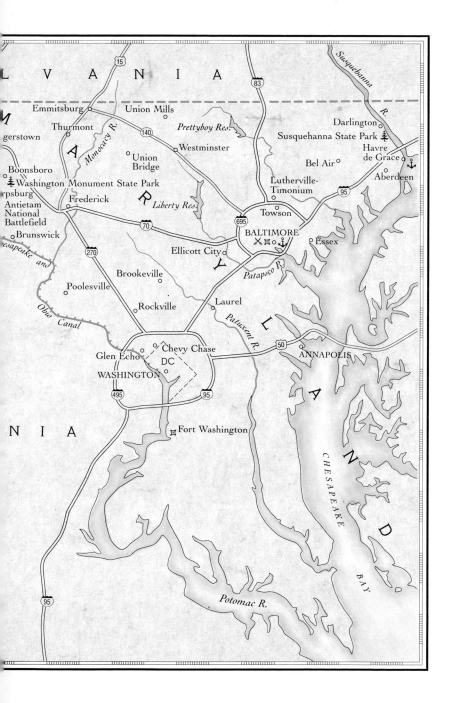

Georgetown to Cumberland; but for all the magnificence of its technical achievements, it was obsolete by the time it was finished. The Baltimore and Ohio Railroad was begun on the same day as the canal and reached Cumberland eight years earlier, in 1842. A decade later the B & O reached the Ohio River at Wheeling, at about two-thirds the cost the canal used to get to Cumberland.

When New York took the lead in the Atlantic trade with England and the rest of Europe, Baltimore merchants expanded their grain and flour trade with South America. By the 1860s the city was a major producer of heavy machinery, iron, clothing, bricks, sailcloth, and copper.

An 1833 literary contest in a Baltimore newspaper played a large part in launching the career of a then-unknown writer, Edgar Allan Poe. One of the judges helped Poe find an editing job in Richmond. Baltimore is also where Poe stopped on September 28, 1849, on his way from Richmond to New York—and promptly vanished. On October 3 an acquaintance discovered him unconscious at a polling place. Possibly, he had been given drugs or liquor in exchange for his vote, but there is no certain evidence of it. Taken to a hospital, he was delirious for four days, and died on October 7, at the age of 40. He was buried at the Presbyterian Cemetery, now called Westminster, under a numbered gravestone. In 1875 the schoolchildren of Baltimore contributed funds to have Poe's remains moved to a prominent spot in the graveyard and to have a proper monument erected over them. The place where he died, now Church Home Hospital at 100 North Broadway, is marked with a plaque.

At the outbreak of the Civil War, Baltimore was strongly secessionist. Abraham Lincoln, on a goodwill tour of the North before his inauguration, was warned that an attempt would be made on his life as he changed trains in Baltimore. His Pinkerton guards, taking the threat seriously, smuggled the president-elect through the city by night. On April 19, 1861, the Sixth Massachusetts Regiment was attacked as it marched through; and mobs tore down railroad bridges and telegraph lines to isolate Washington, DC from the North. General Benjamin Butler had to ferry troops down the Chesapeake to Annapolis, where they repaired a rail line and made their way to the capital. Federal troops occupied the city, and arrested many pro-Southern citizens and officials, including the chief of police, who had been a leader in the destruction of the rail and telegraph lines.

President Lincoln inspecting the headquarters of the Army of the Potomac, October 1, 1862.
General McClellan is sixth from left.

During the war, Baltimore profited from the sale and shipping of supplies, and the economy slumped somewhat after the war. The Panic of 1873 brought on a national depression and induced the B & O Railroad to impose wage cuts. Up and down the line, workers seized control of the railroad. In Baltimore the mayor called out the militia to control crowds of strikers and their families. Rock throwing by the strikers was met by gunfire from the militia, and ten people were killed. A reporter for the *Baltimore Sun* remarked upon the large number of women marching in support of their striking husbands and fathers: "They look famished and wild," he wrote, "and declare for starvation rather than have their people work for the reduced wages." The B & O strike spawned similar work stoppages and bloodshed—the Great Strikes—in the industrial Northeast.

The national economy improved in 1878, and Baltimore's prosperity resumed, fueled by the city's thriving production of iron, steel, textiles, fertilizer, and canned oysters. The late 1870s also saw the establishment of Johns Hopkins University. Endowed by a wealthy Quaker merchant of that name, Johns Hopkins originally occupied two buildings in the Mount Vernon district but moved to its present site in North Baltimore in 1916. Its campus was once part of the Homewood Estate of the Carroll family. The university is internationally renowned for its medical school, which was founded in 1893.

The downtown district suffered a devastating fire in 1904, wiping out nearly all of the district's eighteenth- and nineteenth-century buildings. A shift of wind saved City Hall from the flames, and a residential section farther north, on higher ground, was not damaged. The city immediately set about rebuilding. In June of the following year, Henry James gave a lecture in Baltimore, where he stayed at the Hotel Belvedere, a "quietly affable" landmark that is still standing. He professed himself enchanted by the city— "my sensibility yielded so completely to Baltimore"—finding here in the early summer evening a "perfect felicity."

Baltimore does not have a reputation as a literary center, but it may deserve one. Poe got his start and wrote "The Raven" here; Upton Sinclair was born in Baltimore in 1878; Gertrude Stein studied medicine at Johns Hopkins from 1897 to 1900; and F. Scott Fitzgerald wrote *Tender Is the Night* in a house (now demolished) just north of the city in Towson. He lived in the city itself from 1933 to 1935, saying, "I belong here, where everything is civilized and gay and rotted and polite." In one of his autobiographical sketches, the melancholy "Afternoon of an Author," he describes his apartment at 3337 North Charles Street and a ride through the town on a double-decker bus.

This tour of Baltimore begins at the Washington Monument in Mount Vernon, describes the sites in the center of the city and the northern section, then covers the southern portion of Baltimore and the waterfront.

WASHINGTON MONUMENT

Robert Mills's design for the Washington Monument in Washington, DC was ultimately rejected by the builders who brought that troubled project to completion, but his design for Baltimore's Washington Monument (North Charles Street at Mount Vernon Place) was realized—a towering column, one hundred and sixty-four feet high, with a sixteen-foot-high statue of the hero on the

OPPOSITE: *Robert Mills's Washington Monument is topped by a sixteen-foot statue of the "father of our country," sculpted by Enrico Causici.*

top. Construction began in 1815 and was completed in 1829. (By that time, the farmers of remote, Boonsboro, Maryland had piled up a crude tower of stones in Washington's honor, gaining for themselves the distinction of having completed the first memorial to the nation's first president.) Visitors may climb the steps for a spectacular view of Baltimore. The monument is surrounded by a park donated to the city by the heirs of John Eager Howard, a Revolutionary War hero who owned much of this district. North of the monument, a statue of Howard pays tribute to his courage and leadership at the battle of Cowpens, South Carolina in January 1781. Also north of the monument is a statue of Roger Brooke Taney, chief justice of the Supreme Court. To the south is a monument to Lafayette; to the northeast is **Mount Vernon Place Methodist Church,** a Gothic building dating to the early 1870s.

The surrounding **Mount Vernon District** has been a fashionable residential district since the early 1800s. The remodeling of the **Garrett-Jacobs Mansion** (11 West Mount Vernon Place, private), now occupied by the Engineering Society of Baltimore, was begun in 1884 by Stanford White for Robert Garrett, president of the B & O Railroad, and continued in 1905, by John Russell Pope, for a subsequent owner. Purchase and partial demolition of a neighboring townhouse completed the remodeling in 1915.

MARYLAND HISTORICAL SOCIETY

The society's museum, located in the 1846 brick house of Enoch Pratt and in a modern gallery, is the major repository of Maryland paintings, historical documents, and manuscripts, and displays outstanding collections of furniture, silver, ceramics, and historical artifacts. The exhibits cover four centuries of Maryland history, from the 1600s to the twentieth century, with an emphasis on life in Baltimore from the late 1700s to the Civil War.

The society possesses the world's largest collection of nineteenth-century American silver (including many pieces by the Baltimore firm of Samuel Kirk) and the largest collection—roughly one hundred and fifty canvases—of paintings by the Peale family. The furniture collection includes examples by the important Baltimore makers William Camp and John Needles. The double parlor in the Pratt house, one of four period rooms in that building, displays the largest extant set of Empire furniture made by the New York maker Charles-Honoré Lannuier. Pratt's original Gothic

Revival library, with its furnishings, ranks as one of the finest American rooms in that style, and is also on view. Costumes, textiles, toys, dollhouses, photographs, and prints chronicle daily life in Maryland from the colonial period to the present. In addition, one floor of the gallery building is devoted to collections of Maryland's maritime heritage. A treasured exhibit is Francis Scott Key's handwritten manuscript of "The Star-Spangled Banner."

LOCATION: 201 West Monument Street. HOURS: 10–5 Tuesday– Friday, 9–5 Saturday, 1–5 Sunday. FEE: Yes. TELEPHONE: 410–685–3750.

WALTERS ART GALLERY

During the late nineteenth and early twentieth centuries, William T. Walters and his son Henry, both of whom earned their fortunes in the railroad business, amassed one of the country's largest private art collections. The elder Walters primarily collected contemporary paintings, but also began to procure Chinese porcelain, becoming one of the first Americans to take an interest in that field of art. Henry Walters had broader tastes, including art from ancient Egyptian, Greek, Roman, and Aztec cultures, Islamic coins, Renaissance sculpture, Italian, Flemish, and English paintings, Sèvres porcelain, Limoges enamels, tapestries, and stained glass. He had an affinity for small decorative objects that could be held in the hand. Both father and son bought pieces that appealed to them personally, seeking the advice of connoisseurs only rarely. In 1909 Henry Walters opened a gallery, in an Italian Renaissance–style building, to display his collection. Today the collection is displayed in three buildings, but nine-tenths of the objects on display were acquired by the Walterses themselves. Henry Walters died in 1931 and bequeathed the museum, with its collection, to the city.

LOCATION: 600 North Charles Street. HOURS: 11–5 Tuesday–Sunday. FEE: Yes. TELEPHONE: 410–547–9000.

Old St. Paul's Episcopal Church (North Charles and Saratoga streets) was designed by Richard Upjohn, who incorporated elements of an earlier building that burned in 1854. Built in 1856, it contains mosaic and stained-glass work by Louis Comfort Tiffany and the Tiffany Studios as well as glass by Maitland Armstrong and John LaFarge. Adjacent is a **Masonic Temple** built in 1866, and rebuilt after fires in 1890 and 1908.

B & O RAILROAD MUSEUM

The largest railroad museum in the country, the B & O Museum displays more than eighty locomotives and cars in a roundhouse (built in 1884) and in the surrounding yard. Among the exhibits are a replica of America's first locomotive, the 1830 "Tom Thumb" (which lost a race with a horse-drawn car when its fan belt slipped); the 1832 steamer "Atlantic"; the world's oldest (1838) surviving private passenger car; the 1856 locomotive "William Mason"; a boxcar used to haul supplies during the Civil War; and massive, sleek diesel locomotives of the twentieth century. The museum also preserves a wealth of railroad memorabilia, such as the silver spade used by Charles Carroll in the 1828 ceremony marking the start of construction, uniforms, timetables, clocks, lanterns, and models. The museum's entrance is the 1830 Mount Clare Station, the country's first railroad station. Although the B & O is often referred to as America's first railroad, the Granite Railway was built in Quincy, Massachusetts in 1826, a year before the B & O was chartered. The B & O began regular passenger service in 1830.

LOCATION: Pratt and Poppleton streets. HOURS: 10–5 Daily. FEE: Yes. TELEPHONE: 410–752–2490.

The **Battle Monument** (Calvert and Fayette streets), a Roman fasces topped by the figure of Victory, was built to honor the defenders of Baltimore in the 1814 battle against the British invasion. Baltimore's **City Hall** (100 North Holiday Street, 410–837–5424) was built between 1867 and 1875 in an eclectic style suggesting the French Second Empire, with a mansard roof, portico, and large cupola. The city **Courthouse** (Calvert and St. Paul streets), a French Renaissance building completed in 1899, features historical murals by John LaFarge and Charles Yardley Turner.

BALTIMORE MUSEUM OF INDUSTRY

Housed in an 1865 oyster cannery in south Baltimore, this museum chronicles the city's industrial history with re-created, fully operating workshops (a garment loft, blacksmith shop, machine shop, and print shop); examples of mechanical items invented or produced in Baltimore; and large photo-murals of factories and docks.

LOCATION: 1415 Key Highway. HOURS: Memorial Day through Labor Day: 12–5 Tuesday–Friday, 10–5 Saturday; Labor Day through Memorial Day: 7–9 Wednesday, 12–5 Thursday–Friday and Sunday, 10–5 Saturday. FEE: Yes. TELEPHONE: 410–727–4808.

George Frederick's design for Baltimore's City Hall includes an atrium bathed in light filtered through the building's cupola.

The **Baltimore Streetcar Museum** (1901 Falls Road, 410–547–0264) displays a dozen nineteenth- and twentieth-century horse cars and trolley cars and offers rides on some of them. The city built one of the first electric-streetcar lines in the 1880s, but shut it down because people and animals were getting shocks from the electrified rail. Later, when overhead electrical lines had been perfected, the city reopened and expanded its rail system.

BASILICA OF THE ASSUMPTION

A landmark of both religious and architectural history, the basilica was built between 1804 and 1815 by Bishop John Carroll, America's first Roman Catholic bishop. (Before the Revolution British law forbade the construction of Catholic churches in the colonies, and worship took place in private homes.) The Baltimore cathedral was one of the first Catholic churches built in the first thirteen of the United States, and the first cathedral. In 1804 Bishop Carroll invited Benjamin Henry Latrobe to review plans drawn up by another architect for the basilica. Latrobe advised rejecting the plans, and submitted two of his own, one Gothic and one Classical.

Charles Carroll of Carrollton, one of the signers of the Declaration of Independence, gave the

(Profit was not his motive; it was his practice to design churches free of charge.) The bishop chose Latrobe's Neoclassical plan.

Latrobe designed a cross-shaped building with a spacious interior. There are three domes—the largest of which is seventy-two feet in diameter—and a barrel vault. These domes were fashioned of stone, supported by piers and arches that lend to an interplay of shapes. Nine stained-glass windows enhance the beauty of the basilica. The south tower's clock and bells sound the "Angeles" three times each day. The red hat of Cardinal James Gibbons hung from arches to the left of the altar for seven decades after his death in 1921, and will eventually be displayed again.

LOCATION: Cathedral and Mulberry streets. HOURS: 7–5 Monday–Friday, 7–6:30 Saturday–Sunday. FEE: None. TELEPHONE: 410–727–3564.

Davidge Hall (522 West Lombard Street, 410–706–7454), built in 1812, survives as the oldest building in the United States continuously used for medical education, and contains probably the oldest anatomical theater in the English-speaking world.

elegant country estate of Homewood to his son as a wedding present.

The **Edgar Allan Poe House and Museum** (203 North Amity Street, 410–396–7932) belonged to Poe's aunt Maria Clemm. He lived here from 1832 to 1835, during which time he fell in love with his cousin Virginia Clemm, whom he married in 1836, when she was but 13 years old. Although most of what Poe wrote in this period was not on his best level, he did write two stories that stand out, "Berenice," his first sensational horror story, and another story for a newspaper contest. The *Saturday Visitor* offered a $50 prize for the best short story submitted, and $25 for the best poem. Poe entered and won both, but the judges would award him only one prize, for his story, "MS. Found in a Bottle." One of the judges, lawyer and novelist John Pendleton Kennedy, befriended Poe and recommended him to Thomas Willis White, editor of the *Southern Literary Messenger,* who invited Poe to come to Richmond to work for the publication in August 1835.

HOMEWOOD

An exceptionally beautiful Federal mansion, Homewood was built in the early 1800s by Charles Carroll (a signer of the Declaration of Independence) as a wedding present for his only son, Charles, Jr.,

and his wife, Harriet. Charles, Jr., apparently was his own architect—in the extensive correspondence that has been preserved
there is no mention of a payment to a professional architect, but
the correspondence does relate that a plan was sent from the son to
the father and was approved. The two-story house, at the top of a
knoll, has porticos at two entrances. Charles, Jr., spared nothing in
cost on the construction—expenses ran over $40,000, an enormous
sum—and the result was an interior of great elegance, one of the
finest American expressions of the Adamesque style. Among its
striking elements are the delicately wrought fanlights and side-
lights, the plaster cornices, and the carved fireplace mantels.

The furniture, silver, and porcelain in the house are all period
objects appropriate to a Federal house, and they reflect the great
wealth of the owner. A set of prints, *The City of Philadelphia,* has
been hung in the entrance hall because records show that Charles,
Jr., subscribed to the series when it began publication in 1800. A
portrait of George Washington has been hung in the drawing room
(Charles, Sr., mentioned such a portrait in a letter to his son). The
curators change the furniture arrangements and room settings
four times a year to reflect seasonal changes the Carrolls would
have made. The room arrangements are based on early nineteenth-century prints.

Although its name suggests domestic solidity, Homewood was
not a happy place. Charles, Jr., was an alcoholic who was unable to
control his drinking despite the pleas of his extended family. That
the family may not have handled this problem with sympathy is
evident in a letter written by a nephew, who wrote, "we can't get
him to shoot himself, so must bear with this degradation still
longer." In 1816 Harriet Carroll moved her four daughters to
Philadelphia, with the approval of the family. Charles, Jr., died in
1825, leaving the estate to his son. In the 1890s the house was used
as a boys' school, and it was eventually given to Johns Hopkins
University, which used it as a faculty club and later for offices. A
complete restoration was completed in 1987.

LOCATION: 3400 North Charles Street. HOURS: 11–3 Tuesday–
Saturday, 12–3 Sunday. FEE: Yes. TELEPHONE: 410–516–5589.

BALTIMORE MUSEUM OF ART

Housed in a large, 1929 Neoclassical building designed by John
Russell Pope, the museum is noted for the Epstein Collection of old

master paintings, with works by Botticelli, Raphael, Titian, Rembrandt, Van Dyck, Goya, and others; and for the Cone Collection of French paintings by Delacroix, Manet, Degas, Cézanne, Picasso, Matisse, and others. The museum also exhibits African, Asian, and Pacific art, photographs, prints, and drawings.

The museum's **American Wing** features a large gallery of paintings, a textile gallery, a comprehensive collection of Maryland silver of the eighteenth and nineteenth centuries, and a fine collection of Maryland Federal period furniture. The wing has seven period rooms ranging in date from 1740 to 1817, including a room from the 1771 Samuel Ringgold House in Chestertown, with a finely carved overmantel by a Philadelphia carver, and a 1799 oval room from Willow Brook in Baltimore, with beautiful Adamesque plasterwork. In the garden is the **Oakland Spring House,** designed as a small Greek temple by Benjamin Henry Latrobe for the country estate of a Baltimore lawyer, Robert Goodloe Harper.

LOCATION: Art Museum Drive, Wyman Park. HOURS: 10–4 Wednesday–Friday, 11–6 Saturday–Sunday. FEE: Yes. TELEPHONE: 410–396–7100.

In 1822 Thomas Doughty painted the View of Baltimore from Beech Hill *from the estate of the collector Robert Gilmor, Jr. (detail).*

The **Jewish Museum of Maryland** (15 Lloyd Street, 410–732–6400), one of the nation's largest Jewish museums, occupies a three-building complex in the old Jewish immigrant area of East Baltimore. The **Lloyd Street Synagogue** (1845), oldest in Maryland and third oldest in the country, and built of brick in a Greek Revival style, has the first stained glass window in the United States to feature a Jewish star. **B'nai Israel** (1876), in a Moorish Revival style, is the oldest synagogue in Baltimore still used for regular services. The museum building offers exhibits on Jewish life, history, and art, and has a library and research center.

Lovely Lane United Methodist Church

Known as the Mother Church of American Methodism, this magnificent Romanesque Revival church, completed in 1887, was designed by Stanford White. Construction was begun in 1884, one hundred years after Methodist ministers met in Baltimore and organized the Methodist Episcopal Church. It is one of the few buildings White designed in a Medieval style (most of his work involved architectural classicism). The rough granite exterior is dominated by a massive square tower, 186 feet high, with a conical roof. The church was part of a complex of buildings White designed along St. Paul Street for the Women's College of Baltimore City, founded by the church's minister, Dr. John F. Goucher, and later renamed for him. Goucher asked that the vaulted ceiling of the church be decorated with a sky map, showing the stars and planets exactly as they were at 3:00 AM on the night the church was founded. A professor of astronomy from Johns Hopkins charted the positions, and White illuminated the ceiling with 340 gas jets to make the gold-leaf stars twinkle. However, the stars have fallen off.

LOCATION: 2200 St. Paul Street. HOURS: Guided tours 9–4 Monday–Friday, 11 or 12 Sunday. TELEPHONE: 410–889–1512.

Mencken House

The famed journalist and editor H. L. Mencken (1880–1956), the "Sage of Baltimore," spent most of his life in this rowhouse. Although born at a different house, he lived here from childhood until his marriage, returning after the death of his wife five years later. At the age of eighteen he had begun writing for Baltimore

OPPOSITE: *The 186-foot bell tower of Lovely Lane Methodist Church is modeled after that of a twelfth-century church in Ravenna, Italy.*

newspapers. He edited the monthly magazines *Smart Set* and *American Mercury,* and in 1918 published a landmark study, *The American Language,* describing the idioms and usages of American English. His sitting room, dining room, garden, and second-floor writing room have been preserved. The study faces a church, and he liked to tell visitors that "the Holy Ghost stands beside me, guiding me to the truth." He built the brick wall surrounding the backyard with his own hands, inserting a copy of Beethoven's death masque and a bronze marker commemorating his dog, "Tessie." An audio-visual presentation traces his literary achievements.

LOCATION: 1524 Hollins Street. HOURS: 10–5 Saturday, 12–5 Sunday. FEE: Yes. TELEPHONE: 410–396–7997.

Mount Clare Mansion

The oldest surviving mansion in Baltimore, and a fine example of pre-Revolutionary architecture, Mount Clare was completed in 1760 after four years of construction. It was the home of Charles Carroll the Barrister (so called to differentiate him from other notable Charles Carrolls of Maryland) and his wife Margaret Tilghman Carroll. This branch of the family was Protestant (Charles's father, Dr. Charles Carroll, renounced Catholicism when he arrived in Maryland from Ireland in 1715). He settled in Annapolis, where his house is preserved on the grounds of St. John's College.

Mount Clare stands in city-owned, 110-acre Carroll Park, originally a 2,368-acre plantation, on the Patapsco River, begun by Dr. Carroll. Iron deposits discovered on the land allowed the family to enter the profitable business of ironmaking, which became one of the cornerstones of the family fortune. During the Revolution Charles the Barrister served on the Council of Safety and the Committee of Correspondence. He is credited with the authorship of the Maryland Declaration of Rights and much of the state constitution. He died in 1783. Carroll's heirs occupied the house until 1850. During the Civil War Federal troops were quartered in it; later in the century it was a German social club. The city acquired the house and its remaining land in 1890.

Many Carroll family furnishings have been returned to the house, which has been restored. The drawing room features Louis XV furniture of the 1750s, while other rooms have imported English furniture, Waterford crystal, and fine silver. In the drawing room are portraits of Charles and Margaret Carroll by Charles

Begun about 1754, Mount Clare is the only pre-Revolutionary building still standing in Baltimore.

Willson Peale, whose studies in London were supported in part by gifts from Carroll. The grounds, now undergoing restoration, included a bowling green, vineyard, gardens, and an orangery.

LOCATION: Carroll Park, Washington Boulevard and Monroe Street. HOURS: 11–3 Tuesday–Friday, 1–3 Saturday–Sunday. FEE: Yes. TELEPHONE: 410–837–3262.

Built in 1785, **Old Otterbein United Methodist Church** (West Conway and Sharp streets, 410–685–4703) is the city's oldest church in continuous use.

PEALE MUSEUM

Founded in 1814 by Rembrandt Peale, the museum has forty paintings by members of the Peale family of painters. The father, Charles Willson Peale (1741–1827), was born in Centreville on the Eastern Shore, and worked in Annapolis as a saddler and woodcarver until a group of gentlemen made it financially possible for him to study art in London. After studying there under Benjamin West, he returned to America to become one of the country's most important painters. He had seventeen children by three wives, and bestowed on his sons such names as Raphaelle, Rembrandt, Titian (two boys were given this name), and Rubens. One of the Titians, a naturalist, sailed on the U.S. Exploring Expedition (1838 to 1842) to the Pacific and Antarctic oceans.

The museum displays remnants of the second set of mastodon bones unearthed in America (in 1801), and Charles Willson Peale's superb 1806 painting *Exhuming the First American Mastodon*. Peale himself organized the dig, near Newburgh, New York, with financial help arranged by Thomas Jefferson. It was America's first organized scientific expedition. Jefferson was interested in Peale's mastodon hunt as a way to disprove the claims of French philosophers that the American climate could support only weak forms of life. The museum also displays an excellent collection of prints, paintings, and photographs chronicling the city's history.

LOCATION: 225 Holliday Street. HOURS: April through October: 10–5 Tuesday–Saturday, 12–5 Sunday; November through March: 10–4 Tuesday–Saturday, 12–4 Sunday. FEE: Yes. TELEPHONE: 410–396–3523.

SHOT TOWER

From its construction in 1828 until 1892, the tower was one of the country's leading producers of lead shotgun pellets for hunters and the military. This apparently simple item was difficult to produce. Droplets of molten lead were allowed to fall from a sieve at the top of the 215-foot-tall tower—as they fell the droplets formed themselves into spheres. At the bottom of the tower, the shot landed in a pool of water that rapidly cooled them and cushioned their fall. Because vibration could affect the shape and quality of the shot, the tower had to be very sturdy. The tower's 17-foot-deep foundation rests on rock; and at the base the brick walls are six feet thick. At its peak of production the tower turned out 12.5 million pounds of shot a year. Although this tower is long out of use, its production technique, with some modifications, remains the standard method for producing small shot. The tower features a display of antique guns made or designed in Baltimore, an exhibit on the history of duck hunting, and a demonstration explaining the history and use of the tower. The top is not accessible to the public.

LOCATION: 801 East Fayette Street. HOURS: 12–5 Saturday–Sunday. FEE: None. TELEPHONE: 410–396–3523.

MUSEUM ROW

Sites near the Shot Tower are collectively known as Museum Row, located just east of Harborplace. They are among the eight properties of the **Baltimore City Life Museums**, which preserve and interpret aspects of the city's history.

Exhibits and costumed guides re-create the life of a middle-class artisan and his family in the first half of the nineteenth century at **1840 House**, a reconstructed rowhouse that was the home of a wheelwright. The refurbished **Carroll Mansion** was the winter home of Charles Carroll of Carrollton, signer of the Declaration of Independence. His office is on the first floor; upstairs are the family's living and entertaining quarters.

The **Baltimore Center for Urban Archaeology** exhibits artifacts representing the 12,000-year history of human habitation in Baltimore. The collection of artifacts unearthed in the city includes nineteenth-century glassware and ceramics, and tools made by prehistoric Indians. Visitors can see archaeologists at work in the center's laboratory. The **City Life Exhibition Center** traces Baltimore's past from the 1600s.

LOCATION: 33 South Front Street. HOURS: 10–4 Wednesday–Friday, 10–5 Saturday–Sunday. FEE: Yes. TELEPHONE: 410–396– 3523.

One block south of Museum Row, the **Star-Spangled Banner Flag House** (844 East Pratt Street, 410–837–1793) was the home of Mary Pickersgill, who sewed the enormous thirty-by-forty-two-foot flag that flew over Fort McHenry during the bombardment witnessed by Francis Scott Key. The flag is now displayed at the Smithsonian's National Museum of American History in Washington, DC. Mrs. Pickersgill's Federal house has been preserved.

The **Mother Seton House** (600 North Paca Street, 410–523–3443) is a small, brick, Federal style house where St. Elizabeth Seton established a school for girls in June 1808. Born to an Anglican family in 1774, Mother Seton converted to Catholicism after the death of her husband. At the invitation of Bishop Carroll of Baltimore she came here and opened this school. During her stay in Baltimore, Seton took the vows of a nun and founded the Daughters and Sisters of Charity. She moved to Emmitsburg in 1809. In 1975 she became the first American-born person to be canonized a saint in the Roman Catholic Church.

The **Babe Ruth Birthplace** (216 Emory Street, 410–727–1539), a narrow, brick rowhouse where the famed hitter was born in 1895, has exhibits about his career with the Boston Red Sox and the New York Yankees, including uniforms, bats, gloves, photographs, and other memorabilia. The museum also pays tribute to the exploits of the Baltimore Orioles. Furnishings are of the late nineteenth century.

BALTIMORE MARITIME MUSEUM

Three twentieth-century vessels, two of which saw action in World War II, are moored here. The Coast Guard cutter *Taney* is the last warship still afloat that was in Pearl Harbor during the Japanese attack, on December 7, 1941, that brought the United States into the war. The submarine *Torsk,* launched in December 1944, was responsible for the last sinking in the war when it destroyed a Japanese freighter. Also moored here is the lightship *Chesapeake,* built in 1930. All three ships may be toured.

LOCATION: Pier 3 at Pratt Street. HOURS: Monday–Thursday 11–5, 10–6 Friday–Saturday, 10–5 Sunday. FEE: Yes. TELEPHONE: 410–396–3854.

U.S.S. CONSTELLATION

The sloop-of-war U.S.S. *Constellation,* now in permanent berth in Baltimore's Inner Harbor, bears the same name as the famous frigate of 1797, which saw action in the early days of the republic. In 1799, during the "Quasi-War" with France, the 38-gun *Constellation* utilized superior speed and firepower to capture *L'Insurgente* in the West Indies. The *Constellation* also served in the war against Algeria. The ship was broken up in 1854.

The *Constellation* visitors see today is called a sloop-of-war because she carries her guns on one deck. The 22-gun *Constellation* is the largest sloop-of-war built by the Navy, and its last all-sail ship. Launched in Norfolk, in 1854, she interdicted the slave trade off Africa for two years, capturing three slavers and freeing 700 people. In the Mediterranean during the U.S. Civil War, she attempted without success to capture the Confederate commerce raider *Sumter.* This sloop-of-war is the only ship still in existence that saw Civil War action.

OPPOSITE: *Two details show the care lavished on the* Constellation.

After the war, *Constellation* carried famine relief to Ireland and was a training ship for Naval Academy midshipmen. During World War II she was the flagship of Battleship Group 5. Decommissioned and donated to a not-for-profit group, *Constellation* was reconfigured to resemble her 1797 namesake, and opened to the public. The ship was closed in 1994 for repairs; much of the planking had dry-rotted. The outer planking was to be replaced with a laminated shell of Douglas fir and epoxy glue.

Westminster Church and Burying Ground (Fayette and Greene streets, 410–706–7228) is the burial place of Edgar Allan Poe, his grandfather David Poe, and other figures important in the city's and country's history. The cemetery was first used in 1786, and the church was built over it, in 1852, on arches that created a series of catacomblike passages.

The **Lillie Carroll Jackson Museum** (1320 Eutaw Place; being renovated) honors the Maryland civil rights leader who was president of the Baltimore branch of the National Association for the Advancement of Colored People from 1935 to 1970. Impelled by the lynching of several blacks on the Eastern Shore in the 1930s and by later killings, by overcrowding in Baltimore ghettoes, and by wage inequalities, Jackson fought for the hiring of black police officers, desegregation of stores, schools, and housing, and for equal wages for blacks. As a young girl she had been denied care in a whites-only hospital—as a result, she had to undergo surgery in a doctor's office that left her face permanently disfigured. The museum displays many of her personal items as well as exhibits about the civil rights struggle.

The **Fells Point** district was a shipbuilding center in the 1700s and 1800s—the *Constellation* was launched here in 1797—and was a residential area for sailors and captains. More than three hundred two- and three-story houses of the eighteenth and nineteenth centuries remain. It was named after William Fell, an English Quaker who settled here in 1730. The district has seen a revival in recent years, but it still retains its waterfront atmosphere. The city's oldest surviving urban residence is here, the **Robert Long House** (812 South Ann Street, 410–675–6750).

FORT MCHENRY

On September 13–14, 1814, Francis Scott Key watched a British fleet bombard Fort McHenry in an attempt to force its surrender, which would have left the city of Baltimore open to invasion. For twenty-five hours, the British fired incendiary shells at the fort, which was unable to defend itself because its guns did not have the range to reach the fleet. Nonetheless, the garrison and the fort itself withstood the bombardment, forcing the British to give up the invasion. Key was aboard a ship under a truce flag, negotiating for the release of an American captive. When he went ashore, Key quickly wrote the four verses of "The Star-Spangled Banner" to the tune of an old English song, "To Anacreon in Heaven." The first verse describes the flag, illuminated during the nighttime bombardment by "the rockets' red glare" and the "bombs bursting in air," still fluttering defiantly over the fort in the early light of dawn. Handbills with the verses were immediately distributed throughout the city and to the troops defending it. The song became an unofficial national anthem, and was officially recognized as such by Congress in 1931. The flag that Key watched was sewn in Baltimore at a house now called the Star-Spangled Banner Flag House. The flag itself is preserved at the National Museum of American History in Washington, DC.

An aerial view of Fort McHenry reveals its star shape.

The construction of Fort McHenry, begun in the 1790s, was completed in 1803. With the enlarged barracks, quarters, guardhouses, and gun batteries, the star-shaped fort today looks much as it did during the Civil War, when it was a prison for captured Confederate soldiers and sympathizers.

LOCATION: East Fort Avenue. HOURS: Early June through Labor Day: 8–8 Daily; Labor Day through early June: 8–5 Daily. FEE: Yes. TELEPHONE: 410–962–4299.

NORTHERN MARYLAND

The northern and western regions of Maryland were settled later than the Chesapeake Bay area. It was not until the first half of the 1700s that settlers moved into the interior of the colony in significant numbers. The ruling Calvert family offered inexpensive land to lure German farmers from Pennsylvania. The farmers settled the towns of Frederick and Hagerstown; Cumberland remained the far-western frontier of settlement until after the Revolution. Even after the French and Indian War had removed the French from the scene, the British government, fearful of antagonizing the Iroquois, was reluctant to allow settlement west of the Alleghenies. What finally opened Maryland's frontier was the construction of the National Road and, later, the Baltimore and Ohio Railroad. The westernmost county was named Garrett, not after an early settler or a hero of the Revolution, but after the president of the B & O, John W. Garrett, whose trains facilitated coal mining as well as vacationing. By the second half of the nineteenth century Garrett County already had a reputation for natural beauty—it was one of many regions called, with more enthusiasm than precision, the American Switzerland. The railroad created two classes of mountain people—those who took their ease in elegant hilltop "cottages" and the miners, farmers, and woodsmen who lived in the hollows.

This tour begins with sites northeast of Baltimore, then circles the city to the southwest and west.

HAMPTON NATIONAL HISTORIC SITE

One of the largest late Georgian–style mansions in the state, Hampton was the residence of the Ridgely family for over a century and a half. It was built between 1783 and 1790 by Charles

OPPOSITE: *The silver ewer on the center table in Hampton's Drawing Room is said to have been a gift of Lafayette.*

Ridgely, who amassed a fortune in ironmaking, shipping, trading, and agriculture. He died childless in 1790 just as the house was being completed and bequeathed it to his nephew Charles Carnan with the proviso that Carnan change his name to Ridgely.

Charles Carnan Ridgely, who served in the State Legislature, Senate, and as governor for three terms, earned a reputation as a horse fancier and a gracious host. He built stables and a racecourse on the property. A visitor in 1805 wrote, Ridgely "is very famous for race horses and usually keeps three or four . . . in training. . . . He is a very gentell man and is said to keep the best table in America." A twentieth-century biographer described him as "the typical aristocrat of his day. He had the fortune that enabled him to live like a prince, and he also had the inclination." The princely lifestyle of the Ridgelys of Hampton lasted throughout the nineteenth century. The horticulturist Henry Winthrop Sargent, who visited Hampton in 1850, took note of the "exquisitely kept" gardens and the "foreign air of the house" and concluded that they "quite disturb one's ideas of republican America." By the late 1800s the family fortunes went into decline, yet the Ridgelys were able to keep the house until 1948, when it was acquired by the National Park Service for its historical and architectural significance.

Today the house stands on sixty acres of grounds that include twenty-seven dependencies and farm buildings, as well as landscaped gardens. The main block of the house is flanked by wings, linked to the block by passageways, and topped by a large cupola. The stone house was stuccoed—unusual for the region—with a local sand containing traces of iron, giving the exterior a pinkish hue. The whole effect is one of grandeur rather than grace, with the massive cupola adding to the impression of a public building rather than a private residence. The Great Hall at the center of the house, fifty-one feet long, was used for dinner parties and dances and reflects Ridgely's penchant for entertaining on a grand scale.

Nine rooms in the house have been decorated in the styles popular during the different periods of the Ridgely occupancy, using furniture, paintings, and decorative objects that were owned by the family or are appropriate to the period. The parlor reflects the earliest period at Hampton, 1790 to 1829. The drawing room furnishings, which date from the 1830s, include an original set of Baltimore painted furniture, large gilt mirrors, an imported Chinese gaming table, and a family portrait from 1797 attributed to Rembrandt Peale. The music room is in the later Victorian style, with a Rococo Revival set of chairs, love seat, couch, and table; a Steinway piano made of rosewood; a harp made in London; and a copy of Thomas Sully's 1820 portrait of Charles Carnan Ridgely. Together the furniture, silver, portraits, glassware, and other items represent American styles and tastes from the 1760s to the 1880s.

The grounds of the estate include parterres, terraces planted with roses and peonies, 200-year-old catalpa trees, an imported cedar of Lebanon, a reconstructed orangerie dating to about 1825, and other outbuildings. In 1880 there were more than 4,000 rose plants on the property. Eliza Ridgely, who died in 1867, imported many trees, plants, and flowers and designed some of the gardens. Many family members are buried in a cemetery on the grounds.

LOCATION: 535 Hampton Lane, north from I-695, Exits 27B or 28, in Towson. HOURS: 9–5 Daily. FEE: None. TELEPHONE: 410–823–1309.

In nearby Lutherville, the **Fire Museum of Maryland** (1301 York Road, 410–321–7500) displays fifty pieces of firefighting equipment from the 1820s to the 1960s, along with photographs and other memorabilia.

Two of the state's oldest gristmills are in Harford County, northeast of Baltimore. **Jerusalem Mills** (Jerusalem Road seven miles southwest of Bel Air) was built in 1772. **Amos Mill** (Amoss Mill Road, three miles east of Norrisville) is believed to have been built at the time of the Revolution. The mills have not been restored and do not have facilities for visitors, but they are of architectural interest and preserve some eighteenth- and nineteenth-century machinery.

U.S. ARMY ORDNANCE MUSEUM

This open-air museum displays the world's most complete collection of tanks, artillery, and other weapons. The collection was started just after World War I when an army review group called the Calibre Board evaluated different types of artillery used in that war. In 1973 a private foundation took over the operation of the museum. The collection includes a massive German railroad gun that pounded the American beachhead at Anzio in World War II; a German V-2 rocket; the American T-12 bomb, weighing 43,600 pounds, which was developed to penetrate the concrete shells of German submarine pens; an atomic cannon designed to fire both

The Susquehanna Museum of Havre de Grace.

conventional and atomic shells; and weapons of the Chinese and
Soviet armies. The museum displays rifles, carbines, and helmets.
Some prototype weapons that were failures are also displayed.

> LOCATION: Route 22 (Aberdeen Thruway), Aberdeen. HOURS:
> 10–4:45 Daily. FEE: None. TELEPHONE: 410–278–3602.

The industrial port city of **Havre de Grace** preserves the 1829
Concord Point Lighthouse (Lafayette Street, 410–939–1498) and a
lock on the Susquehanna & Tidewater Canal. Adjacent to the lock
is an 1840 lockhouse, now called **Susquehanna Museum of Havre
de Grace** (Conesteo and Erie streets, 410–939–5780), with exhibits
about the history of the canal.

SUSQUEHANNA STATE PARK

The park contains several historic sites. The **Rock Run Grist Mill,**
a four-story mill built in 1794, preserves much of its original
milling machinery, including a twelve-ton water wheel. The **Carter
Mansion,** a thirteen-room house built in 1804, displays some nineteenth-century furnishings and a collection of antique dolls. The

Jersey Toll House was built about 1818 to collect tolls for the crossing of a bridge over the Susquehanna River. The bridge was knocked down by ice floes in 1856. The **Steppingstone Museum** (461 Quaker Bottom Road, 410–939–2299) displays a large collection of nineteenth-century tools and household items.

> LOCATION: Route 155, three miles north of Havre de Grace. HOURS: Sunrise to Sunset, Daily; *Mill and Mansion:* May through October. FEE: None. TELEPHONE: 410–557–7994.

North of the park in Darlington is the 1850 **Stafford Furnace** (Stafford Road), used in the production of white flint.

NORTHWESTERN MARYLAND

In Elkridge a handsome granite railroad bridge, **Thomas Viaduct,** crosses the Patapsco River on eight arches. The sixty-foot-high span, built in 1833 by the B & O Railroad, can be seen from Levering Avenue. Designed by Benjamin H. Latrobe, son of architect Benjamin Henry Latrobe, the bridge has served the railroad for a century and a half.

ELLICOTT CITY

Thirteen miles from Baltimore, Ellicott City was founded in the 1770s by the Ellicott family, who established mills on the Patapsco River. Andrew Ellicott assisted in the design of Washington, DC; Joseph Ellicott aided in the surveying of the Erie Canal and founded Buffalo, New York. Some of the town's early stone buildings, along Route 144, are preserved. The B & O Railroad built its first passenger terminal in Ellicott City in 1831. The **B & O Railroad Station Museum** (Maryland Avenue and Main Street, 410–461–1944) displays train models and offers a light-and-sound presentation about the history of the railroad, including the first run of the locomotive "Tom Thumb" from Ellicott City to Baltimore. The impressive **Howard County Courthouse** (Court House Drive, 410–313–2111) was built of granite in 1843. The Howard County Historical Society (Court Avenue, 410–461–1050) maintains a free library and museum in a building erected in the 1890s on the site of the collapse of the First Presbyterian Church.

CLARA BARTON NATIONAL HISTORIC SITE

After heroically tending the wounded on Civil War battlefields and in Europe, Clara Barton battled government bureaucracies and the

antifeminist prejudices of her day to found the American Red Cross. During the Civil War she gave aid to the wounded at the Second Battle of Manassas, Antietam, the Wilderness, Fredericksburg, and Spotsylvania. After the war she spent several years identifying the graves of unknown soldiers of Andersonville Prison. Suffering from a nervous breakdown, she traveled to Europe, where she nursed the wounded during the Franco-Prussian War and learned of the activities of the International Red Cross. She persuaded the U.S. government to sign the Treaty of Geneva, which established the American Red Cross.

This house was built in 1891 to serve as a warehouse for American Red Cross supplies. It became Barton's home in 1897 and continued as the first permanent headquarters of the American Red Cross until Barton's resignation as the organization's president in 1904. She died here in 1912 at the age of 90. The house displays some of her furniture and personal possessions.

LOCATION: 5801 Oxford Road, Glen Echo. HOURS: Tours 10:30–4:30 Daily. FEE: None. TELEPHONE: 301–492–6245.

CHESAPEAKE & OHIO CANAL NATIONAL HISTORICAL PARK

The entire 184 miles of the C & O Canal, from Georgetown to Cumberland, have been preserved as a national park. Begun on July 4, 1828, when President John Quincy Adams turned a ceremonial shovelful of dirt, the canal reached Cumberland in 1850. Because Cumberland stands 605 feet above sea level, seventy-four locks had to be built along the canal to lift or lower barges to different levels. The canal was a major engineering achievement, but the Baltimore & Ohio Railroad took much of its business. The canal operated until 1924. A visitor center in a nineteenth-century tavern has exhibits about the canal and a model of a lock. Barge tours of the canal are available in the summer months. Other information centers along the canal are located in Georgetown, Antietam Creek, Four Locks, Hancock, and Cumberland.

LOCATION: 11710 MacArthur Boulevard, Potomac. HOURS: Call to confirm hours at information centers. FEE: Yes, for Great Falls and barge tours. TELEPHONE: 301–739–4200; call 301–299–3613 for barge tours.

OPPOSITE: *The wooden galleries of the Clara Barton House were designed to resemble an elegant riverboat.*

ROCKVILLE

An 1815 brick house where Lafayette visited in 1824, the **Beall-Dawson House** (103 West Montgomery Avenue, 301–762–1492), has been restored with furniture from the mid-1800s. A doctor's office on the grounds has exhibits of nineteenth-century medical items. The house is the headquarters of the Montgomery County Historical Society. Residences from the late eighteenth to the early twentieth century, including those of the Victorian style, are preserved in the **West Montgomery Avenue Historic District.** The authors F. Scott and Zelda Fitzgerald are buried in **St. Mary's Catholic Church Cemetery** (520 Veirs Mill Road). Scott Fitzgerald died of a heart attack in 1940; Zelda was killed in a fire in 1948 at a North Carolina mental hospital where she was a patient.

CARROLL COUNTY FARM MUSEUM

Nineteenth-century agricultural methods are demonstrated in a complex of buildings that include a broom shop, blacksmith shop, wagon shed, and a mansion built in 1852. The staff demonstrates quilting, spinning, weaving, tinsmithing, pottery making, and other crafts.

> LOCATION: Center Street off Route 140, south of Westminster. HOURS: April through June and September through October: 12–5 Saturday–Sunday; July through August: 10–4 Tuesday–Friday, 12–5 Saturday–Sunday. FEE: Yes. TELEPHONE: 410–876–2667.

Several miles north of Westminster, the **Union Mills Homestead** (Route 97 in Union Mills, 410–848–2288) preserves the twenty-three-room house and gristmill of the Shriver family. Before the Battle of Gettysburg, both Union and Confederate generals stopped here, separately, to eat. The author Washington Irving also spent a night here. The mill and the oldest portion of the house were both built in 1797. The house displays many furnishings and household items used by six generations of Shrivers.

FREDERICK

The town of Frederick was laid out in 1745 when western Maryland was being rapidly settled by German farmers from Pennsylvania. The immigrants were lured by the low cost of this fertile farm land, which Lord Baltimore and other proprietors were eager to see settled. Frederick was established by Daniel Dulany, an Annapolis lawyer and land speculator, who anticipated a rise in land values as the town grew. In 1748 the town was named the seat of Frederick County and it soon became the commercial center of the surrounding farm region. In the 1782 census this county was the most populous in Maryland, surpassing even Baltimore County.

General Edward Braddock, on his ill-fated march into Pennsylvania in 1755, stopped at Frederick to gather horses, wagons, and other supplies. He met with so much resistance from the town residents that Benjamin Franklin had to come to Frederick to cajole the farmers. Anti-British feelings grew stronger in the 1760s, when the town refused to pay the tax imposed by the Stamp Act. During the Revolution the townspeople contented themselves with hanging three Loyalists. Hessian prisoners were confined at a barracks in the town but were well treated by the German populace.

After the Revolution, Frederick prospered as a center of milling and the manufacture of glass, iron, paper, and whiskey. Improved toll roads linked it with Baltimore, Harper's Ferry, and, to the west, Hagerstown and Cumberland Its importance as a transportation center grew when the National Road was constructed west from Cumberland. Two notable residents of this period were Francis Scott Key, who wrote the words to the national anthem (he had a legal practice here), and Key's brother-in-law, Roger Brooke Taney, the chief justice of the Supreme Court who handed down the 1857 Dred Scott decision and administered the presidential oath of office to Lincoln in 1861.

During the Civil War, wounded soldiers from the Battle of Antietam were tended at makeshift hospitals in the town. In 1864 Confederate general Jubal Early marched into town and extracted a ransom of $200,000, which was financed by a bond issue that was not paid off until 1970. Later, General Early clashed with Federal troops outside of Frederick, as townspeople watched in fascination from the rooftops. (The Federal commander professed to be amazed at their detached interest in the carnage.) In 1862 Frederick was the scene of one of the most famous episodes of the war, Barbara Fritchie's defiant flag-waving, which was celebrated—perhaps largely invented—by the poet John Greenleaf Whittier. Her house was torn down after the war, but it has been reconstructed as a tribute to her patriotism.

Whittier's description of the town itself—"The clustered spires of Frederick stand / Green-walled by the hills of Maryland"—

remains an accurate one. The spires he limned were those of the courthouse and five churches, which still stand—All Saints Episcopal Church, the Evangelical Reformed Church, Trinity Chapel, the Evangelical Lutheran Church, and Saint John's Roman Catholic Church—their steeples illuminated at night. Frederick preserves a large number of eighteenth- and nineteenth-century buildings. A revitalization program of the 1970s focused on the historic district, which now has a number of shops and restaurants. There is a **visitor center** at 19 East Church Street (301–663–8687).

At the center of the town is **Courthouse Square.** In 1765 residents burned an effigy of the royal tax collector to protest the Stamp Act, and twelve county judges declared that they would continue to process legal transactions without the required stamp on documents. President Lincoln, standing on the steps of 119 Record Street, where a wounded general was being treated, addressed a crowd here in October 1862 after visiting the Antietam battlefield. The brick houses at **103–105 Council Street** were built in 1817. Lafayette was a guest at number 103 during his 1824 tour of the United States. Architect Robert Mills designed the first two stories of **100 North Court Street.** The third story is a later addition.

Opposite the end of Record Street, 110–112 West Church Street is known locally as the **Spite House** (private) because it was hastily built in 1814 by the landowner to prevent the town from extending Record Street. The owner, Dr. John Tyler, took advantage of a state law forbidding the taking of land if a house stood on it. When he had exhausted other legal measures to prevent the construction, he had workmen dig a foundation overnight and sat down in the midst of the workers in his rocking chair, declaring himself to be at home. One of this country's earliest eye specialists, Dr. Tyler is credited with conducting the first successful operation to remove cataracts. His papers show that patients came from Europe to consult him.

At 108 West Church is the oldest house still standing on the square, **All Saints Episcopal Rectory,** built by Dr. Tyler in 1790. The iron dog on the front steps was stolen by Confederate troops. A Hagerstown man found the dog on the field at Antietam and recognized it from newspaper advertisements seeking its recovery. One of the finest small Gothic structures in the country, **All Saints Episcopal Church** (106 West Church Street) was designed by Richard Upjohn and completed in 1855. The interior features four

OPPOSITE: *Federal townhouses line a street in Frederick.*

styles of stained glass, including a Bavarian triptych over the altar. The neighboring parish hall (21–25 North Court Street), a two-story stuccoed building, was built as a church in 1813 and converted to a parish hall when the current church was completed. In the colonial period this Anglican parish covered all of western Maryland and was supported by taxes from that large region. In 1768 Bennett Allen was appointed its minister by Lord Baltimore. The townspeople locked him out, but Allen managed to take possession of his church by force, then promptly hired a replacement for himself while he continued to collect his salary. Francis Scott Key and Thomas Johnson, the first governor of Maryland, were members of this parish.

The **Frederick County Court House,** which gives the square its name, is the third to stand on this site. It was built in 1862 after its predecessor was destroyed the previous year in a fire started by a law clerk. Working late one night, the tired clerk had left a candle burning and it ignited some papers.

Two of Frederick's ecclesiastical landmarks are across the street from one another. The cornerstone of **Trinity Chapel** was laid in 1763, but its clock tower is a replacement dating to 1807. The clock's works have been removed and deposited in the Smithsonian Institution as an important example of nineteenth-century technology; the clock is now electrified. On the Sunday before the Battle of Antietam, Stonewall Jackson attended services at the **Evangelical Reformed Church.** The minister had posted the subject of his sermon—a plea for divine aid for the Union cause—and General Jackson napped during the oration. North on Market Street is the **City Hall,** where General Early extracted his ransom from the town. The building has since been greatly altered.

Kemp Hall, a three-story brick building at the corner of North Market and East Church streets, was the meeting place of the Maryland General Assembly during its debate on the question of secession in 1861. Unionists, in the minority, managed to delay a vote until Federal troops arrived and arrested the secessionists. The Greek Revival–style **Winchester Hall** (12 East Church Street) was used as a hospital during the Civil War. The **Historical Society of Frederick County** (24 East Church Street, 301–663–1188) is headquartered in an early-nineteenth-century house displaying local historical items. To the north at Second Street and Chapel Alley is **St. John's Roman Catholic Church,** completed in 1837.

Frederick's other historic sites are located away from the Court Square area. In the northern part of the city is **Rose Hill Manor**

Children's Museum (1611 North Market Street, 301–694–1648), a museum of nineteenth-century life with tours and hands-on activities in the mansion, blacksmith shop, carriage museum, log cabin, farm museum, and gardens. It is designed for children and located on the grounds of the eighteenth-century estate of George Washington's friend Thomas Johnson. The city's other sites are located to the south and west.

Barbara Fritchie House and Museum

In September 1862 a Confederate column marched through Frederick past the house of Barbara Fritchie, whose husband, by then deceased, had run a glove-making business in an attached shop. There is no reliable record as to what actually happened, but Mrs. Fritchie, then 95 years old, may have stood in her doorway waving a small, silk American flag. Possibly the elderly lady's eyes had deceived her into thinking that the troops were Federal. Apparently, Barbara Fritchie resisted efforts to persuade or force her to put the flag away. Reports of the incident inspired the Massachusetts abolitionist poet John Greenleaf Whittier to write "Barbara Fritchie," which appeared in *The Atlantic Monthly* of October 1863.

In Whittier's version the Confederate commander was none other than Stonewall Jackson, who orders his men to fire upon the flag. Whittier's famous couplet records Fritchie's response: "'Shoot if you must this old gray head, / But spare your country's flag,' she said." Ashamed, Jackson calls out to his men: "'Who touches a hair of yon gray head / Dies like a dog! March on!' he said." The poem was widely popular in its day and has been memorized by generations of schoolchildren. Whittier later said that while he may have been mistaken "in the details" of the incident, he made no mistake about Fritchie's "noble character, her loyalty, and her patriotism." Winston Churchill, who had a keen interest in the Civil War, visited the Fritchie House during World War II with President Roosevelt. With some prompting, Churchill recited the entire poem.

The original Fritchie House, damaged by a flood, was torn down in 1867. This replica, built in 1927, displays some of her furniture, china, quilts, a family Bible, and a dress and doll clothes sewn by her. The original flag is owned by a descendant.

LOCATION: 154 West Patrick Street. HOURS: April through September: 10–4 Monday, Thursday–Saturday, 1–4 Sunday; October through November: 1–4 Saturday–Sunday. FEE: Yes. TELEPHONE: 301–698–0630.

On the grounds of the Maryland School for the Deaf (South Market and Clarke streets, 301–662–4159) are the **Hessian Barracks,** where Hessian prisoners were confined during the Revolution. Some of the prisoners decided to settle here after the war. In the southern part of the town, at the end of Market Street, is **Mount Olivet Cemetery,** burial place of Francis Scott Key, Barbara Fritchie, and 875 Confederate soldiers who died at Antietam and Monocacy. There is a large monument to Key, dedicated in 1893.

Schifferstadt Architectural Museum

Completed in 1756 by German settlers, Schifferstadt is the oldest surviving house in Frederick and one of the best examples of colonial German architecture. It was the farmhouse of Joseph Brunner, who named it after the German town where he had lived. Many original architectural features are intact. Of interest are the original door locks, knobs, and hinges, all in a variety of shapes. The two-and-a-half-story house was built of quarried stones—the walls are thirty inches thick—with hand-hewn beams of oak. The interior walls were insulated with a mixture of clay, dried husks and weeds, and horsehair. Under the northern half of the house is a vaulted cellar for food storage. Another original item is a cast-iron stove, dated 1756, made in Pennsylvania. The stove bears the saying, "Where your treasure is, there is your heart," in German.

LOCATION: 1110 Rosemont Avenue at Route 15. HOURS: Early April through mid-December: 10–4 Tuesday–Saturday, 12–4 Sunday. FEE: None. TELEPHONE: 301–663–3885.

THURMONT

The **Catoctin Iron Works** (Cunningham Falls State Park, Catoctin Hollow Road, 301–271–7574) preserves an iron furnace built in 1774 and used until 1904. Adjacent are the ruins, now stabilized, of the ironmaster's large mansion. Stone cottages (private) occupied by iron workers are nearby.

Near Thurmont is **Apple's United Church of Christ** (Roddy and Apple's Church roads), a two-story, one-room stone church built in 1826 that may be seen during regular Sunday services. Also near Thurmont are two covered bridges dating from the 1850s— **Loy's Station Bridge** (Old Frederick Road off Route 77) and **Roddy Road Covered Bridge** (Roddy Road).

Schifferstadt, the oldest surviving house in Frederick. The farmhouse was named after the German hometown of its builder, Joseph Brunner, and is constructed in the colonial German style of architecture.

HAGERSTOWN

The city preserves the house built by its founder, Jonathan Hager, in 1739. The **Jonathan Hager House and Museum** (City Park, 301–739–8393), a restored, two-and-a-half-story stone building, displays period furnishings and archaeological artifacts from around the state. If the veranda is original, and it seems to be, it is one of the earliest in America. The **Miller House** (135 West Washington Street, 301–797–8782) displays the collections of the local historical society, including clocks and dolls. **Rose Hill Cemetery** (South Potomac Street) is the burial place of some two thousand Confederate soldiers.

WASHINGTON MONUMENT STATE PARK

The park is the location of the country's first monument erected to honor George Washington. On July 4, 1827, the people of Boonsboro put up a fifteen-foot-high tower of stones, fifty-four feet in circumference. Its completion at the end of the day was marked when three Revolutionary War veterans fired a salute from the top. During the Battle of Antietam the Signal Corps used it as an observation point. The monument was rebuilt and enlarged in 1882 and again in the 1930s. Near the entrance to the park is the **Old South Mountain Inn,** a stone structure built in 1730 and still functioning as a restaurant.

LOCATION: Three miles southeast of Boonsboro. HOURS: 8–Dusk Daily. FEE: None. TELEPHONE: 301–791–4767.

The town of **Boonsboro,** settled in 1774, was the site of several skirmishes during the Civil War. General Stonewall Jackson, walking his horse down a road, was nearly captured here by Federal troops. Another Confederate officer spotted the Northerners and saved Jackson through a ruse: He yelled orders as if he had troops hiding in the woods, when in fact he had only a few men with him. The Federals were deceived and ran off. The early road through town became the National Pike. The **Boonsboro Museum of History** (113 North Main Street, 301–432–6969) displays weapons, Civil War artifacts, and other historical items.

BRUNSWICK

In the 1880s this small town was selected as the site for a B & O Railroad repair shop, bringing on a local economic boom. The town preserves many buildings from the 1890s and a brick round-house built in 1907. The **Brunswick Railroad Museum** (40 West Potomac Street, 301–834–7100) displays train models and railroad equipment, uniforms, and memorabilia.

ANTIETAM NATIONAL BATTLEFIELD

After his victory at Manassas, General Robert E. Lee launched an invasion of Maryland intending to bring that state to the Confederate side. But when Lee's men marched into this staunchly Unionist section they met a cold reception. The army's parade through

OPPOSITE: *A monument to the 132nd Pennsylvania Regiment keeps watch over now-peaceful Bloody Lane at Antietam.*

Casualties of the Battle at Antietam Creek lie near the Dunker Church, 1862.

Frederick provoked Barbara Fritchie's famous display of the Stars and Stripes. Outside of Frederick, a Confederate officer dropped a copy of Lee's plans in a field, where it was found and carried to General McClellan. With the plans in his hand McClellan proclaimed, "If I cannot whip Bobbie Lee, I will be willing to go home."

The two armies met at Antietam Creek outside the town of Sharpsburg on September 17, 1862. That day of battle was the bloodiest in any American war. Fierce fighting took place along a sunken road called Bloody Lane, where some 5,000 men fell. It presented, in the words of a newspaper reporter on the scene, a "ghastly spectacle. . . . Confederates had gone down as the grass falls before the scythe." About 40,000 Confederates fought 87,000 Federal troops. By the end of the day the dead and wounded of both sides numbered over 23,000. McClellan failed to carry out his orders to destroy Lee's army once and for all, and he was dismissed on November 7 by President Lincoln for refusing to pursue Lee aggressively after the battle. However, Antietam was a strategic

Today, Dunker Church sits quietly on a hillside on the site of the battle.

victory for the North. His invasion a failure, Lee retreated to Virginia. Confederate hopes for aid from Great Britain were dashed. The victory is also credited with providing Lincoln with the political strength to issue the Emancipation Proclamation.

The major points of the fighting are preserved in the battlefield park, including **Dunker Church, The Cornfield, Bloody Lane,** and **Burnside Bridge,** where a northern corps was held off by a few hundred Georgia riflemen. At **Antietam National Cemetery** 4,776 Federal soldiers are buried. A visitor center has exhibits and an audio-visual presentation about the battle.

> LOCATION: Routes 34 and 35 in Sharpsburg. HOURS: Memorial
> Day through Labor Day: 8:30–6 Daily; Labor Day through late May:
> 8:30–5 Daily. FEE: Yes. TELEPHONE: 301–432–5124.

The small town of **Samples Manor** is the location of the restored **Kennedy Farmhouse** (Chestnut Grove Road, 301–963–3300), from which the abolitionist John Brown departed on his famous raid on Harper's Ferry in October 1859.

The tomb of Elizabeth Ann Seton is now a shrine to the first American-born saint.

The **National Shrine of St. Elizabeth Ann Seton** (333 South Seton Avenue, Emmitsburg, 301–447–6606) contains a chapel and the gravesite of Elizabeth Ann Seton (1774–1821), who in 1975 became the first American woman to be canonized by the Roman Catholic Church. There is also a museum, a Revolutionary-era stone house, and the "White House" with a replica of a classroom of the period. A widow who had converted to Catholicism, Seton founded a girls' school here in 1809 and established a religious community.

FORT FREDERICK

Completed in August 1756, this stone fortress was built to protect the Maryland frontier from attacks by the French and their Indian allies. The massive walls, 120 feet long, 20 feet high, and 4 feet thick, overlook the Potomac River from a high point on Fairview Mountain. The fort was never attacked, but it did serve as an important supply base. During the Revolutionary War thousands of British and Hessian prisoners were confined here. The park's museum displays artifacts from the site. On some summer weekends there are musters and other military demonstrations.

> LOCATION: Route 56 near Indian Springs. HOURS: *Park:* April through October: 8:30–Sunset Daily; November through March: 10–4 Wednesday–Sunday; *visitor center:* May through September: 8–4 Monday–Friday, 9:30–5:30 Saturday–Sunday. FEE: None. TELEPHONE: 301–842–2155.

The **Paw Paw Tunnel** (Route 51 outside Paw Paw, WV) was one of the construction feats of the C & O Canal, a 3,118-foot-long cut through solid rock.

CUMBERLAND

Situated on a bend of the Potomac River and surrounded by the Allegheny Mountains, Cumberland began in 1749 as a trading post called Will's Creek. Just west of the town is **The Narrows,** a gap in the Alleghenies crossed by the Indians of the Ohio Valley and, later, white settlers heading west. The commerce of the Ohio Valley was transported eastward, and vice versa, through this gap. Cumberland's location near The Narrows would make it an important transportation hub in early road, canal, and railroad systems. built in the nineteenth century.

In 1754 Will's Creek was the starting point for George Washington's expedition against the French, which culminated in his surrender at Fort Necessity in Pennsylvania. Governor Sharpe ordered the construction of a log fort, which was strengthened in 1755 and named Fort Cumberland. It stood on the hill above the intersection of Washington and Greene streets, a site now occupied by **Emmanuel Parish Church,** a Gothic Revival structure built in 1851. General Edward Braddock's disastrous 1755 expedition against the French departed from Fort Cumberland, and Washington commanded the fort's garrison in 1756. His small headquarters, **Washington's Cabin** (Riverside Park, 301–777–8214), was moved from its original site in 1921 and has been restored. In 1794 Washington again visited Cumberland to review the troops assigned to suppress the Whiskey Rebellion.

In 1785 a new town was laid out around the fort. Coal from the hills around Cumberland was transported by boat down the Potomac. In 1811 the construction of the National Road, authorized by Congress five years earlier to facilitate commerce and settlement, was begun at Cumberland. By 1818 the road reached Wheeling on the Ohio River and ultimately extended to Illinois. The next three decades saw the simultaneous construction of the Chesapeake & Ohio Canal and the Baltimore & Ohio Railroad. The railroad reached Cumberland in 1842, the canal in 1850. The advantages of the railroad quickly became apparent, and it was extended westward. The canal, which never got beyond Cumberland, was made obsolete by rail transportation.

During the Civil War the town was garrisoned by Federal troops. In 1865 Confederate raiders captured two Union generals and spirited them out of town. The prisoners (one of them was General George Crook, who later won fame as the nemesis of Geronimo) were taken to Richmond.

The **Chesapeake & Ohio Canal National Historical Park** has a visitor center in Cumberland (Canal Street, 301–722–8226) housed in a 1913 railroad station that displays photographs and memorabilia about the canal and the B & O Railroad. Five miles south of the town on the canal is the **C & O Canal Boat Replica** (301–722–8226). Nearby is one of the canal's original stone locks.

The **Washington Street Historic District** preserves many nineteenth-century houses (private), as well as the 1894 **Allegany County Courthouse** (30 Washington Street) and the 1850 **Allegany County Public Library** (31 Washington Street).

History House (218 Washington Street, 301–777–8678) is the headquarters of the Allegany County Historical Society. The society has renovated the three-story 1867 townhouse and furnished a parlor, dining room, ballroom, music room, bedrooms, and kitchen with items from the Victorian period.

West of Cumberland at the junction of routes 40A and 55 is the **Clarysville Bridge,** a stone arch bridge built to carry the National Road. The **Clarysville Inn** (Route 40A, 301–722–3900) was built in 1807 along the National Road. Southwest of Cumberland is the **Lonaconing Iron Furnace** (East Main Street in Lonaconing, 301–463–2920), built in 1837.

East of Grantsville the **Casselman Bridge,** which crosses the Casselman River just north of Route 40, was built in 1813 as part of the
National Road. At the time of its construction the eighty-foot-long
stone arch bridge was the longest of its type in the country. Nearby
is the region's oldest (1797) gristmill, **Stanton's Mill** (Route 40,
301–895–3332), now owned by Spruce Forest Artisan Village. In
the town of **Grantsville,** some of whose inhabitants are descended
from Amish and Mennonite settlers, the 1824 **Casselman Hotel**
(Main Street, 301–895–5055) still functions as an inn.

OAKLAND

Oakland grew from a tiny settlement to a small town in the 1850s
after the B & O Railroad announced that it was building a station
here in the heart of western Maryland's mountains. The **B & O
Railroad Station,** built on Liberty Street in 1884, is a local architectural landmark. The scenic beauty of the area attracted wealthy
summer residents, including two notable generals—George Crook,
who pursued Geronimo, and Lew Wallace, who wrote *Ben Hur.*
Many late-nineteenth-century summer houses (private) can be seen
in the town of **Mountain Lake Park** east of Oakland off Route 135.

The beautiful Queen Anne-style Oakland B & O Railroad Station.

DELAWARE

OPPOSITE: *Built in 1892, New Castle's Old Library houses exhibits concerning Delaware's history.*

The history of Delaware is a remarkably placid one. Its only colonial-era Indian "massacre" was the result of a misunderstanding on the part of the attackers, from whom the white settlers chose not to exact any vengeance. The Dutch, Swedes, and English contended for possession of the colony, but they managed to live in harmony with each other once the English gained control. The state's only battle of the Revolution was a minor engagement near Newark.

Before exploring the New York river that now bears his name, Henry Hudson had made a tentative approach to Delaware Bay on the *Half Moon,* in August 1609, but he went no farther than the entrance because of its dangerous shoals. The bay was named in honor of the governor of Virginia, Lord De La Warr, by the English explorer Samuel Argall, who took refuge in it during a storm in 1610.

The colony's first European settlement, a commercial venture backed by Dutch investors, was established at Lewes in 1631. All but one of the first group of settlers were killed by the relatives of an Indian who had been executed by the tribe itself for a theft from the Dutch. (Though the Dutch had complained to the chief, they had not wanted the man killed.) The next group of settlers chose to overlook the massacre in the hope of maintaining a friendly trade. As it turned out, the colony quickly failed: The rival Dutch West India Company was violently opposed to competition in the fur trade, and the colonists were unable to capture enough whales to make a profit on oil.

The Indians in northern Delaware were a branch of the Lenni Lenape, who provided furs to the agents of the Dutch West India Company in exchange for weapons, liquor, clothing, and metalware. This was profitable to both sides until the beaver population was exhausted. Another tribe was the Nanticoke, who may have moved into southern Delaware from Maryland's Eastern Shore. After both tribes were reduced by European diseases, the surviving members headed west in the 1750s. (A few Nanticoke still live in the vicinity of Oak Orchard.)

Delaware's first permanent settlement, another commercial venture, was established in 1638, at what would later be named Wilmington, by Swedes under the leadership of the Dutchman Peter Minuit. In 1651, the Dutch asserted their claim to the region by building Fort Casimir nearby, at the future site of New Castle. The Swedes drove out the Dutch; the Dutch returned and drove

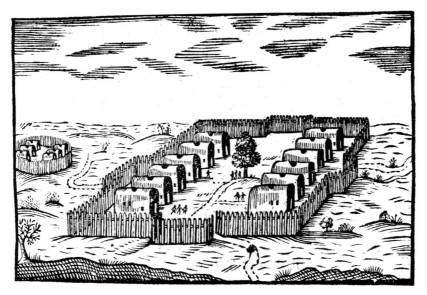

Each Lenni Lenape village, consisting of several hundred people, had its own government and was independent of the others.

out the Swedes; finally, the English, in the service of the Duke of York, took firm possession of the colony by blasting at Fort Casimir and routing its score of defenders.

In 1664 King Charles II granted his brother James, duke of York, all the territory between the Delaware and the Connecticut rivers. Although the Dutch holdings on the western bank of the Delaware did not fall within this domain, the duke took them anyway. Further confusion resulted when Charles granted the colony of Pennsylvania to William Penn in 1681, and in the following year the duke ceded Delaware to Penn. The Calverts, proprietors by royal charter of the colony of Maryland, also claimed portions of Delaware. Mason and Dixon surveyed the boundary in the 1760s, but the Maryland border was not agreed upon until 1776. A similar dispute with New Jersey was settled in court in 1912.

Although battle barely touched Delaware during the Revolution, this state produced some of the best fighters. Delaware's Continental regiment, known as the Blue Hens for the brood of fighting cocks kept for sport in the regiment's camps, distinguished

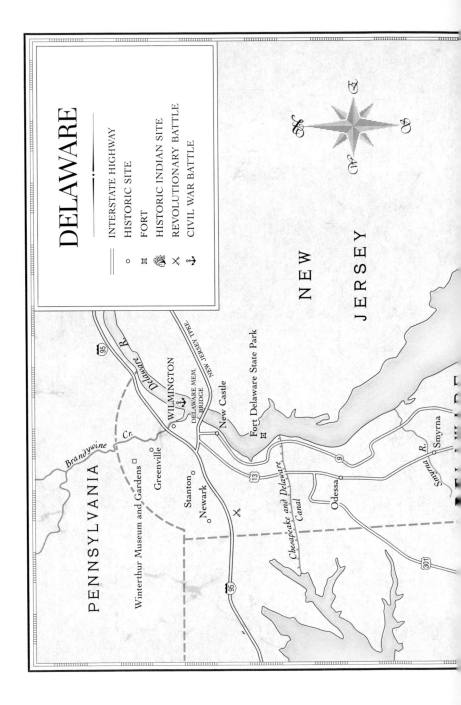

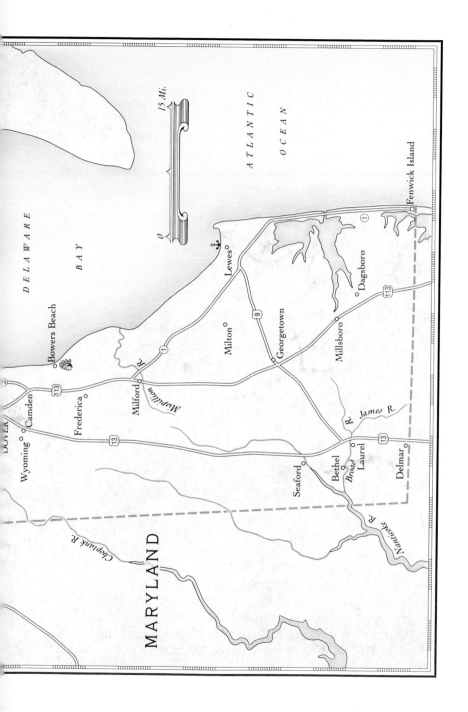

itself throughout the war. Captain Robert Kirkwood was extolled by General Light Horse Harry Lee as a man who had risked his life thirty-three times for his country, finally losing it in action. Delaware also produced the Revolutionary theorist John Dickinson, known (as is Virginia's George Mason) as "the pen of the Revolution," who successfully pressured the reluctant Pennsylvania delegation to accept the Declaration of Independence. Delaware's origins as a separate state date back to 1704, when Pennsylvania allowed its three counties to have their own legislature, but it did not actually become a separate political entity until it adopted a state constitution in 1776. On December 6, 1787, that legislature became the first to ratify the United States Constitution, earning Delaware its nickname, the First State.

In 1785 a Delaware inventor, Oliver Evans, devised automatic milling machinery that greatly improved the efficiency of flour mills. The machinery was put to use in a number of new mills that rose in the Brandywine River Valley north of Wilmington, but Evans died poor. A family that had considerably better luck arrived in Delaware in 1800. Irénée duPont, who had fled Revolutionary France with his father and brother in 1799, persuaded his father to finance the establishment of a gunpowder mill on the Brandywine, preserved today as the Hagley Museum. Their company flourished almost immediately, derived large profits from the War of 1812 and the Civil War, and, by the late nineteenth century, produced over 90 percent of the country's gunpowder. After World War I the company began producing chemicals, fertilizers, and synthetic fabrics, among other products. The manufacture of one synthetic material at the duPont factory in Seaford led to that town's sobriquet, the "nylon capital of the world." The duPont fortune also created one of the country's most important museums of Americana: Winterthur, located in the mansion of Henry I. duPont.

While portions of the northern county became heavily industrialized in the first half of the nineteenth century, the two southern counties remained agricultural. The Delaware Railroad reached the southern counties in the 1850s. A blight began to sweep through the region's peach trees, but the farmers were able to shift back to their original cash crops—corn, wheat, and berries. The town of Delmar, divided by the border of Delaware and Maryland after the Mason-Dixon line turned south for this purpose, was founded in 1859, when the railroad reached this edge of the state. The railroad brought manufacturing to southern Delaware, but extracted its tribute in the form of high rates. The

The facade of City Hall, Wilmington.

railroad had no competition until 1924, when the first modern highway breached the isolation of the southern counties.

This tour of Delaware begins with Wilmington and the other sites under the curve of the northern border, and then proceeds to New Castle and the southern counties.

WILMINGTON

Swedish settlers arrived here in 1638 and built Fort Christina, named after the Swedish queen, on a site at the foot of Seventh Street by the Christina River. They traded furs and tobacco and raised corn, barley, and other grains. Dutch forces, led by Peter Stuyvesant, took over the settlement in 1655, only to be ousted, in turn, by the English in 1664. Nonetheless, the Swedes prospered under English rule, attracting even more Swedish immigrants. The town was laid out in a grid in the 1730s and became the region's marketplace for agricultural trade, milling, and shipping. The 1730s also saw the arrival of Pennsylvania Quakers, who built more markets, wharves, and breweries and fitted out ships to carry the region's flour, meat, butter, and barrel staves to the West Indies. A resident of the nearby port of New Castle grumbled about the competition, referring to Wilmington as "an upstart village on a neighboring creek."

During the Revolution, George Washington camped at Wilmington with 11,000 Continentals before the battle of Brandywine in Pennsylvania. The British occupied the town in September and October 1777, following their victory at Brandywine, but Wilmington did not suffer any destruction. In the nineteenth century the town prospered amid a boom in the manufacture of textiles, paper, and gunpowder along the Brandywine. Mid-century saw Wilmington's own factories producing railroad cars and iron-hulled ships, and late in the century the duPont company made the city its headquarters, where it remains today. The city has also profited from Delaware's liberal incorporation and banking laws, which have attracted many lawyers and financial institutions.

Delaware History Museum

The museum occupies a renovated Art Deco Woolworth five-and-ten-cent store. Operated by the Historical Society of Delaware, it has three galleries and features changing exhibitions devoted to Delaware's history through displays of everyday life, costumes, toys, regional decorative arts, and paintings. A nine-foot-tall folk-art statue of George Washington is a prominent exhibit.

LOCATION: 504 Market Street Mall. HOURS: 12–4 Tuesday–Friday, 10–4 Saturday. FEE: None. TELEPHONE: 302–655–7161.

The society also operates **Old Town Hall** (512 Market Street, 302–655–7161). The two-story brick building, with arched first-floor windows, a clock set in its pediment, and a cupola, was built between 1798 and 1800. It was probably designed by Pierre Bauduy, a French architect, painter, and early partner of the duPonts. The city moved to new offices in 1916. The town hall doubled as Wilmington's jail, and the original cells can be seen. The building was closed for renovation in the late 1990s.

Adjacent to the Old Town Hall is **Willingtown Square,** a cluster of eighteenth-century houses now used as offices (private). Six blocks away is **Rodney Square,** named for Caesar Rodney, whose statue, unveiled in 1923, stands in its midst. He is depicted on a horse galloping toward Philadelphia, as he was on July 1, 1776, when he cast the deciding vote that put the colony's delegation in favor of adopting the Declaration of Independence.

Delaware Art Museum

Internationally acclaimed for its collection of Pre-Raphaelite paintings, the Delaware Art Museum also maintains an extensive collection of American paintings and illustrations from 1840 to the present. The seeds of this collection were planted in 1912 with the effort to keep works of illustrator Howard Pyle in Wilmington. The American illustration collection has grown around this preeminent core of Pyle's works and archives to include works by N. C. Wyeth, Elizabeth Shippen Green, and Maxfield Parrish.

Branching out from this collection, permanent and traveling exhibits give an overview of the development of American painting. Works in the permanent collection include those of Thomas Eakins, John Sloan, Winslow Homer, Edward Hopper, and Childe Hassam as well as major works by such contemporary artists as Grace Hartigan and Paul Wiesenfeld. The museum also maintains a Children's Gallery, which encourages art and design experimentation through its exhibits. A research library, containing 40,000 volumes and open to the public, houses reference, archival, and scholarly sources.

LOCATION: 2301 Kentmere Parkway. HOURS: 10–5 Tuesday–Saturday, 12–5 Sunday. FEE: Yes. TELEPHONE: 302–571–9590.

Delaware Academy of Medicine

At the corner of Lovering Avenue and Union Street stands the Delaware Academy of Medicine. The building formerly stood at the corner of Fourth and Market streets as the National Bank of Delaware and in an early movement toward historic preservation was carefully dismantled, moved, and rebuilt in 1930. The building may have been designed for its original site in 1815 by Pierre Bauduy, the same man who designed the Old Town Hall. The move to its new site was orchestrated by Charles O. Cornelius, former curator of the American Wing of the Metropolitan Museum of Art, with particular care. From the wooden pegs in the rafters to the marble flooring, from the interior trim to the exterior bricks dismantled one by one, the structure was rebuilt to stand virtually as it did in 1816; and apart from an addition dedicated in 1958, it still does. The finest Neoclassical building in the state, the Academy shows the influence of Benjamin Henry Latrobe.

Exhibition space in the first floor of the building provides insight into historical and contemporary medicine and dentistry through books, brochures, and artifacts dating from the 1700s. Displays encompass subjects such as the history of health in Delaware schools and patient education information.

Three historic churches are preserved in Wilmington. **Old Swedes Church** (606 Church Street, 302–652–5629), the oldest church in the state, was begun in 1698. Its porches and brick tower were added later. The pews are replicas installed in 1899, but the black-walnut pulpit is original. Adjacent to the church are a graveyard with many seventeenth- and eighteenth-century burials, and the **Hendrickson House Museum,** a 1690s stone farmhouse that was moved to this site from Pennsylvania. It is typical of the farmhouses built by the Swedes. **Old Asbury Methodist Church** (226 North Walnut Street) was dedicated in 1789 by Francis Asbury, the country's first Methodist bishop. **First Presbyterian Church** (Park Drive and West Street, 302–656–3994) dates to the 1740s.

Rockwood Museum

After thirty-two years as a successful merchant banker in England, Joseph Shipley retired to his native Delaware and built this country estate between 1851 and 1857. He hired an English architect, George Williams, to build him a fifty-room mansion in the Rustic-Gothic style. After Shipley's death in 1867, the house passed to his sisters. When Hannah Shipley died in 1892, Rockwood was acquired by a nephew, Edward Bringhurst, whose descendants occupied Rockwood until 1972. The house has been restored as an "upstairs-downstairs" museum of the 1890-to-1920 period. Fourteen rooms are open for the display of furnishings of the Shipleys and Bringhursts; other exhibits show the working lives of the servants. The museum's interpretation of daily life is based on manuscripts, letters, and photos that belonged to the occupants.

LOCATION: 610 Shipley Road. HOURS: March through December: 11–3 Tuesday–Sunday; January through February: 11–3 Tuesday–Saturday. FEE: Yes. TELEPHONE: 302–761–4340.

OPPOSITE: *Regularly used for services, the Old Swedes Church in Wilmington was built in 1698, making it one of the oldest still-active churches in the U.S.*

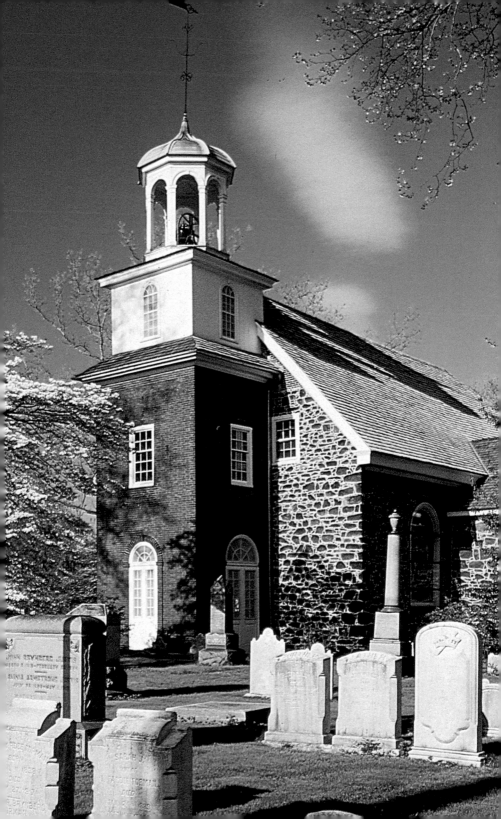

The conservatory at Rockwood. OPPOSITE: *The spectacular gardens at Nemours were designed with those of Versailles in mind.*

Nemours Mansion and Gardens

This three-hundred-acre estate, with formal French gardens and a 102-room Louis XVI–style house, was built by Alfred I. duPont in 1910 as a tribute to his French forebears. DuPont also included on the estate a children's medical facility that opened in 1940 and continues to provide services today. The house, designed by the New York firm Carrère & Hastings, features antique furnishings, Oriental rugs, tapestries, and outstanding works of art. On the grounds are cast iron gates made for the Russian empress Catherine the Great. DuPont, who died in 1935, is buried beneath a granite bell tower on the estate.

LOCATION: Rockland Road, between routes 202 and 141. HOURS: May through November: Guided tours every two hours 9–3 Tuesday–Saturday, 11–3 Sunday. FEE: Yes. TELEPHONE: 302–651–6912.

Hagley Museum and Eleutherian Mills

Irénée duPont's 1802 gunpowder mills, in use until 1921, are preserved at this 230-acre site on the Brandywine River, as are workers' houses and a school. An 1814 cotton mill contains exhibits about the technology of producing flour, paper, and iron, with a model of the important milling machinery invented by Oliver Evans. Also on the grounds is Eleutherian Mills, the duPont family's home for five generations, designed by Pierre Bauduy.

LOCATION: Route 141. HOURS: Mid-March through December: 9:30–4:30 Daily; January through mid-March: 9:30–4:30 Saturday–Sunday, Guided tour 1:30 Monday–Friday. FEE: Yes. TELEPHONE: 302–658–2400.

WINTERTHUR MUSEUM

Although today it is the premier museum of American furniture and decorative arts, Winterthur was formerly the private residence of Henry Francis duPont. Opened to the public in 1951, the nine-story mansion has nearly two hundred period rooms, all purchased or salvaged from actual houses from Georgia to New Hampshire. The rooms range in date from 1640 to 1840 and are completely furnished with paintings, prints, silver, pewter, glassware, textiles, and ceramics. The whole collection numbers 89,000 items.

A room taken from an Essex, Massachusetts, house built in the 1680s displays plain pine tables and chairs for everyday use along with a fine carved-oak cupboard that held the family's most treasured possessions. The Readbourne Parlor, with panelling taken from a 1733 house of that name on Maryland's Eastern Shore, is furnished with a chest made in Boston, painted to imitate Chinese lacquerwork; a tea table and chairs made in Philadelphia; and a painting by the noted colonial portraitist John Wollaston. The Blackwell Parlor has an elaborately carved chimneypiece, doorways, and cornice. There are rooms taken from houses in Chestertown, Maryland, and Albany, New York; a stair hall of sensuous elegance, which may be in whole or in part from Montmorenci, a North Carolina house; a Charleston, South Carolina, room with Chippendale furniture; a bedroom with furniture in the style of

OPPOSITE: *The Hagley Museum. DuPont mills provided 40 percent of all the gunpowder used by the Allied Forces in World War I.* OVERLEAF: *The Azalea Woods of the Winterthur Gardens.*

Lined with panelling from a 1744 Maryland plantation home, Winterthur's Marlboro Room also features paintings by Charles Willson Peale.

the Salem, Massachusetts, architect and woodcarver, Samuel McIn-tire; a parlor of Baltimore furniture; and a room of Empire-style furniture by the New York cabinetmaker Duncan Phyfe. In con-trast to the elegance of these rooms, the museum has a frugally furnished Shaker dwelling room; a stair hall decorated with an 1831 painted landscape by an artist from rural upstate New York; and a cabinetmaker's shop from East Hampton, New York, with its eighteenth- and nineteenth-century tools.

Born in 1880, duPont passed many of his early years in the quiet occupation of managing the family farm at this country estate, living in the psychological shadow of his dynamic father, a Civil War veteran and U.S. senator. In 1923 he began collecting American ceramics and furniture, inspired by a visit to Beauport, the Gloucester, Massachusetts, house that the collector Henry David Sleeper had furnished with antiques. Upon the death of his father in 1926, duPont inherited the Winterthur estate and a fortune of fifty million dollars. He began buying rooms of old houses and added a wing to his mansion to accommodate twenty-three period rooms and their furnishings. By 1946 he had increased the number of rooms to eighty. He moved into a smaller house on the grounds and opened the mansion to the public. The house is set amidst a 980-acre park landscaped by duPont himself.

LOCATION: Route 52, Winterthur. HOURS: 9–5 Monday–Saturday, 12–5 Sunday. FEE: Yes. TELEPHONE: 302–888–4600.

NEWARK

The only fighting of the Revolution in Delaware took place on September 3, 1777, at a spot south of Newark called **Cooch's Bridge,** marked by a granite monument at Route 4, east of Route 896. A British force commanded by Lord Cornwallis was met here by light-infantry units that failed to stem the British advance toward Pennsylvania. Local legend holds that the thirteen-star American flag was first flown in battle at this engagement.

In nearby **Stanton,** the **Hale-Byrnes House** (606 Stanton-Christina Road, 302–998–3792) is an early eighteenth-century brick house where George Washington held a council of war with generals Lafayette, Wayne, and Green prior to engaging the British at Chadd's Ford, Pennsylvania.

The 1822 Montmorenci Staircase at Winterthur comes from a North Carolina home.

NEW CASTLE

The old capital of New Castle, six miles south of Wilmington on the Delaware River, preserves a beautiful grouping of eighteenth- and early nineteenth-century buildings—public edifices, a church, and private houses—around a green believed to have been laid out by Peter Stuyvesant in the 1650s. Portions of the rest of the town also date to the eighteenth and early nineteenth centuries, and in addition, New Castle boasts an extraordinarily fine eighteenth-century house built by George Read II. Its interior plasterwork ranks among the finest half-dozen examples in America.

In 1651 Peter Stuyvesant, governor of the Dutch settlement at New Amsterdam (later New York), intending to take control of the bay from the Swedes at Fort Christina (Wilmington), landed here with two hundred men and built a fort. He called the place New Amstel. In 1654 a Swedish ship took possession of New Amstel, but Stuyvesant returned again in 1655 and reasserted Dutch rule. Finally, in 1664, Sir Robert Carr, with two frigates, fired upon the Dutch fort, killing three of the twenty defenders. He seized the region for England's Duke of York, changing its name to New Castle. The Swedes, Finns, and Dutch were soon joined by English settlers and, in 1682, by William Penn, who carried authorization from the Duke of York to include the former Swedish and Dutch possessions in his domain of Pennsylvania.

In 1704 New Castle was made the seat of government for Pennsylvania's "Lower Counties," the three counties that, in 1776, joined to form the state of Delaware. The convention that formed the state met here and selected New Castle as the capital; fear of British attack prompted the government's eventual move to Dover.

Revolutionary spirit was strong in this region: Before the Revolution, New Castle's residents collected £200 to send to Boston when that city's port was ordered closed in reprisal for the Boston Tea Party. At the outbreak of the Revolution, the royal portraits that had adorned the courthouse chambers were publicly burned in bonfires on the green. Any Loyalists were kept silent by the presence of the Delaware Regiment, which had marched from Wilmington to oversee the demonstration. British warships were often in sight off New Castle, and one of them swooped down on the shore in 1777 and seized John McKinly, president of the state.

After the Revolution, New Castle stood at the junction of an important trade and travel route between Philadelphia, Annapolis,

Baltimore, and Washington. Stagecoaches traversed a turnpike across the Delmarva Peninsula from Frenchtown on the Chesapeake Bay to New Castle's wharves on the Delaware. In 1832 a railroad line was opened alongside the turnpike, but new roads and railroad lines created direct links between Philadelphia and Baltimore and ended New Castle's importance as a stopping point.

Old Court House

Standing with its back to the green is the Old Court House, Delaware's colonial capitol. Built in 1732, the simple two-and-a-half-story brick building is unadorned but for a cupola and a small balcony over the central entrance. A large courtroom on the first floor has been restored to its eighteenth-century appearance. A small adjacent room holds a few display cases with artifacts unearthed locally. Information on walking tours is available here.

LOCATION: Delaware Street. HOURS: 10–3:30 Tuesday–Saturday, 1:30–4:30 Sunday. FEE: None. TELEPHONE: 302–323–4453.

New Castle's Old Courthouse. The octagonal cupola served as the focus from which surveyors drew the arc forming the state's northern border.

New Castle green with the spire of Immanuel Episcopal Church. The church's serene interior, opposite, has been restored to its ca. 1820 appearance.

Adjacent to the Old Court House is the 1823 **Town Hall,** a square brick building with an arched arcade through its first floor. The arcade once gave access to market stalls behind the hall, but these stalls were torn down in the 1880s.

New Castle's **green** is dominated by the sturdy square tower and spire of **Immanuel Episcopal Church,** built in 1703 and restored in the early 1980s after it was heavily damaged in a fire. The interior is a reconstruction of the original, with a high vaulted ceiling and arched windows. The church is surrounded by a graveyard with many eighteenth- and nineteenth-century burials. On the south side of the green stands the **Arsenal** (now a restaurant), built by the federal government in 1809, and the **New Castle Presbyterian Church** (25 Second Street, 302–328–3279) built in 1707. Facing the church from the north side of the green across Third Street is the **Old Library Museum** (302–322–2794), a hexagonal brick building put up in 1892 as the town library. It now houses exhibits about the history of the town and the state.

Facing the green along Third Street is a row of brick houses dating to the eighteenth and early nineteenth centuries. All are

private except the **Old Dutch House** (32 Third Street, 302–322–2794). Its steeply pitched roof and overhanging eaves are distinctly Dutch in style. Town records indicate it was standing as early as 1704, but no record of its construction survives.

One block north of the green, the **Amstel House Museum** (Fourth and Delaware streets, 302–322–2794) has several rooms of eighteenth-century household artifacts. The earliest portion of the building may date to the 1680s; the main section was constructed in the 1730s. George Washington attended a wedding here in 1784.

One block south of the green is **The Strand,** lined with a group of brick houses constructed after a fire swept the street in 1824. From The Strand, Alexander's Alley and Packet Alley once led down to wharves at the river. The Strand is also the location of New Castle's finest house, the George Read II House.

George Read II House and Garden

The house was built between 1797 and 1804, in the style of an elegant Philadelphia townhouse, by George Read II. He hired a Philadelphia carpenter, Peter Crouding, to work out detailed plans for the house and to supervise its construction. The first-floor rooms have thirteen-foot-high ceilings, marble fireplaces, softwood floors, profuse plaster ornamentation, and finely carved woodwork. The color scheme has been restored to the original bright colors—salmon pink, Prussian blue, and light yellow among them. The decoration of the dining room dates to the 1920s, when the house was refurbished. The restorers decided to maintain this room—which features scenic wallpaper painted in 1927—as both a tribute to the twentieth-century owners and an example of Colonial Revival taste. The restored taproom in the basement also dates to the 1920s. The gardens were designed in 1847 by Robert and David Buist in the style of the landscape architect Andrew Jackson Downing.

George Read II, who was an attorney, began work on the house when he was 32, apparently expecting it to be the headquarters for a brilliant political career. In fact, he never attained the influence and power of his father, a signer of the Declaration of Independence and one of Delaware's leading political figures.

LOCATION: 42 The Strand. HOURS: March through December: 10–4 Tuesday–Saturday, 12–4 Sunday; January through February: 10–4 Saturday, 12–4 Sunday. FEE: Yes. TELEPHONE: 302-322-8411.

FORT DELAWARE STATE PARK

Located on Pea Patch Island, a mile off Delaware City, Fort Delaware is a massive pentagonal fortress that was completed in 1859 and used in the Civil War as a prison for captured Confederates. At one time, 12,500 men were held in the fort and on the island. During the war some 2,700 prisoners died here from cholera and other diseases. The granite walls are surrounded by a moat, yet numerous prisoners escaped to the Delaware shore where they were given aid by Southern sympathizers.

LOCATION: Pea Patch Island. Access to park by boat only; boat leaves from park office on Clinton Street, Delaware City. HOURS: Wednesday–Sunday, phone for specifics. FEE: Yes, for boat. TELEPHONE: 302–834–7941.

Two cannon at Fort Delaware. OVERLEAF: *The moat, which gives the fort the appearance of hovering over Pea Patch Island, proved only a slight obstacle to Confederate prisoners who were intent on escape.*

Old Drawyer's Church, Odessa.

ODESSA

A busy commercial center in the eighteenth and nineteenth centuries, Odessa then went into a decline after it was bypassed by the
railroad. In the 1930s a former resident, H. Rodney Sharp, began
purchasing and restoring historic houses in the town and moving
other historic buildings here. Sharp donated several properties to
Winterthur Museum from 1958 to 1966, and the museum acquired
others from Odessa.

Historic Houses of Odessa

Three buildings under the auspices of Winterthur are regularly
open to the public. The **Corbit-Sharp House,** completed in 1774
for a very successful tanner named William Corbit, is a two-and-a-
half-story brick mansion with an elegant facade, dormer windows,
and a roof balustrade with Chinese Chippendale fretwork. It is an
unusually well-documented property since the family saved the
original bills for its construction, along with room-by-room inven-
tories. The house is furnished with many original family heirlooms
as well as regional pieces of the period. The house is also notable

Barn on the grounds of the Corbit-Sharp house.

for its fine woodwork. The **Wilson-Warner House,** while not as elegant as its neighbor, has been restored according to an 1828 bankruptcy-sale document. **Brick Hotel Gallery** across the street displays a large collection of Rococo Revival furniture by the well-known New York cabinetmaker John Henry Belter.

> LOCATION: Second and Main Streets. HOURS: March through December: 10–4 Tuesday–Saturday, 1–4 Sunday. FEE: Yes. TELE-PHONE: 302–378–4069.

North of Odessa is one of the state's finest eighteenth-century churches, the **Old Drawyer's Church** (Route 13). The church was begun in 1773, but portions of the interior were built in the 1830s.

    Old St. Ann's Episcopal Church (Route 14, west of Odessa, 302–378–2401) is a simple brick church built in 1768. The interior includes a slave gallery. South of Odessa, the town of **Smyrna,** a prosperous commercial center in the eighteenth and early nineteenth centuries, declined in the latter part of the century. Several houses (private) built in the late 1700s can be seen along Main and Mt. Vernon streets. The **Allee House** (southeast of Smyrna on Route 9, just south of Route 6, 302–653–9345) is a mid-eighteenth-century plantation house open to the public for limited hours.

DOVER

The fear that the British would invade northern Delaware in 1777 caused the state capital to be moved from New Castle to a succession of safer sites. Political pressure from the southern counties led to Dover being selected as the permanent capital in 1781. This Kent County community was laid out according to William Penn's plan in 1718. Court House Square, part of Penn's original plan, is now called the **Green** and is still the town's center of activity. From there, in 1775, Delaware's hard-fighting Continental Regiment marched off to the Revolutionary War. On December 7, 1787, in the Golden Fleece Tavern located on the Green, Delaware became the first state to ratify the United States Constitution.

On the eastern side of the Green stand court buildings and the **Old State House.** This building, completed in 1792, served as the state capitol for over 140 years. The gambrel-roofed Georgian brick building—with a Palladian window over the doorway and an octagonal cupola housing a bell cast in 1763—was extensively restored in 1976. The work included reconstruction of a curving

The graceful double staircase in the first-floor courtroom of the Old State House, Dover.

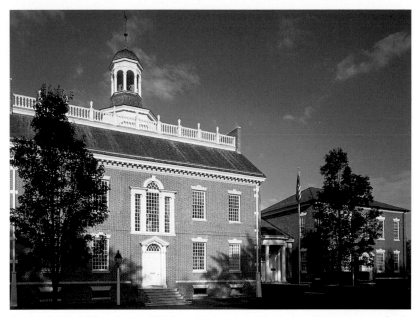

During the Civil War, Dover's Old State House was briefly used by Union troops to detain some local leaders who espoused secession.

staircase in the courtroom on the first floor and the furnishing of the house and senate chambers with pre-1815 antiques and reproductions in the style of that period. Tours of the State House begin at the **Visitor Center** behind the Old State House (302–739–4266). The center has exhibits concerning state history and also provides information about tours of all the state museums as well as the **Hall of Records** (Duke of York Street), where the colony's royal charter is displayed along with a large painting of the departure of the Continental troops from the Green.

One block south of the Green is **Christ Episcopal Church** (Water and South State streets, 302–734–5731), built in 1734 but extensively altered in the late 1850s, when the original pews were removed, and in 1876, when its tower was added. North of the Green, the governor's mansion, a 1791 house named **Woodburn** (151 Kings Highway, 302–739–5656) is open by appointment.

West of the green are **Delaware State Museums** properties. The Meeting House Galleries in the 1790 Presbyterian Church and the 1880 Sunday School building are on Meeting House Square, part of Penn's plan. One features archaeology, the other life in the early 1900s. The Johnson Victrola Museum honors Eldridge Johnson, founder of the Victor Talking Machine Company in 1901. Exhibits include Victrolas and early records.

Delaware Agricultural Museum

This reconstruction of a typical nineteenth-century Delaware farm features buildings and structures that were moved to, or replicated on, the museum's grounds; they include an 1893 farmhouse, a barn built in the late 1800s, a blacksmith shop of the 1850s, and a reconstructed mill. The museum sponsors numerous special events, some focusing on seasonal activities such as planting and harvesting, and demonstrations of milling and blacksmithing.

> LOCATION: 866 North duPont Highway. HOURS: April through December: 10–4 Tuesday–Saturday, 1–4 Sunday; January through March: 10–4 Monday–Friday. FEE: Yes. TELEPHONE: 302–734–1618.

JOHN DICKINSON PLANTATION

John Dickinson, known as the "pen of the Revolution," grew up in this plantation house built by his father in 1740. Dickinson set forth

The John Dickinson Plantation, also known as Kingston-upon-Hull.

the American view on the Stamp Act and England's tax policies in the "Declaration of Rights and Grievances," the "Petition to the King," and the fourteen "Farmer's Letters." Although he decided to vote against the Declaration of Independence, he volunteered for military duty at the outbreak of the Revolution. His plantation house, one of the largest in the colony, has been restored. The plantation is a property of the Delaware State Museums.

LOCATION: Kitts Hummock Road, six miles south of Dover. HOURS: March through December: 10–3:30 Tuesday–Saturday, 1:30–4:30 Sunday. FEE: None. TELEPHONE: 302–739–3277.

The small agricultural town of **Camden** was laid out in 1783 by a Quaker named Daniel Mifflin. Several late-eighteenth-century brick houses (private) may be seen in the town, off Route 113.

BARRATT'S CHAPEL

In November 1784 sacramental bread and wine were administered by two Methodist ministers to an American congregation for the first time, an event that marked the beginning of Methodism in this country. The ministers were acting on the instructions of Methodism's English founder, John Wesley. Present in the chapel was Francis Asbury, a preacher who had done much to spread the sect in America. Richard Allen, a former slave from the Dover area, later organized in Philadelphia one of the first Africa Methodist Episcopal churches. Barratt's Chapel, a sturdily handsome brick building, was built in 1780.

LOCATION: Route 113, about a mile north of Frederica. HOURS: 1:30–4:30 Saturday–Sunday; other times by appointment. FEE: None. TELEPHONE: 302–335–5544.

LEWES

The Delaware Bay maritime town of Lewes was settled by twenty-eight Dutchmen in 1631. They planted crops, raised cows, traded with the Indians for furs, and hunted whales. Their little settlement, called Zwaanendael ("the place of swans"), was wiped out by an Indian attack soon after its establishment. Only one man survived. The **De Vries Monument** (Pilottown Road) is a memorial, erected in 1909, to the men killed in the attack. In 1659 a fort was built here to prevent the English from settling on the site, but the English seized the town in 1664. For the rest of that century, and into the eighteenth, the town prospered from its trade in grain, meat, and timber. Its subsequent history was peaceful, except for a bombardment by the British during the War of 1812 when the townspeople refused to provide supplies. Throughout its history, however, the nearby shore has been the scene of shipwrecks. In 1987 salvagers raised the hull of the *De Braak*. Originally a Dutch cutter, it was captured and outfitted as a brig by the British, but it sank during a sudden storm in 1798. The ship's cargo of copper and cocoa was lost and half the crew plus the captain, James Drew, were drowned; the captain is buried in the Presbyterian cemetery. When the railroad reached Lewes in 1869, the town's shipping business declined, but it continued to be the home port of pilots who guided ships up the Delaware Bay and River to Philadelphia.

In 1931, to commemorate the three-hundredth anniversary of the Dutch settlement, the state built a replica of the town hall of Hoorn, in the Netherlands. Called the **Zwaanendael Museum** (Savannah Road and King's Highway, 302–645–1148), it houses a museum of local history. The gambrel-roofed **Fisher-Martin House** (Zwaanendael Park), a valuable example of the colony's rural architecture, was built about 1728 in the nearby town of Cool Spring. From 1736 to 1959 it was occupied by members of the Martin family. Moved to this site in 1980, it now serves as a visitor center. Six eighteenth-century structures are in the **Lewes Historical Society Complex** (Third and Shipcarpenter streets, 302–645–7670), including the **Thompson Country Store Museum Shops** and the **Rabbit's Ferry House,** home of the Tricia Hurt Gallery of Fine Arts. The Society also owns the **Coast Guard Lifesaving Station** and the *Overfalls* **Lightship,** which is docked at the foot of Shipcarpenter Street; the **Doctor's Office,** which exhibits antique medical items, on Market Street; and the **Cannonball Maritime Museum** on Front Street, in a house hit during the War of 1812 bombardment. The **Burton-Ingram House** displays furniture of the eighteenth and nineteenth centuries. Georgetown's 1839 Greek Revival courthouse (The Circle) is the site of a biannual ceremony known as Return Day. After the reading, the winners and losers parade through the town in antique carriages and cars.

Christ Church Broad Creek (Route 24, three miles east of Laurel) is unchanged since it was built of unpainted heart-of-pine in 1771. By 1850 this Episcopal church had ceased to hold services because its members had moved to the more conveniently located St. Philip's Church in Laurel or had joined the Methodist church.

MILLSBORO

The **Nanticoke Indian Museum** (Route 24, 302–945–7022) displays spears, arrowhead, corn baskets, and regalia used by the tribe that have been gathered to preserve their heritage. Most of the tribe departed the region by the mid-1800s; today only a few hundred remain. The Nanticoke hold an annual powwow in Oak Orchard during the weekend after Labor Day. South of Millsboro, in Dagsboro, is **Prince George's Chapel** (Route 26, 302–732–6835), which has been altered only slightly since 1757.

The **Fenwick Island Lighthouse** (Fenwick Island, off Route 54, 302–539–8129), built in 1859, was in use until 1979. On the south side of the light stands a colonial boundary marker, set in place in 1751 to denote the border between Delaware side of the stone bears the crest of the proprietor, William Penn; on the Maryland side is the crest of the Calverts. It was at this spot that Charles Mason and Jeremiah began their survey of the boundary line in 1763.

Notes on Architecture

EARLY COLONIAL

In the eastern colonies, Europeans first built houses using a medieval, vertical asymmetry, which in the eighteenth century evolved toward classical symmetry. Roofs were gabled

and hipped, often with prominent exterior chimneys. Small casement windows became larger and more evenly spaced and balanced on each facade. Early English settlers in Virginia and Maryland built with stone or brick, rather than with wood.

GEORGIAN

Beginning in Boston as early as 1686, and only much later elsewhere, the design of houses became balanced about a central axis, with only careful, stripped detail. A few large houses incorporated

double-story pilasters. Sash windows with rectilinear panes replaced casements. Hipped roofs accentuated the balanced and strict proportions inherited from Italy and Holland via England and Scotland.

FEDERAL

The post-Revolutionary style sometimes called "Federal" was more flexible and delicate than the more formal Georgian. It was rooted in archaeological discoveries at Pompeii and Herculaneum in Italy in the 1750s, as well as in contemporary French interior planning principles. As it evolved toward the Regency,

rooms became shaped as polygons, ovals, and circles and acquired ornamentation in the forms of urns, garlands, and swags. Lacking the strong color of English and Scottish prototypes, this style was sweetly elegant; a fan-shaped window over the door is its most characteristic detail.

GREEK REVIVAL

The Greek Revival manifested itself in severe, stripped, rectilinear proportions, occasionally a set of columns or pilasters, and even in a few instances

Greek-temple form. It was used in official buildings and in many private houses. It combined Greek and Roman forms—low pitched pediments, simple moldings, rounded arches, and shallow domes.

GOTHIC REVIVAL

After about 1830, darker colors, asymmetry, broken skylines, verticality, and the pointed arch began to appear. New machinery produced carved

and pierced trim along the eaves. Roofs became steep and gabled; "porches" or "piazzas" became more spacious. Oriel and bay windows became common and there was greater use of stained glass.

ITALIANATE

The Italianate style began to appear in the 1840s, both in a formal, balanced "palazzo" style, and in a picturesque "villa" style. Both had round-headed windows and arcaded porches. Commercial structures were often made of cast iron, with a ground floor of large arcaded windows, and smaller windows on each successive rising story.

387

SECOND EMPIRE

After 1860, Parisian fashion inspired American builders to use mansard roofs, dark col-

ors, and varied textures, including shingles, tiles, and increasing use of ironwork, especially on balconies and skylines. With their ornamental quoins, balustrades, pavilions, pediments, columns, and pilasters, Second Empire buildings recalled many historical styles.

QUEEN ANNE STYLE

The Queen Anne style emphasized contrasts of form, texture, and color. Large encircling verandas, tall chimneys, turrets, towers, and a multitude of textures are

typical of the style. The ground floor might be of stone or brick, the upper floors stucco, shingle, or clapboard. Specially shaped bricks and plaques were used for decoration. Panels of stained glass outlined or filled the windows. The steep roofs were gabled or hipped, and

other elements like pediments, Venetian windows, and front and corner bay windows were typical.

SHINGLE STYLE

The Shingle Style bore the stamp of a new generation of professional architects led by Henry Hobson Richardson (1838-1886). Sheathed in wooden shingles, its forms were smoothed and unified. Verandas, turrets, and complex roofs were sometimes used, but thoroughly integrated into a whole that emphasized uniformity of surface rather than a jumble of forms. The style was a domestic and informal expression of what became known in town mansions and official buildings as Richardson Romanesque.

RICHARDSON ROMANESQUE

Richardson Romanesque made use of the massive forms and ornamental details of the Romanesque: rounded arches, towers, stone and brick facing. The solidity and gravity of masses were accentuated by deep recesses for windows and entrances, by rough stone masonry, stubby columns, strong horizontals, rounded towers with conical caps, and botanical, repetitive ornament.

RENAISSANCE REVIVAL OR BEAUX ARTS

Later in the 1880s and 1890s, American architects who had studied at the Ecole des Beaux Arts in Paris brought a new Renaissance Revival to the United States. Sometimes used in urban mansions, but

generally reserved for city halls and academic buildings, it borrowed from three centuries of Renaissance detail, much of it French, and put together picturesque combinations from widely differing periods.

Illustrations: Column One: Adam Thoroughgood House (top), Westover (bottom); Column Two: Homewood (top), Basilica of the Assumption (bottom); Column Three: Old City Hall, Richmond; Column Four: Old Executive Office Building (top), Oakland B & O Railroad Station (bottom); Column Six: U.S. Naval Academy Chapel.

I N D E X

Numbers in italics indicate illustrations; numbers in boldface indicate maps.

Aberdeen, MD, 330
Abram's Delight, 230
Accokeek, MD, 284
Adams, Henry, 74, 76, 96
Adams, John, 65
Adams, John Quincy, 35, 333
Adams, Marion Hooper "Clover," 96
African Art Museum. *See* National Museum of African Art
Agecroft Hall, 164
Air and Space Museum. *See* National Air and Space Museum
Alexandria, VA, 20, 118-23, *118, 119, 121*
All Saints Episcopal Rectory and Church, Frederick, MD, 337-38
Allee House, 379
Allegany County: Courthouse, 348; Public Library, 348
American Art Museum. *See* National Museum of American Art
American History Museum. *See* National Museum of American History
Amos Mill, 329
Amstel House Museum, 374
Anacostia Museum, 43
Anderson, Larz, House/Society of the Cincinnati, 94-95, *94*
Anderson, Marion, 64
Annapolis, MD, *255,* **258-59,** *260,* 263, *264,* 265-68, *269, 270,* 271-72, *273,* 274-75, *274,* 276, 277, *278,* 279, *279,* 280, *281*
Antietam Creek, MD, 333; National

Battlefield, 342, *343,* 344-45, *344;* National Cemetery, 345
Apple's United Church of Christ, Thurmont, MD, 340
Appomattox Court House National Historical Park, VA, 241
Appomattox Manor Plantation, 178
Argall, Samuel, 352
Arlington, VA, 105-07, *106, 108-09*
Arlington House, 105-07, *106*
Arlington National Cemetery, 106, 107, *108-09*
Arnold, Benedict, 148, 173, 212
Arts and Industries Building, Washington, DC, 50
Ash Lawn—Highland, 247

Bachelor's Hope, 285, *285*
Bacon, Nathaniel, 100
Bacon's Castle, 223
Bacon's Rebellion, 100, 206, 223
Ball's Bluff, VA, Battle of, 110
Baltimore, Cecil, Lord. *See* Calvert, Cecil
Baltimore, MD, *298,* 300-01, **302-03,** 304-06, *307,* 308-16, *311, 312-13, 317,* 318-22, *319, 323,* 324-26, *325;* City Hall, 310, *311;* Courthouse, 310
Baltimore Center for Urban Archaeology, 321
Baltimore Maritime Museum, 322
Baltimore Museum of Art, 314-15
Baltimore Museum of Industry, 310

Baltimore & Ohio Railroad, 304, 305, 326
Baltimore & Ohio Railroad Museum, Baltimore, MD, *298,* 310
Baltimore & Ohio Railroad Station, Oakland, MD, 349, *349*
Baltimore & Ohio Railroad Station, Museum, Ellicott City, MD, 331
Baltimore Streetcar Museum, 311
Bancroft, George, 265, 274
Banks, Nathaniel P., 226, 227, 234
Banneker, Benjamin, 26, 262, 267
Banneker-Douglass Museum of Afro-American Life and History, 267
Barras, Admiral de, 212
Barratt's Chapel, Frederica, DE, 383-84
Bartholdi Fountain, Washington, DC, 37
Barton, Clara, National Historic Site, 331, *332,* 333
Basilica of the Assumption, Baltimore, MD, 311-12, *386*
Bassett Hall, 191
Battle Monument, Baltimore, MD, 310
Bauduy, Pierre, 358, 359, 365
Beall-Dawson House, 334
Beauregard, Pierre, 113, 174
Bel Air, MD, 329

Belle Grove Plantation, 230, *232*, 233
Berkeley, William, 100, 206
Berkeley Plantation, 183-84
Blair-Lee House, 74
Blandford Church, Petersburg, VA, 173, 177, *177*
B'nai B'rith Klutznick National Jewish Museum, 95
B'nai Israel Synagogue, Baltimore, MD, 316
Boonsboro, MD, 342
Boonsboro Museum of History, 342
Booth, John Wilkes, 80, 284
Botetourt, Governor, 189, 198
Bowers Beach, DE, 383
Braddock, Edward, 120, 335, 347
Brandon Plantation, 178
Brandy Station, VA, Battle of, 140
Brick Hotel Gallery, Odessa, DE, 379
Brookneal, VA, 239
Brown, John, 345
Brumidi, Constantino, 33, 34
Brunswick, MD, 342
Brunswick Museum, 342
Brush-Everard House, 197
Bruton Parish Church, Williamsburg, VA, 196, *196, 197*

Building Museum. *See* National Building Museum
Bulfinch, Charles, 32
Bull Run, VA: First Battle of, 113-14; Second Battle of, 113, 114-15

Burnside, Ambrose, 135, 136, 175
Burton-Ingram House, 385
Byrd, William II, 148, 173, 184
Byrd, William III, 239

Calhoun, John C., 35, 91
Calvert, Cecil, 256; portrait of, *257*
Calvert, Leonard, 256, 287, 288, 289
Calvert, Philip, 288
Calvert family, 260, 288, 326
Calvert Marine Museum, 287
Cambridge, MD, 296
Camden, DE, 383
Cannonball Maritime Museum, 385
Capitol, U.S., *28*, 29, *30-31*, 32-35, *32, 33*
Capitol Hill, Washington, DC: Anacostia Museum, 43; Capitol, U.S., *28*, 29, *30-31*, 32-35, *32, 33;* Cedar Hill, 43; Folger Shakespeare Library, 40, *40, 41;* Library of Congress, 38, *39;* Sewall-Belmont House, 37; Supreme Court Building, *36*, 37
Capitol Square, Richmond, VA, 153-56, *154, 155*
Carlyle House Historic Park, 119-20, *119*
Carroll, Charles, of Carrollton, 260, 263, 280, 313, 321; House (Annapolis, MD), 280; Mansion (Baltimore, MD), 321
Carroll, Charles, the Barrister, 267, 318; House (Annapolis, MD), 267

Carroll County Farm Museum, 334
Carroll Park, Baltimore, MD, 318, 319
Carter, George, 112
Carter, Robert "King," 145
Carter family, 179
Carter Mansion, Havre de Grace, MD, 330
Carter's Grove, Williamsburg, VA, 203
Casemate Museum, 218
Casselman Bridge, 349
Casselman Hotel, 349
Catoctin Iron Works, 340
Cedar Creek, VA, Battle of, 226, 230, 233
Cedar Hill, Washington, DC, 43
Centre Hill Mansion, 176
Centreville, MD, 291
Chanceford, 297
Chancellor's Point Natural History Area, St. Mary's City, MD, 289
Chancellorsville, VA, Battle of, *134*, 136-37, *137*
Chantilly, VA, 110
Chaptico, MD, 285, *285*
Charles City, VA, 183
Charlottesville, VA, 243, *244-45*, 246-47, *246;* environs of, 247-50, *248-49, 250, 251*, 252-53, *253*
Chase, Samuel, 263, 271
Chase-Lloyd House, 271
Chatham, 139-40
Chesapeake City, MD, 290
Chesapeake & Ohio Canal, 301, 304
Chesapeake & Ohio Canal Boat Replica, Cumberland, MD, 348
Chesapeake & Ohio Canal National Historical Park,

Cumberland, MD,
348
Chesapeake & Ohio
Canal National
Historical Park,
Potomac, MD, 89,
333
Chesapeake Bay
Maritime Museum,
295, *295*
Chesapeake, 322
Chestertown, MD,
290-91, *291*
Chickahominy Bluff,
Richmond, VA,
172
151, 168
Chippokes Plantation
State Park, 223
Christ Church,
Alexandria, VA, 120
Christ Church,
Irvington, VA, 145
Christ Church,
Washington, DC, 42
Christ Church Broad
Creek, Laurel, DE,
385
Christ Episcopal
Church, Dover, DE,
381
Chrysler Museum, 220-
21, *220*
Cincinnati, Society of
the, 94
City Point National
Cemetery, Hopewell,
VA, 178
Civil War, 24, 79, 92-93,
105, 112, 118, 121-22,
129, 178, 179, 183,
184, 190, 218, 219,
220, 226, 234, 267,
275, 290, 304, 318,
326, 334, 335, 339,
348, 375; Antietam
Creek, MD, 342, *343*,
344-45, *344*; Ball's
Bluff, VA, 110;
Brandy Station, VA,
140; Bull Run, VA,
113-15; Cedar Creek,
VA, 226, 230, 233;

Chancellorsville, VA,
134, 136-37, *137*; Cold
Harbor, VA, 172; Fort
Darling, VA, 173;
Fredericksburg, VA,
131, 135-36; Gaines'
Mill, VA, 172;
Hampton Roads, VA,
216-17; Malvern Hill,
VA, 172; Manassas,
VA, 113-15; New
Market, VA, 234, 236;
Peninsula Campaign,
172, 214; Petersburg,
VA, 174-76, *174*;
Richmond, VA, 168,
169, 172-73; Savage
Station, VA, 172;
Sayler's Creek, VA,
239, 241; Seven Pines,
VA, 172; Spotsylvania
Court House, VA,
139; Wilderness, VA,
137-38; Winchester,
VA, 226-27, 230;
Yorktown, VA, *208*,
209, 214
Clarksville, VA, 239
Clarysville Bridge, 348
Clarysville Inn, 348
Clay, Henry, 35, 74
Clinton, MD, 282
Codman House, 95
Cold Harbor, VA, Battle
of, 172
College of William and
Mary, 188, 200, *201*
Colonial National
Historical Park,
Jamestown, VA, 206,
207, 208, *210-11*, 212,
214
Colonial Williamsburg.
See Williamsburg, VA
Colton's Point, MD, 287
Columbia Historical
Society, Washington,
DC, 93
Colvin Run Mill, 110
Concord Point
Lighthouse, 330
Constellation, 322, *323*,
324
Cooch's Bridge, 369

Coolidge, Calvin, 27, 67
Corbit-Sharp House,
378, *379*
Corcoran Gallery of Art,
71-72
Cornwallis, Charles, 104,
173, 212, 369;
painting of, *213*
Courthouse Square,
Fredericksburg, MD,
337-38
Courtyard Exhibition
Center, 321
Critz, VA, 238
Cross Keys, VA, 235
Culpeper, VA, 139
Culpeper Museum of
History, 140
Cumberland, MD, 301,
333, 347-48
Custis, George Washington
Parke, 105, 106
Dagsboro, DE, 385
Danville, VA, 238
DAR Museum,
Washington, DC, 71
Darlington, MD, 331
Davidge Hall, 312
Davis, Jefferson, 151,
153, 156, 159, 172,
176, 218, 238
De La Warr, Lord, 352
De Vries Monument,
Lewes, DE, 384
Decatur, Stephen, 74,
75, 76, 275
Decatur House, 75-76,
75
Delaware, **8-9**, *350*, 352-
53, **354-55**, 356-60,
357, *361*, 362, *362*,
363, *364*, 365, *366-67*,
368-72, *368*, *369*, *371*,
372, *373*, 374-75, *375*,
376-77, 378-85, *378*,
379, *380*, *381*, *382*
Delaware Academy of
Medicine, 359-60
Delaware Agricultural
Museum, 382
Delaware Art Museum,
359
Delaware City, DE, 375

Delaware State Museum, 381-82
Dewey, George, 277
Dickinson, John, 356, 382-83; Plantation, 382-83, *382*
Discovery, 207
District Court House, Washington, DC, 83
Douglass, Frederick, 26, 43, 267
Dover, DE, 380-83, *380, 381, 382;* Old State House, 380-81, *380, 381*
Drewry's Bluff, VA, 168, 173
Dumbarton House, 90
Dumbarton Oaks, *90, 91, 91*
Dunker Church, Sharpsburg, MD, *344, 345, 345*
Dunmore, Governor, 189, 196, 198, 219
duPont, Henry Francis, 365, 368-69
duPont, Samuel Francis, 92-93
Dupont Circle, Washington, DC, 92-93

Earleville, MD, 290
Early, Jubal, 24, 227, 230, 233, 234, 235, 335
Eastern Shore, MD, 262, 290-91, *291, 292-93, 294-97, 295, 297*
Easton, MD, 294
Edgewood, 183
Edinburg, VA, 234
1840 House, Baltimore, MD, 321
Eisenhower, Mamie, 67
Eleutherian Mills, 365
Elkridge, MD, 331
Ellicott City, MD, 331
Emmanuel Parish Church, Cumberland, MD, 347
Emmitsburg, MD, 346
Evangelical Reformed Church, Frederick, MD, 338

Farrand, Beatrix, 91
Federal Triangle, Washington, DC, 79
Fells Point, Baltimore, MD, 324
Fenwick Island Lighthouse, 385
Fire Museum of Maryland, 329
First Presbyterian Church, Wilmington, DE, 360
Fisher-Martin House, 384
Fitzgerald, F. Scott, 306, 334
Fitzgerald, Zelda, 334
Flagg, Ernest, 71, 275, 277
Flowerdew Hundred Foundation Museum, 178
Fluvanna County Courthouse, 243
Folger Shakespeare Library, 40, *40, 41*
Ford's Theater, 80
Fort Darling, VA, Battle of, 173
Fort Delaware State Park, DE, 375, *375, 376-77*
Fort Frederick, MD, 347
Fort Gilmer, VA, 173
Fort Harrison, VA, 172-73
Fort Lee, VA, 176
Fort Loudoun, VA, 230
Fort McHenry, MD, 300, 321, 324-26, *325;* aquatint of, *301*
Fort Monroe, VA, 218
Fort Severn, MD, 265, 274
Fort Stedman, VA, 176
Fort Stevens, Washington, DC, 24
Fort Ward Museum and Historic Site, VA, 123
Fort Washington Military Historical Park, MD, 282, *283*
Fort Wool, VA, 218-19
Four Locks, MD, 333

Franklin, Benjamin, 335
Frederica, DE, 384
Frederick County Court House, 338
Frederick, MD, 301, 334-35, *336,* 337-40
Fredericksburg, VA, 130-36, *132, 133, 135;* Battle of, 135-36
Fredericksburg and Spotsylvania National Military Park, 134-40, *134, 135, 137, 138*
Freer Gallery of Art, 57
French, Daniel Chester, 62, 64, 93
French and Indian Wars, 120, 226, 230, 335, 347
Fritchie, Barbara, 335, 339, 340; House and Museum, 339
Front Royal, VA, 234
Furnace Town, MD, 297

Gadsby's Tavern Museum, 120, *121*
Gaines' Mill, VA, Battle of, 172
Garber, Paul E., Facility, 282
Garfield, James A., 67
Geddes-Piper House, 291
Geddy, James, House Foundry and Silversmith Shop, 196
Georgetown, DE, 385
Georgetown, Washington, DC, 20, 88-92, *88, 90, 91,* 333
Georgetown University, 89
Gilbert, Cass, 37, 77
Glen Echo, MD, 333
Gloucester, VA, 215, *215*
Grant, Ulysses S., 24, 46, 79, 137, 138, 139, 172, 173, 174, 175, 178, 241; photograph of, *169*
Grant Memorial, 46
Grantsville, MD, 349
Great Falls Park, VA, 107

Guinea, VA, 142
Gunston Hall, 129-30, *129*

Hadfield, George, 42, 83, 86, 89, 105, 106
Hager, Jonathan, House and Museum, 341
Hagerstown, MD, 341
Hagley Museum, *364,* 365
Hale-Byrnes House, 369
Hamilton, Alexander, 212
Hammond-Harwood House, 265, 268, *269, 270,* 271
Hampton, VA, 218
Hampton National Historic Site, MD, 326, *327,* 328-29
Hampton Roads, VA, 216-23, *217, 219, 220, 222;* Battle of, 216-17
Hampton University, 218
Hancock, MD, 333
Harrison, Benjamin, 67, 184
Harrison, William Henry, 183-84, 185
Harrisonburg, VA, 235
Haupt, Enid A., gardens, Smithsonian Institution, *48-49*
Havre de Grace, MD, 330, *330,* 331
Hay, John, 74, 76
Hay-Adams Hotel, 76
Hayes, Rutherford B., 67
Hendrickson House Museum, 360
Henry, Joseph, 49-50
Henry, Patrick, 142, 148, 196, 198, 239; National Memorial, 239
Henry House Hill, Manassas, VA, 113, 115
Hessian Barracks, Frederick, MD, 340
Hillsman House, 241

Hirshhorn Museum and Sculpture Garden, 50-51
Historic St. Mary's City. *See* St. Mary's City
Historic Triangle. *See* Jamestown; Williamsburg; Yorktown
Historical Society of Washington, DC, 93
History House, Cumberland, MD, 348
Hoban, James, 66, 67
Hollingsworth Mill House, 230
Hollywood, MD, 287
Hollywood Cemetery, Richmond, VA, 153
Homewood, *312-13,* 313-14, *386*
Hooker, Joseph "Fighting Joe," 136, 137, 139
Hopewell, VA, 178
Howard County Courthouse, Ellicott City, MD, 331

Immanuel Episcopal Church, New Castle, DE, 372, *372, 373*
Ironsides, MD, 284
Irvington, VA, 145

Jackson, Andrew, 29, 67
Jackson, Lillie Carroll, Museum, 324
Jackson, Thomas J. "Stonewall," 113, 114, 136, 137, 142, 226, 227, 234, 236, 338, 339, 342; Headquarters Museum, 230, *235;* Memorial Cemetery, 235; photograph of, *233;* Shrine, 142; townhouse of, 235

James River plantations, *146,* 178-79, *180-81, 182,* 183-85, *185*
Jamestown, VA, *14-15,* 100, 188, **191,** 203-04, 206, *207,* 208; Church Tower, *205;* Island, *14-15,* 206
Jamestown Settlement, 206, *207,* 208
Jefferson, Thomas, 26, 86, 165, 178, 189, 198, 233, 236, 267, 320; and Monticello, 247-48, 249, 250, 252, 253; at Poplar Forest, 241-42; portrait of (Peale), *227;* and the University of Virginia, 243, 246; and Virginia's state capitol, 153-54; and Washington, DC, 21, 29, 38; and the White House, 65, 66, 67
Jefferson Memorial, *18,* 64, *65*
Jersey Toll House, 331
Jerusalem Mills, 329
Jewish Museum, Baltimore, MD, 316
Johns Hopkins University, 305-06
Johnson, Andrew, 79, 284
Johnston, Joseph E., 172, 214
Jones, John Paul, 272, 277, 279

Kalorama, Washington, DC, 92, 93-97, *94, 97*
Kemp Hall, Frederick, MD, 338
Kenmore, 132-33, *133*
Kennedy, Jacqueline, 67-68
Kennedy, John F., 107
Kennedy Farmhouse, 345
Kernstown, VA, 226
Key, Francis Scott, 300, 324, 325, 335, 338, 340
King, Martin Luther, Jr., 64

Korean War Veterans Memorial, 61

LaFarge, John, 96, 309, 310
Lafayette, 165, 173, 190, 197, 212
Lafayette Square, Washington, DC, 74-77, *75*
Latrobe, Benjamin H.,331
Latrobe, Benjamin Henry, 42, 92, 121, 246, 311-12, 315; and Lafayette Square (Washington, DC), 74, 75, 76; and U.S. Capitol, 29, 32, 35; and White House, 67
Laurel, DE, 385
Lee, Light Horse Harry, 104, 107, 120, 143, 145, 179, 300, 356
Lee, Robert E., 74-75, 105, 106, 115, 120, 121, 135, 145, 151, 179, 218, 235, 236; at Antietam, 342, 344, 345; at Appomattox Court House, 241; Boyhood Home, 120; at Chancellorsville, 136, 137; Memorial, 105; and the Peninsula Campaign, 172; at Petersburg, 174, 175, 176; at Spotsylvania Courthouse, 139; statue of, *152;* at Wilderness, 138
Lee, Thomas, 110, 142, 143
Lee family, 143
Lee-Fendall House, 121
Leesburg, VA, 110
L'Enfant, Pierre Charles, 20, 29, 34, 44
Lewes, DE, 352, 384-85
Lewes Historical Complex, Lewes, DE, 385
Lewis, Meriwether, 68
Lexington, VA, 235, *235,* 236

Library of Congress, 38, *39*
Lincoln, Abraham, 24, 80, 113, 114, 135, 136, 151, 178, 219, 227, 304, 337, 344, 345; photograph of, *305*
Lincoln, VA, 112
Lincoln Memorial, 45, 62, *63,* 64
Lincoln Park, Washington, DC, 42
Linden Row, Richmond, VA, 149
Lloyd Street Synagogue, Baltimore, MD, 316
Lonaconing, MD, 348
Lonaconing Iron Furnace, 348
Long, Robert, House, 324
Lorton, VA, 128-30, *129*
Loudoun Museum, 110
Lovely Lane Methodist Church, Baltimore, MD, 316, *317*
Loy's Station Bridge, 340
Lutherville, MD, 329
Lyceum, Alexandria, VA, 119
Lynchburg, VA, 242

MacArthur, Douglas, Memorial, 221-22
McClellan, George B., 114, 135, 172, 179, 184, 214, 227, 344; photograph of, *305*
McDowell, Irvin, 113, 227
Macedonian Monument, U.S. Naval Academy, 275
McKim, Charles, 67, 68
McLean House, *240*
MacMillan Commission, 27, 45
Madison, Dolley, 66, 74, 87, 90, 140
Madison, James, 87, 140, 233; Museum, 142
Mall, The, Washington, DC, **23,** 27, 44-52, *44-45, 47, 48-49, 51, 53,*

54-55, 56-59, *58, 60,* 61-62, *62, 63,* 64-72, *65, 66, 68, 69, 73,* 74
Malvern Hill, VA, Battle of, 172
Manassas National Battlefield, VA, 113-15, *114, 115, 116-17*
Marbury, MD, 284
Marine Barracks, Washington, DC, 42
Marine Corps Air-Ground Museum, Quantico, VA, 130
Marine Corps Historical Center, Washington, DC, 43
Mariners' Museum, Newport News, VA, 217, *217*
Market House, Annapolis, MD, 280
Marshall, George C., Museum and Library, VMI, 236
Marshall, John, House, 162
Marye's Heights, VA, 135, 136, 137, *138,* 139
Maryland, **8-9, 258-59, 302-03;** eastern, 256, 260, *260,* 262; northern, 326, *327,* 328-31, *330;* northwestern, 331, *332,* 333-35, *336,* 337-42, *341, 343,* 344-49, *344, 345, 346, 349;* southern, *261,* 282, *283,* 284-85, *285, 286,* 287-90, *289;* state house, 263, *264,* 265-66. *See also* Annapolis; Baltimore; Eastern Shore
Maryland Dove, 288-89
Maryland Historical Society, 308-09
Mason, George, 129-30
Masonic Temple, Baltimore, MD, 309
Maymont, 164
Meadow Run Grist Mill, 247

Mencken House, 316,
318
Mercer, Hugh,
Apothecary, 131, *132*
Meredith House & Neild
Museum, 296
Michie Tavern, 247
Middletown, VA, 230,
232, 233
Miller House, 341
Mills, Robert, 59, 77, 82,
149, 156, 306, 337
Millsboro, DE, 385
Minuit, Peter, 352
Monroe, James, 32, 67,
130, 153, 247;
Museum, 131
Monticello, VA, *224*,
247-49, *248-49*, 250,
250, *251*, 252-53, *253*
Montpelier, VA, 140,
141, 142
Monument Avenue,
Richmond, VA, 153
Monumental Church,
Richmond, VA,
148-49
Moore House, 214
Morgan, Daniel, 104,
230
Morris, Robert, Inn, 295
Morse, Samuel F. B., 35,
50
Morven Park, 110, 112
Mount Clare Mansion,
318-19, *319*
Mount Harmon
Plantation, 290
Mount Hebron
Cemetery,
Winchester, VA, 230
Mount Jackson, VA, 234
Mount Olivet Cemetery,
Frederick, MD, 340
Mount Vernon, VA, *98*,
124, 125, *126-27*, 128
Mount Vernon District,
Baltimore, MD, 308
Mount Vernon Place
Methodist Church,
Baltimore, MD, 308
Mountain Lake Park,
MD, 349
Mudd, Dr. Samuel A.,

House, 284
Museum of the
Confederacy, 159
Museum of Hounds and
Hunting, 112
Museum Row,
Baltimore, MD, 321
Myers, Moses, House,
221

Nanticoke Indian
Museum, 385
Narrows, The,
Cumberland, MD, 347
Nassawango Iron
Furnace, 297
National Air and Space
Museum, 51-52, *51*
National Archives, *78*, 79
National Building
Museum, 82-83, *84-85*
National Cemetery,
Winchester, VA, 230
National Colonial Farm
Museum, 284
National Gallery of Art,
46-47, *47*
National Geographic
Society, 86
National Museum of
African Art, 58, *58*
National Museum of
American Art, 82
National Museum of
American History, *54-
55*, 56-57
National Museum of
Natural History, 52,
53, 56
National Portrait
Gallery, 81, *81*
Natural Bridge, VA,
236, *237*
Natural History
Museum. *See* National
Museum of Natural
History
Naval Academy. *See* U.S.
Naval Academy
Navy Museum,
Washington, DC, 42
Nelson House, 214
Nemours Mansion and
Gardens, 362, *363*

New Castle, DE, *350*,
370-72, *371*, *372*, *373*,
374; Old Court
House, 371, *371*;
Presbyterian Church,
372; Town Hall, 372
New Market Battlefield
Park, VA, 234
Newark, DE, 369
Newport News, VA, 217
Newton Historic District,
Salisbury, MD, 296
Nicholson, Francis, 188,
260, 263, 288
9 North Front Street,
Baltimore, MD, 321
Norfolk, VA, 216, 217,
219-22, *219*
Norrisville, MD, 329
Northern Neck, VA,
142-43, *144*, 145

Oak Hill Cemetery,
Washington, DC, 89
Oakland, MD, 349, *387*
Oakland Spring House,
315
Oatlands, 112
Ocean Hall, 285
Octagon House,
Washington, DC, 87, *87*
Odessa, DE, 378-79, *378*,
379
Old Asbury Methodist
Church, Wilmington,
DE, 360
Old City Hall,
Richmond, VA, 156,
157, *386*
Old Drawyer's Church,
Odessa, DE, *378*, 379
Old Durham Church,
Marbury, MD, 284
Old Dutch House, New
Castle, DE, 374
Old Executive Office
Building, Washington,
DC, 72, *387*
Old Library Museum,
New Castle, DE, *350*,
372
Old Lock Pump House,
Chesapeake City, MD,
290

Old Lutheran Church, Winchester, VA, 230
Old Otterbein United Methodist Church, Baltimore, MD, 319
Old Patent Office, Washington, DC, 82
Old Presbyterian Meeting House, Alexandria, VA, 121
Old St. Ann's Episcopal Church, Odessa, DE, 379
Old St. Paul's Episcopal Church, Baltimore, MD, 309
Old South Mountain Inn, 342
Old Stone House, Washington, DC, 89
Old Stone Jail, Palmyra, VA, 243
Old Swedes Church, Wilmington, DE, 360, 361
Old Town, Alexandria, VA, 118, 118
Old Town Hall and Market House, Fredericksburg, VA, 130-31
Old Trinity Church, St. Mary's City, MD, 289
Old Trinity Episcopal Church, Cambridge, MD, 296
Old Wye Church, Wye Mills, MD, 294
Olmsted, Frederick Law, 33
Orange, VA, 142
Overfalls Lightship, 385
Oxford Museum, 295
Oxford, MD, 295

Paca, William, 263; House, 254, 265, 272, 273
Palmyra, VA, 243
Parris, Alexander, 156, 159
Pasteur and Galt Apothecary Shop, 193
Paw Paw, WV, 347

Paw Paw Tunnel, 347
Pea Patch Island, DE, 375, 375, 376-77
Peale, Charles Willson, 125, 318-19, 319-20
Peale Museum, 319-20
Pemberton Hall, 296
Peninsula Campaign, 172, 214
Penn, William, 294, 370, 380
Pershing Park, 79
Petersburg, VA, 173-77, 174, 177; National Battlefield, 174-76
Petersen House, 80
Phillips Collection, 93
Poe, Edgar Allan, 148, 218, 247, 304, 306, 324; House and Museum (Baltimore, MD), 313; Museum (Richmond, VA), 168
Pohick Church, Lorton, VA, 128
Point Lookout State Park, 290
Polk, James K., 67
Pope, John Russell, 64, 308, 314
Poplar Forest, Lynchburg, VA, 241-42, 242
Poplar Hill Mansion, Salisbury, MD, 296
Port Republic, VA, 235
Port Tobacco, MD, 284-85
Port Tobacco Courthouse, 285
Potomac, MD, 333
Presbyterian Church, Fredericksburg, VA, 131
Prestwould Plantation, 239
Prince George's Chapel, Dagsboro, DE, 385
Princess Anne, MD, 296, 297
Prospect Hill, VA, 135, 135, 136
Purnell, Julia A., Museum, 297

Quantico, VA, 130
Queen Anne's County Courthouse, MD, 291

Raleigh Tavern, 193
Ramsay House, 119
Randolph, Peyton, House, 197
Read, George II, House and Garden, 374
Red Hill Shrine—The Patrick Henry National Memorial, 239
Renwick, James, 49, 72, 87, 89
Renwick Chapel, Washington, DC, 89
Renwick Gallery, 72, 73, 74
Revolutionary War, 104, 148, 165, 190, 196, 197, 218, 242, 252-53, 266, 277, 335, 340, 347, 353-54, 358, 370, 380; Newark, DE, 369; Norfolk, VA, 219-20; Petersburg, VA, 173; Yorktown, VA, 208, 210-11, 212, 213, 214-15
Reynolds Homestead, 238
Richmond, VA, 4, 105, 148-49, **150**, 151, 152, 153-54, 154, 155, 156, 157, 158, 159, 160-61, 162, 163, 164-65, 165, 166-67, 168, 169, 170-71, 172-73; environs of, 173-78, 174, 177; Governor's Mansion, 4, 156; James River plantations near, 146, 178-79, 180-81, 182, 183-85, 185; National Battlefield Park, 168, 172-73
Rifles, Warren, Confederate Museum, 234
Rising Sun Tavern, 131
Rochambeau, Comte de, 197

Rock Creek Cemetery, Washington, DC, 96
Rock Run Grist Mill, 330
Rockefeller, Abby Aldrich, Folk Art Center, 200
Rockville, MD, 334
Rockwood Museum, 360, *362*
Roddy Road Covered Bridge, 340
Rodney Square, Wilmington, DE, 358
Rolfe, John, 100, 204
Roosevelt, Edith Galt, 67, 68
Roosevelt, Franklin Delano, 64
Roosevelt, Theodore, 27, 67, 275
Rose Hill Cemetery, Hagerstown, MD, 341
Rose Hill Manor Children's Museum, Frederick, MD, 338-39
Rosewell, 215, *215*
Ruth, Babe, Birthplace, 322

Sackler, Arthur M., Gallery, 57, 58
St. Anne's Church, Annapolis, MD, 266-67
St. Clements Island, MD, 256, 287
St. Clements Island— Potomac River Museum, 287
St. Elizabeth Ann Seton, 321, 346; House, 321; National Shrine of, 346
St. Ignatius Roman Catholic Church, St. Inigoes, MD, 290
St. Inigoes, MD, 290
St. John's Church, Hampton, VA, 218
St. John's Church, Richmond, VA, 148
St. John's Church, Washington, DC, 74, 76

St. John's College, Annapolis, MD, 267
St. John's Episcopal Church, Washington, DC, 89
St. John's Roman Catholic Church, Frederick, MD, 338
St. Luke's Church, Isle of Wight County, VA, 223
St. Mary's Catholic Church Cemetery, Rockville, MD, 334
St. Mary's Church, Annapolis, MD, 280
St. Mary's Church, Washington, DC, 87
St. Mary's City, MD, 288-89, *281, 289;* State House, 288, *289*
St. Mary's Square Museum, St. Michaels, MD, 294-95, *295*
St. Paul's Episcopal Church, Alexandria, VA, 121
St. Paul's Episcopal Church, Norfolk, VA, *219*, 220
St. Paul's Episcopal Church, Richmond, VA, 151
St. Peter's Parish Church, New Kent County, VA, 185
Saint-Gaudens, Augustus, 96
Salem Church, Chancellorsville, VA, *137*
Salisbury, MD, 296
Samples Manor, MD, 345
Savage Station, VA, Battle of, 172
Sayler's Creek Battlefield Historical State Park, 239, 241
Schifferstadt, 340, *341*
Scotchtown, VA, 142
Seven Pines, VA, Battle of, 172
Sewall-Belmont House, 37

Sharpsburg, MD, 342, *343*, 344-45, *344, 345*
Shenandoah National Park, 226
Shenandoah Valley, VA, 226-27, **228-29**, 230, *231, 232,* 233-36, *235, 237*
Shepherd, Alexander, 24, 45
Sheridan, Philip H., 95, 178, 226, 227, 230, 233, 234, 235, 241; photograph of, *233*
Sheridan Circle, Washington, DC, 95
Sherman Monument, 79
Sherwood Forest, 185
Shiplap House, 280
Shirley Plantation, *146*, 179, *180-81, 182,* 183
Shockoe Slip, Richmond, VA, 153
Shot Tower, Baltimore, MD, 320
Siege Museum, Petersburg, VA, 176
Sinclair, Upton, 306
Skyline Drive, 226
Smallwood State Park, 284
Smith, John, 223
Smith's Fort Plantation, VA, 223
Smithson, James, 47-48, 50
Smithsonian Building, *48-49,* 49-50
Smithsonian Institution, 47-52, *48-49, 51, 53, 54-55,* 56-58, *58*
Smyrna, DE, 379
Snow Hill, MD, 297
Solomons, MD, 287
Sotterley, *261,* 262, *286,* 287
Sousa, John Philip, 42
Spotswood, Governor, 196-97
Spotsylvania Court House, VA, Battle of, 139
Spray, Godiah, Tobacco Plantation, 288

Stabler-Leadbeater
  Apothecary Shop, 121
Stafford Furnace, 331
Stanton, DE, 369
Stanton Square,
  Washington, DC, 42
Stanton's Mill, 349
Star-Spangled Banner
  Flag House, 321
Stein, Gertrude, 306
Steppingstone Museum,
  331
Steuben, Friedrich von,
  173
Stonewall Cemetery,
  Winchester, VA, 230
Strand, The, New Castle,
  DE, 374
Strasburg, VA, 234
Stratford, VA, 143, *144*,
  145
Stratford Hall, 143, *144*,
  145
Stuart, J. E. B., 153, 183
Stuyvesant, Peter, 357,
  370
Suitland, MD, 282
Sully Historic Site, 110
Sumner, Charles,
  School, 86
Supreme Court
  Building, *36*, 37
Surratt House, 282
Surrender Field,
  Yorktown, VA, 214
Surrender Triangle,
  Appomattox, VA, 241
Surry, VA, 223
Susan Constant, 206
Susquehanna Museum
  of Havre de Grace,
  330, *330*
Susquehanna State Park,
  MD, 330-31
Sutherlin House, 238

Taft, William Howard,
  62, 107
Taney, 322
Tariff Commission
  Building, Washington,
  DC, 82
Tarleton, Banastre, 203,
  253

Teackle Mansion, 296,
  297
Textile Museum,
  Washington, DC, 96
Third Haven Friends
  Meetinghouse, 294
Thomas Viaduct, 331
Thornton, William, 29,
  87, 92, 128
Thoroughgood, Adam,
  House, 222, *222*, *386*
Thurmont, MD, 340
Tiffany, Louis Comfort,
  177, 277, 309
Tobacco Warehouse,
  Annapolis, MD, 280
Tomb of the Unknowns,
  Arlington National
  Cemetery, 107
Torsk, 322
Towson, MD, 306
Trapezium House,
  Petersburg, VA, 176
Treasury Annex,
  Washington, DC, 77
Treasury Building,
  Washington, DC, 77,
  77, 79
Trinity Chapel,
  Frederick, MD, 338
Tripoli Monument, U.S.
  Naval Academy, 277
Truman, Harry S, 67
Tuckahoe Plantation,
  165
Tucker House, 291
Tudor Place, 92
Tyler, John, 153, 184,
  185

Union Mills, MD, 334
Union Mills Homestead,
  334
Union Station,
  Washington, DC, 27
U.S. Army Ordnance
  Museum, Aberdeen,
  MD, 329-30
U.S. Army
  Quartermaster
  Museum, Petersburg,
  VA, 176
United States Chamber
  of Commerce

building, Washington,
  DC, 77
U.S. Naval Academy,
  Annapolis, MD, 272,
  274-75, *274*, *276*, 277,
  278, 279-80, *279*, *387;*
  Museum, 275
University of Virginia,
  243, *244-45*, 246-47,
  246
Upjohn, Richard, 309,
  337

Valentine Museum,
  159, *160-61*, 162
Van Buren, Martin, 67
Victualling Warehouse
  Maritime Museum,
  280
Vietnam Memorial, 62,
  62
Virginia, **8-9, 102-03,
  228-29;** northern, *98*,
  100-01, 104-07, *106*,
  108-09, 110, *111*, 112-
  15, *114*, *115*, *116-17*,
  118-23, *118*, *119*, *121*,
  122-23, *124*, 125, *126-
  27*, 128-40, *129*, *132*,
  133, *134*, *135*, *137*,
  138, *141*, 142-43, *144*,
  145; southern, 238-39,
  241-42; state capitol,
  153-54, *154*, *155*. *See
  also* Charlottesville;
  Hampton Roads;
  Jamestown;
  Richmond;
  Shenandoah Valley;
  Williamsburg;
  Yorktown
Virginia Beach, VA, 222
Virginia Company of
  London, 203, 204
Virginia Historical
  Society, Richmond,
  VA, 162, 164
Virginia House, 164,
  165, *166-67*
Virginia Military
  Institute, 236
Virginia Museum of
  Fine Arts, Richmond,
  VA, 162

Waldorf, MD, 284
Walker, Maggie L.,
    House, 162, *163*
Wallace, DeWitt,
    Decorative Arts
    Gallery, 200, *202*
Walter, Thomas U., 32,
    33, 221
Walters Art Gallery, 309
War of 1812, 218, 280,
    282, 294-95, 300, 324-
    25, 384; Washington,
    DC, 21, 32, 38, 66-67
Warren-Sipe Museum,
    235
Washington, Booker T.,
    64, 238; National
    Monument, 238
Washington, George,
    101, 104, 105, 107,
    118, 120, 122, 123,
    125, 129, 185, 226,
    236, 282, 347, 348,
    358, 369; at
    Annapolis, 263, 266;
    Birthplace National
    Monument, 143;
    Cabin (Cumberland,
    MD), 347-48; in
    Fredericksburg, 130,
    133-34; Grist Mill,
    122-23, 123; Masonic
    National Memorial,
    122-23; at Mount
    Vernon, 125, 128; on
    the Northern Neck,
    VA, 142, 143; Office
    Museum, 230; statue
    of, *154*; and
    Washington, DC, 20,
    29, 34; at Yorktown,
    208, 212
Washington, Mary,
    House, 133-34
Washington, DC, **8-9,**
    18, 20-27, *21,* **22, 23;**
    Capitol Hill, *28,* 29,
    30-31, 32-35, *32, 33,*
    36, 37-38, *39,* 40, *40,*
    41, 42-43; downtown,
    74-77, *75, 77, 78,* 79-
    83, *81, 84-85,* 86-87,
    87; Dupont Circle and
    Kalorama, 92-97, *94,*

97; Georgetown, 88-92,
    88, *90, 91;* the Mall, 44-
    52, *44-45, 47, 48-49, 51,*
    53, 54-55, 56-59, *58,*
    60, 61-62, *62, 63,* 64-72,
    65, 66, 68, 69, 73, 74

Washington College, 291
Washington Hotel,
    Princess Anne, MD,
    296
Washington and Lee
    University, 236
Washington Monument,
    Baltimore, MD, 306,
    307, 308
Washington Monument,
    Richmond, VA, 154
Washington Monument,
    Washington, DC, 45,
    59, *59, 60,* 61
Washington Monument
    State Park,
    Boonsboro, MD, 342
Washington Street
    Historic District,
    Cumberland, MD, 348

Waterford, VA, *111,* 112
Waynesboro, VA, 235
Webster, Daniel, 35, 74;
    portrait of (Healy), *35*
West Montgomery
    Avenue Historic
    District, Rockville,
    MD, 334
Westminster, MD, 334
Westminster Church
    and Burying Ground,
    Baltimore, MD, 324
Weston Manor, 178
Westover, 179, 184, *185,*
    386
Westover Church, VA,
    185
White, Andrew, 256, 285
White, Stanford, 96,
    246, 308, 316
White House, The, 65-
    70, *66, 68, 69*
White House of the
    Confederacy, 156,
    158, 159

Whittier, John
    Greenleaf, 335, 339
Wickham-Valentine
    House, 159, *160-61,*
    162
Wilderness, VA, Battle
    of the, 137-38
Williamsburg, VA, 100,
    101, 105, *186,* 188-93,
    190, 191, *192, 194-95,*
    196-98, *196, 197, 199,*
    200, *201, 202,* 203;
    Capitol, *192,* 193, *194-*
    95; Governor's Palace,
    186, 188, 198, *199*
Willingtown Square,
    Wilmington, DE, 358
Willoughby-Baylor
    House, 221
Wilmington, DE, 352,
    357-60, *357;* Old
    Town Hall, 358
Wilson, Woodrow,
    House, 95
Wilson-Warner House,
    379
Wilton, 164-65
Winchester, VA, Battles
    of, 226-27, 230
Winchester Hall,
    Frederick, MD, 338
Winterthur Museum,
    DE, 365, *366-67,* 368-
    69, *368, 369*
Wolstenholme Towne,
    VA, 203
Woodburn, 381
Woodlawn, 128
Wright's Chance, 291
Wye Mill, 294
Wye Mills, MD, 294
Wythe, George, House,
    198

Yorktown, VA, 104,
    188, **191,** 208, *208,*
    209, 210-11, 212, *213,*
    214-15; Civil War and,
    208, 209, 214; Victory
    Center, 214; Victory
    Monument, 215

Zwaanendael Museum,
    384

M. Romanelli/Image Bank: **60**
A. M. Rosario/Image Bank: **387 (top left)**
Photo by Joseph Szaszfai/© Yale University Art Gallery: **213**
David E. Tripp/ Homewood, Johns Hopkins University: **312-313, 386 (top center)**
Michael Ventura/Folio Inc.: **264**

University of Virginia Library: **246** (Thomas Jefferson Papers, Manuscripts Division)
Jonathan Wallen: **78, 283, 298, 307, 317, 327, 330, 332, 386 (bottom center)**
M. E. Warren, Baltimore: **254, 274, 278, 289, 291, 297, 319, 323 (top), 341, 349, 387 (bottom left and top right)**
Bill Weems/Woodfin

Camp: **44-45**
Western Reserve Historical Society: **231** (Palmer Collection)

The editors gratefully acknowledge the assistance of Ann J. Campbell, Ferris Cook, Amy Hughes, Carol A. McKeown, Cathy Peck, Klaske Piebenga, Martha Schulman, and Patricia Woodruff.

Cover credits

Main photo: © Robert Llewellyn.

Inset 1: Everett C. Johnson/Folio Inc.

Inset 2: Map by Guenther Vollath.

Inset 3: "Mock-Bird" by Catesby; Colonial Williamsburg Foundation.

Inset 4: © Michael Freeman.

Composed in Basilia Haas and ITC New Baskerville by Graphic Arts Composition, Inc., Philadelphia, Pennsylvania. Printed and bound by Toppan Printing Company, Ltd., Tokyo, Japan.